New Ways in Teaching With Music

Jean L. Arnold and Emily Herrick, Editors

This book has a companion website. Go to www.tesol.org/teachingwithmusic for additional resources.

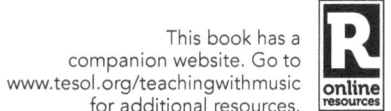

www.tesol.org/bookstore

TESOL International Association
1925 Ballenger Avenue
Alexandria, Virginia, 22314 USA
www.tesol.org

Director of Publishing: Myrna Jacobs
Copy Editor: Tomiko Breland
Production Editor: Kari S. Dalton
Cover Design: Citrine Sky Design
Layout and Design: Capitol Communications, LLC

Copyright © 2017 by TESOL International Association

All rights reserved. Copying or further publication of the contents of this work are not permit-ted without permission of TESOL International Association, except for limited "fair use" for educational, scholarly, and similar purposes as authorized by U.S. Copyright Law, in which case appropriate notice of the source of the work should be given. Permission to reproduce material from this book must be obtained from www.copyright.com, or contact Copyright Clearance Center, Inc., 222 Rosewood Drive, Danvers, MA 01923, 9787508400.

Every effort has been made to contact copyright holders for permission to reprint borrowed material. We regret any oversights that may have occurred and will rectify them in future printings of this work.

ISBN 9781942799856
Library of Congress Control Number 2017941701

....

Page 154 ["You Needed Me": The Simple Past Tense in Action]
You Needed Me
Words and Music by Randy Goodrum
Copyright © 1975 (Renewed) Chappell & Co., Inc.
All Rights Administered by Chappell & Co., Inc.
All Rights Reserved
Used by Permission of ALFRED MUSIC

Page 235 [Tying It Together: Music, Reading, and Writing]
Tie a Yellow Ribbon 'Round the Old Oak Tree
Words and Music by Irwin Levine and L. Russell Brown
Copyright © 1972 (Renewed) Irwin Levine Music and Peermusic, Ltd.
All Rights for Irwin Levine Music Controlled and Administered by Spirit One Music (BMI)
All Rights Reserved
Used by Permission of Alfred Music

Page 247 [Songs and Memories for Expanding Vocabulary and Grammar]
The House That Built Me
Words and Music by Tom Douglas and Allen Shamblin
Copyright © 2009 Sony/ATV Music Publishing LLC, Tomdouglasmusic and Built On Rock Music
All Rights on behalf of Sony/ATV Music Publishing LLC and Tomdouglasmusic Administered by
　　Sony/ATV Music Publishing LLC, 424 Church Street, Suite 1200, Nashville, TN 37219
All Rights on behalf of Built On Rock Music Administered by ClearBox Rights
International Copyright Secured
All Rights Reserved
Reprinted by Permission of Hal Leonard LLC

Contents

Note: The lessons in each section are arranged according to level, low to high.

Introduction ix

Part I: Music for Reading

Introduction 3
Line Quest: Underline the Answer, *Katherine Riebe* 5
Tell Me More: *Wh–* Question Formation, *Katherine Riebe* 8
Storytelling Songs, *Fergal Kavanagh* 10
Speed Reading About Music, *Jean L. Arnold* 12
In Other Words, *Tamara Guy* 18
Paraphrase Match Me Up, *Tamara Guy* 20
Identifying POVs, *Tamara Jones* 22
An Interview With a Songwriter, *Elena Shvidko* 24

Part II: Music for Writing

Introduction 29
Collaborative Storytelling, *Tamara Jones* 31
Opera for English, *Haley P. Vickers and Jace Vickers* 33
Emotional Involvement: Using Music as the Writing Muse,
   Patrick T. Randolph 35
Music and Word-Go-Round, *Lilika Couri* 37
Life's a Happy Song: Figurative Language, *Ann Bouma* 38
Getting to Know You, *Lilika Couri* 40
The Back Story, *Emily Herrick* 42
Musical Paraphrasing, *Tamara Jones* 43
A Special Place, *Sally La Luzerne-Oi* 45
Telling Images, *Jovana Milosavljevic Ardeljan* 47
Want to Be a Songwriter?, *Nadezda Pimenova* 49
Don't Mess With Genres!, *Elena Shvidko* 52
Writing a Report: Music in Koolistan, *Alan S. Weber and Vincent Corver* . . . 55
Every Song Tells the Story: Using Musicals to
   Practice Summarizing, *Emily Beccketti and Jessica Sarles* 57
Elements of a Narrative, *Ann Bouma* 60

Part III: Music for Listening

Introduction 65
Chorus Reconstruction, *Jacob Huckle* 67
Dueling Kazoos, *Paul Keyworth* 69
Listen for Your Line, *Rebecca Palmer* 72
Aural to Visual: Turning Songs Into Tableau Vivant, *Joseph V. Dias* 74
Find and Fix the Mistakes!, *Timothy R. Janda* 76
Rhyming Words in Lyrics: Exploring Student Creativity in TESOL,
    Vander Viana and Sonia Zyngier 78
Close Listening: What'd He Say?, *Jean L. Arnold* 80
Irony, *Arlyn Mañebo-Baron* 82
Sound Scavenger Hunt, *Walcir Cardoso, Ross Sundberg, and Tiago Bione* 84
Lyrical Visualization and Interpretation, *Nathan Galster* 87
Lyrics: Dictation and Note-Taking, *Jon Noble* 89
Taylor Swift Lyrics Gap Fill, *Christopher Pond and Sean H. Toland* 91
A Musical Tribute to Vincent Van Gogh, *Stacie A. Swinehart* 94
Affix Awareness, *Rita M. Van Dyke-Kao* 96
Islamic Songs and the Mastery of Listening Skills,
    Mohamed A. Yacoub 98
Listening for and Noting Large Numbers: "The Galaxy Song,"
    Jean L. Arnold 100
This Is an Important Announcement!, *Jim Cracraft* 102
Polite Apologies in American English, *Lisa Leopold* 105
Lady Mondegreen Rides Again!: How to Use Mondegreens
    (Misheard Song Lyrics) to Further Listening Skills
    and Understand Phonetic Features, *Chris Walklett* 107

Part IV: Music for Speaking

Introduction 111
Singing to Develop Rhythm and Linking, *Marsha J. Chan* 112
Desert Island Songs, *Peter McDonald* 114
Learning to the Beat: Improving Speaking Fluency and
    Pronunciation With a Metronome, *Ildiko Porter-Szucs* 116
Do You Hear What I Hear? Discussing the Pieces in a
    Musical Ensemble, *Christopher Stillwell* 119

Let's Make Rhymes, *Mike de Jong* 121

Rap 101: Keeping It Real, *Tom Lackaff* 123

Rocking out for Better Pronunciation and Spelling, *Marie Webb* 126

Character in Music, *Matthew Kobialka* 129

Battle of the Planets, *James Broadbridge* 131

Movie Theme Songs, *Islam M. Farag* 133

My Musical Autobiography, *Nathan Galster* 135

Karaoke Presentations, *Meaghan Harding* 137

Impromptu Speaking, *Lauren Lesce* 140

Music Festival: Looking for a Headliner and Opening Act!,
   Simon Thomas and Sean H. Toland 142

Fast Song Sing-Along, *Benjamin J. White* 144

Part V: Music for Grammar

Introduction 149

What About Me? Pronouns, *Ann Bouma* 150

My Daily Routine, *Juan Manuel Rivas* 151

And His Momma Cries: Present Tense, *Ann Bouma* 152

"You Needed Me": The Simple Past Tense in Action, *Jacqueline Foster* . . 154

What Would You Do if You Had $1,000,000?, *Eman Elturki* 156

"Cheap Thrills" by Sia: Identifying Compound-Complex
   Sentences, *Diana Hemmelgarn* 158

Using Music for Verb Structure Review, *Jolene Jaquays* 161

Singing Your Love With Adjective Clauses, *Sara Okello,*
   Wendy Wang, and Allison Piippo 163

Songs of Regret, *Josefina C. Santana* 165

Grammar Karaoke: Singing Along With *Wh*– Noun Clauses,
   Wendy Wang, Sara Okello, and Allison Piippo 167

Song Parodies, *Carrie K. Bach* 169

Clause Comparison, *Allison Piippo, Wendy Wang, and Sara Okello* . . 171

Part VI: Music for Vocabulary

Introduction 175

Graded Music: Analyzing Lyrics by Vocabulary Level,
   Ross Sundberg, Walcir Cardoso, and Tiago Bione 177

Activating Learner Recognition of Vocabulary Through Music,
Gene Thompson 180

Hi De Ho: Vocabulary Call-and-Response, *Kevin McCaughey* 182

Cloze Clues, *Timothy R. Janda* 184

The New Year Class, *Deniz Şalli-Çopur* 186

The "Happy Friday" Song Project, *Sibel Taşkin Şimşek* 188

This Song Is as Sad as a Wet Puppy, *Emily Herrick* 190

Do You Know *X*?, *Priscila Leal* 191

Chunking Song Lyrics, *Laura Murphy* 193

Listening Between the Lines, *Ha Hoang* 195

About Time, *Sally La Luzerne-Oi* 197

Teaching Collocations, Phrasal Verbs, and Idioms
Through Songs, *Friederike Tegge* 199

Part VII: Music for Cultural Exploration

Introduction 203

Looking at the Great Depression Through Song, *Jacqueline Nenchin* . . 205

Weekly Worldly Warm-Up, *Crystal Bock-Thiessen* 207

Community Radio Collaboration, *Emily Herrick* 210

American History Through Folk Songs, *Timothy R. Janda* 211

Music Video for Cultural Exploration, *Kevin Knight* 213

National Anthems, *Elizabeth J. Lange* 215

America's National Pastime, *Constance Leonard* 217

Make a Music Video With a Social Message,
Sean H. Toland and Simon Thomas 219

What's in a Song? From Peace to Protests: Culture Abounds,
Joshua Wedlock 222

Part VIII: Music for Integrated Skills

Introduction 227

Song Dictogloss, *Friederike Tegge* 228

All I Want to Be . . . , *Hayriye Ulaş Taraf* 230

Drawing a Tale, *Ha Hoang* 233

Tying It Together: Music, Reading, and Writing,
Eleanora (Nonie) S. Bell and Xiaowei (Vivian) Shi 235

"Nobody's Home," *Joyce Cunningham* 238

It's Not Easy Being Born This Way, *Thomas Fast* 240

"Tom's Diner," *Thomas Fast* 242

Content Connection: Environment and Climate Change,
Lisa G. Harris 244

Songs and Memories for Expanding Vocabulary and Grammar,
Ruth Ann Marotta and Theresa McGarry 247

Sing Our Song, *Rebecca Palmer* 249

Studying Literature With Music, *Mike Hammond* 251

INTRODUCTION

Learning and music have enjoyed a long and intimate connection. Ancient Greek and Chinese philosophers viewed music as a vital educational tool; medieval poets sang their verses and, more recently, language teachers have used approaches from Suggestopedia to jazz chants. Teachers have seemed to intuit that music can facilitate language learning, and now new research in neuroscience provides scientifically based confirmation for some of these intuitions and may support a more consistent use of music in the classroom. In fact, some theorists propose that language is one kind of music and that, at least for human infants, musical cognition is the foundation for language learning (Brandt, Gebrain, & Slevc, 2012).

Increasing numbers of recent studies from Australia, Europe, Japan, and the United States suggest a link between how the brain processes language and music. Both language and music require processing syntax (musical and grammatical structures) and both require remembering seemingly random items (vocabulary and sequences of notes; Miranda & Ullman, 2007). Neuroimaging and behavioral studies have shown the brain uses the same structures to process both musical and linguistic rules or syntax (Fiveash & Pammer, 2014; Levitin & Menon, 2003; Patel, 2003). In addition, investigations into brain wave patterns have shown that a second region of the brain is used for memorization of both linguistic and musical information (Miranda & Ullman, 2007).

More specifically, additional studies suggest a link between music and grammar (Gordon et al., 2015); music and vocabulary (De Groot, 2006; Legg, 2009; Ludke, Ferreira, & Overy, 2014); music and reading (Slater et al., 2014; Zeromskaite, 2014); and music and phonology, listening, speech, and pronunciation (Chobert & Besson, 2013; Slevc, 2012; Tanaka & Nakamura, 2004). It's no wonder that, when it comes to language learning, as Lems (2005, p. 13) wrote, "Music works."

Using music, especially music that is chosen in collaboration with students, invigorates both students and teacher. It can reduce the fear factor, increase interest and participation, and create fun. Music can decrease students' anxiety levels while increasing motivation and retention (Cunningham, 2014; Dolean, 2015; Speh & Ahramjian, 2011). When students are engaged, their creative juices flow, they become more receptive, and learning becomes more memorable, whether the instructional goal is grammar or cultural understanding.

Music can be included in all curricular areas, including listening, speaking, reading, writing, vocabulary, grammar, and cultural exploration. Listening to music sharpens students' ability to identify sounds, words, and suprasegmental patterns, which can in turn be applied in speaking. Reading about composers, artists, and genres can generate extended activities, and writing assignments can follow from this. Music lyrics provide authentic texts for grammatical analysis and vocabulary acquisition. Because music is an expression of culture, it provides a window to understanding the target language and its culture. Finally, music can be used as a tool to integrate many language skills in one lesson.

Each of the following areas constitutes one section of *New Ways in Teaching with Music*: reading, writing, listening, speaking, grammar, vocabulary, cultural exploration, and integrated skills. The lessons are a sampling of how music is used in the English language classroom by teachers in Africa, Asia, Australia, Europe, the Middle East, New Zealand, and North and South America—every continent except Antarctica is represented. The 87 contributors include not only full-time teachers, but also musicians; students; writers; administrators; producers (of both film and music); and, finally, a journalist, a photographer, and a poet. The types of music they use for teaching are equally as diverse: from nursery rhymes to opera, from classical to hip hop, and from national anthems to pop. We offer all of the contributors our most sincere thanks for their creativity, expertise, and generosity in sharing their work.

In a review of the literature on using music for learning the English language, Engh (2013) reports that there is not much written about how music is actually being used in the English language classroom, despite his conclusion that "From an educational standpoint, music and language not only can, but should be studied together" (p. 121). *New Ways in Teaching with Music* offers you 101 different ways that you can incorporate music into your language classroom. Additionally, we hope that you will visit our companion website, www.tesol.org/teachingwithmusic. You will find short biographies of our contributors; a bibliography of articles, books, and recent theses and dissertations that are related to music and language learning; an annotated list of websites helpful for classroom teachers who want to integrate music in their classrooms; MP3s; PowerPoint presentations; and other material mentioned in this book.

> When you see this icon, go to www.tesol.org/teachingwithmusic to access these valuable resources.

Each of the activities in this book lists the level of proficiency for which the activity is best suited, the activity's aims, time required for preparation and in class, and materials needed. Here are a few things to keep in mind as you make your way through this book:

- Only you know your students and your context: Please preview all songs and videos before using them in class to see if they are appropriate for your students. Note that you can always mute a video and play only the audio version if the images in a video aren't suitable for your group.
- We know that the materials and resources available to each educator vary; however, for the sake of simplicity, the activities in this book assume that all teachers have access to a blackboard or whiteboard, paper and writing utensils, and audio equipment.

We have used music first as language learners and now as language teachers. We are happy to compile this book of the best ideas and resources from practicing teachers about how they use music in their English language teaching, and we hope you'll enjoy trying some of these creative techniques.

REFERENCES

Brandt, A., Gebrain, M., & Slevc, L. R. (2012). Music and early language acquisition. *Frontiers in Psychology, 3*, 1–17. doi: 10.3389/fpsyg.2012.00327

Chobert, J., & Besson, M. (2013). Musical expertise and second language learning. *Brain Sciences, 3*, 923–940. doi: 10.3390/brainsc3020923

Cunningham, C. (2014). Keep talking: Using music during small group discussions in EAP. *ELT Journal, 68*(2), 179–191. doi:10.1093/elt/ccto97

De Groot, A. (2006). Effects of stimulus characteristics and background music on foreign language vocabulary learning and forgetting. *Language Learning, 56*(3), 463–506.

Dolean, D. D. (2015). The effects of teaching songs during foreign language classes on students' foreign language anxiety. *Language Teaching Research, 20*(5), 638–653. doi: 10.1177/1362168815606151

Engh, D. (2013). Why use music in English language learning? A survey of the literature. *English Language Teaching, 6*(2), 113–127. doi: 10.5539/elt.v6n2p113

Fiveash, A., & Pammer, K. (2014). Music and language: Do they draw on similar syntactic working memory resources? *Psychology of Music, 42*(2), 190–209.

Gordon, R. L., Shivers, C., Wieland, E., Kotz, S. A., Yoder, P. J., & McAuley, J. D. (2015). Musical rhythm discrimination explains individual differences in grammar skills in children. *Developmental Science, 19*(4), 653–644. doi: 10.111/desc.1230

Legg, R. (2009). Using music to accelerate language learning: An experimental study. *Research in Education, 82*(1), 1–12.

Lems, K. (2005). Music works: Music for adult English language learners. *New Directions for Adult and Continuing Education, 107*, 13–21.

Levitin, D., & Menon, V. (2003). Musical structure is processed in "language" areas of the brain: A possible role for Brodmann Area 47 in temporal coherence, *NeuroImage, 20*, 2142–2152. doi: 10.1016/j.neuroimage.2003.08.016

Ludke, K. M., Ferreira, F., & Overy, K. (2014). Singing can facilitate foreign language learning. *Memory & Cognition, 42*, 41–52. doi:10.3758/s13421-013-0342-5

Miranda, R. A., & Ullman, M. T. (2007). Double dissociation between rules and memory in music: An event-related potential study. *NeuroImage, 38*, 331–345. doi: 10.1016/j.neuroimage.2007.07.034

Patel, A. D. (2003). Language, music, syntax and the brain. *Nature Neuroscience, 6*(7), 674–681.

Slater, J., Strait, D. L., Skoe, E., O'Connell, S., Thompson, E., & Kraus, N. (2014). Longitudinal effects of group music on literacy skills in low-income children. *PLoS One. 9*(11). 1–9. doi: 10.1371/journal.pone.0113383

Slevc, L. R. (2012). Language and music: Sound, structure, and meaning. *WIRE's Cognitive Science, 3*(4), 483–492. doi: 10.1002/wcs.1186

Speh, A. J., & Ahramjian, S. D. (2011). Teaching without a common language; synchronicities between the pedagogies of music and language acquisition. *Bulletin of the Transilvania University of Brasov, 4*(53), 77–82.

Tanaka, A., & Nakamura, K. (2004). Auditory memory and proficiency of second language speaking: A latent variable analysis approach. *Psychological Reports, 95*(3), 723–734.

Zeromskaite, I. (2014). The potential role of music in second language learning: A review article. *Journal of European Psychology Students, 5*(3), 78–88. doi: 10.5334/jeps.ci

FURTHER READING

Coyle, Y., & Gomez Garcia, R. (2014). Using songs to enhance L2 vocabulary acquisition in preschool children. *ELT Journal, 68*(3), 276–285. doi:10.1093/elt/ccuo15

Johns Hopkins Medicine. (2014, February 19). The musical brain: Novel study of jazz players shows common brain circuitry processes both music, language. *ScienceDaily*. Retrieved from https://www.sciencedaily.com/releases/2014/02/140219173136.htm

Koelsch, S., Gunter, T. C., von Cramon, D. Y., Zysset, S., Lohmann, G., & Friederici, A. D. (2002). Bach speaks: A cortical "language-network" serves the processing of music. *NeuroImage, 17*, 956–966. doi: 10.1006/nimg.2002.1154

Lee, H. (2014). Social media and student learning behavior: Plugging into mainstream music offers dynamic ways to learn English. *Computers in Human Behavior, 36*, 496–501. doi: 10.1016/j.chb.2014.02.019

Maess, B., Koelsch S., Gunter, T. C., & Friederici, A. D. (2001). Musical syntax is processed in Broca's area: An MEG study. *Nature Neuroscience, 4*(5), 540–545.

Medina, S. L. (1993). The effect of music on second language vocabulary acquisition. *FLESNews, 6*(3), 1–8.

Northwestern University. (2014, December 16). How music class can spark language development. *ScienceDaily*. Retrieved from https://www.sciencedaily.com/releases/2014/12/141216175711.htm

Schön, D., Boyer, M., Moreno, S., Besson, M., Peretz, I., & Kolinsky, R. (2008). Songs as an aid for language acquisition. *Cognition, 106*, 975–983. doi:10.1016/j.cognition.2007.03.005

Schön, D., Gordon, R., Campagne, C., Magne, C., Astesano, C., Anton, J., & Besson, M. (2010). Similar cerebral networks in language, music and song perception. *NeuroImage, 51*, 450–461. doi: 10.1016/j.neuroimage.2010.02.023

Slevc, L. R., & Miyake, A. (2006). Individual difference in second-language proficiency: Does musical ability matter? *Psychological Science, 17*(8), 675–681.

Weinberger, N. M. (1997). The musical hormone. *MuSICA Research Notes, 4*(2). Retrieved from http://www.musica.uci.edu/mrn/V4I2F97.html

Part I

Music for Reading

Part I: Music for Reading

Although this is the shortest chapter in *New Ways in Teaching with Music*, music has a great part to play in helping English language learners (ELLs) with reading. To tackle academic reading tasks, students need to be able to combine bottom-up reading skills, such as decoding written symbols, and top-down processes, that is, using prior experiences and knowledge to make sense of a text. Just as there is great variety in written prose texts, musical texts come in many types and genres that students can identify. Reading strategies such as prediction; confirming expectations; reading for gist, general understanding, or detailed comprehension; scanning; and interpreting the text can be applied to the lyrics of popular songs. Reading necessarily involves understanding vocabulary, and songs can provide a context for the vocabulary, giving students a way to create and test hypotheses about the meaning. English songs can serve as an enticement to understand this language, and they are readily heard around the world in this digital age.

Lyrics to popular songs can be accessed online and scrutinized by ELLs. This alluring, authentic resource can be tapped easily, even for beginner ELLs. In her recent doctoral dissertation, Tegge (2015) reports that "songs can and do serve as an 'entry level' authentic and unsimplified text genre that can be used as teaching material in the classroom and that overall meets the needs of language learners in terms of vocabulary demand" (p. 125). Songs can be used to consolidate words already learned and deepen a learner's knowledge of the word. Additionally, using songs has several advantages over other types of authentic texts because they are short; therefore, they can be used more easily, the context is complete and clear, and they can be repeated within one class period—perhaps focusing on a different skill with each repetition (Tegge, 2015, pp. 128–129). Music and language overlap in terms of rhythm and emphasis, and this overlap facilitates students' noticing how words are used together. This type of "chunking" may help the learner retain the information as an integrated whole (Tegge, 2015, pp. 179–180).

The first musical offering in this chapter is from Katherine Riebe. Her "Line Quest" activity is a musical take on a traditional "find the answer in the text" activity, providing scanning practice. This activity can incorporate choral reading, which helps develop reading fluency and rhythm (Richards, 1993, p. 99). Riebe's second contribution about forming *wh–* questions gets students reading closely, analyzing, and comprehending text to a greater extent. In the third activity, Fergal Kavanagh offers a kinesthetic activity in which students reconstruct a text—the story of a song—in chronological order. Following this, Jean Arnold describes a daily practice of speed reading and offers a sample text and comprehension questions on a musical topic.

The next two contributions from Tamara Guy help students with close reading skills and paraphrasing. The first activity uses national anthems as the target language: The words need to be carefully rephrased as their message carries great import, representing an entire country. The second activity is more kinesthetic, requiring students to match original wording with correct paraphrases, which were created by different class teams. The next activity by Tamara Jones requires students to think critically and identify bias and point of view in songs, and summarize them. Finally, Elena

Shvidko has students locate main ideas and details, then work critically with the text and apply the knowledge in a practical activity.

Students are interested in classroom activities that utilize lyrics from songs they know, and they can also be drawn in by songs with meaningful, clearly articulated messages. Teachers need to select music carefully. Salcedo (2002), in her dissertation, concludes that to be most effective, the songs used for teaching ELLs need to

- be popular and meaningful;
- be slow enough to be comprehensible;
- be clearly-enunciated;
- have no difficult idioms, slang, or vulgar language;
- use normal speech and word order;
- be catchy and geared to right age; and
- have a strong connection between the text and characteristics of the music (pp. 125–126).

Of course, these are general guidelines, but if you're just starting out using music in the classroom, they may be helpful.

Besides using music for classroom activities, using appropriate music in the background while learners read can boost their concentration and facilitate verbal memory (Jensen, 2000). The books by Brewer (2008) and Jensen (2005) listed in the references list can give you more specific information on successfully choosing the right background music for the task.

Whether using songs with lyrics or without, bring on the tunes!

REFERENCES

Brewer, C. B. (2008). *Soundtracks for learning: Using music in the classroom.* Bellingham, WA: LifeSounds Educational Services.

Jensen, E. (2000). *Music with the brain in mind: Enhance learning with music.* San Diego, CA: Corwin Press.

Jensen, E. P. (2005). *Top tunes for teaching: 977 song titles and practical tools for choosing the right music every time.* San Diego, CA: Corwin Press.

Richards, R. G. (1993). *LEARN: Playful techniques to accelerate learning.* Tucson, AZ: Zephyr Press.

Salcedo, C. S. (2002). *The effects of songs in the foreign language classroom on text recall and involuntary mental rehearsal* (Doctoral dissertation). Retrieved from http://etd.lsu.edu/docs/available/etd-1111102-204823/unrestricted/Salcedo_dis.pdf

Tegge, F. (2015). *Investigating song-based language teaching and its effect on lexical learning* (Unpublished doctoral dissertation). Victoria University of Wellington, New Zealand. Retrieved from http://researcharchive.vuw.ac.nz/handle/10063/4577

Line Quest: Underline the Answer

Katherine Riebe

Levels	Beginner to intermediate
Aims	Improve reading skills
	Find answers from a text
	Work on answering yes/no and information questions
Class Time	20 minutes
Preparation Time	10–15 minutes
Resources	Audio recording of selected song
	Handout of song lyrics
	Handout of comprehension questions based on the song

It is important to provide students with various sources of reading material in addition to textbooks and articles. Using music in a reading class is novel and may create excitement and interest. In addition, having students underline their answers in a text can be beneficial as it gets them in the habit of returning to the text when doing reading comprehension activities. This underlying task is an active reading skill, which is useful even for college students.

PROCEDURE

1. Prepare and copy the song lyrics and a list of comprehension questions about the song.
2. Hand out the song lyrics and read them; answer general questions about background, vocabulary, etc.
3. Play the song.
4. Hand out comprehension questions about the song.
5. Have students answer the questions by going back to the reading, finding the answers, and underlining them.
6. Go over the answers, asking students to identify where they were located.

CAVEATS AND OPTIONS

1. Provide the song lyrics for homework the day before, or in class as silent reading or an oral class reading.
2. Show the comprehension questions on a screen or write them on the board. You can also have students read the questions silently or have everyone read together as a class.
3. Have students find the answers by themselves or in pairs.

4. This activity could be an opportunity to teach students how to direct others to a location in a song using words like *verse/stanza*, *chorus*, *line*, and *sentence*.

5. Focus on just *yes/no* questions or just information questions, or a combination of both. Give students tips on what kind of information they are looking for when dealing with each type of question.

6. Follow the reading activity with a discussion of the song. Some students may like to hear it again and sing along.

7. For homework, give students the lyrics of another song. After they listen to the song and read its lyrics, ask them to write comprehension questions based on the lyrics. Go over the questions they write in class the next day or collect them for evaluation later.

APPENDIX A: *Examples of Songs*

- "Tie a Yellow Ribbon Round the Ole Oak Tree," Dawn featuring Tony Orlando
- "Piano Man," Billy Joel
- "Cat's in the Cradle," Harry Chapin
- "The Gambler," Kenny Rogers
- "Earth Song," Michael Jackson
- "Man in the Mirror," Michael Jackson
- "Copacabana," Barry Manilow
- "Dancing Queen," ABBA
- "I Finally Found Someone," Bryan Adams with Barbra Streisand
- "Christmas Shoes," NewSong
- "Ding-Dong the Witch Is Dead," from *The Wizard of Oz* movie
- "God Must Have Spent a Little More Time on You," NSYNC
- "Isn't She Lovely," Stevie Wonder
- "Don't Worry, Be Happy," Bobby McFerrin
- "Lately," Stevie Wonder
- "Dance with My Father," Luther Vandross
- "One Sweet Day," Mariah Carey and Boyz II Men
- "Grown-up Christmas List," Amy Grant
- "Wind Beneath My Wings," Bette Midler
- "Love Song," Sara Bareilles
- "Home," Michael Bublé
- "Butterfly Kisses," Bob Carlisle
- "Cinderella," Steven Curtis Chapman
- "Who Are the People in Your Neighborhood?," Sesame Street
- "Don't Give Up," Bruno Mars/Sesame Street

- "See You Again," Wiz Khalifa
- "7 Years," Lukas Graham
- "Fight Song," Rachel Platten
- "I Believe I Can Fly," R Kelly
- "The Climb," Miley Cyrus

APPENDIX B: *Sample Questions*

"Tie a Yellow Ribbon ('Round the Ole Oak Tree)"

1. Which phrase tells where the songwriter has been?
2. When did the author see his girlfriend last?
3. What will the author do if his girlfriend doesn't want a relationship with him anymore?
4. Will the author be upset with his girlfriend if she wants to be done with him?
5. Is the author confident of his reception?
6. How does the author feel before he finds out how his girlfriend feels?
7. How do you know others in the bus know his story?
8. Did the author expect to see what he saw?
9. What did he see?

"The Christmas Shoes"

1. Where was the songwriter?
2. Was he in a happy mood?
3. Who was standing in front of the boy?
4. Describe the boy.
5. What did the boy want to buy and for whom?
6. What day was it?
7. Who was sick?
8. How do we know that this person was seriously ill?
9. What problem did the boy have when it was his turn to pay?
10. How was the problem resolved?

Tell Me More: *Wh–* Question Formation

Katherine Riebe

Levels	High beginner to intermediate
Aims	Improve reading skills
	Establish relationship between reading a text and the comprehension questions asked about it
	Work on creating and answering information/wh– questions
Class Time	20–30 minutes
Preparation Time	10–15 minutes
Resources	Audio recording of a song (preferably a song that is easy to understand and/or tells a story)
	Handout of song lyrics

Asking questions is a basic part of communication, and learning how to ask good questions will be valuable to students. Students improve reading skills when they see the relationship between what they've just read and the comprehension questions they are asked. Having students formulate and answer their own *wh–* questions requires them to read a text more closely. Students come to realize that most information included in a text is included for a reason. For higher level students, this exercise allows them to practice writing and grammar skills as well as to analyze and comprehend a text. Doing this activity with a song introduces variety into the class and may serve to energize students.

PROCEDURE

1. Prepare a handout with the song lyrics and make copies for the students.
2. Hand out the song lyrics and play the song.
3. Read the song lyrics and answer general questions about background, vocabulary, etc.
4. Have students write six *wh–* questions about the text along with the answers (one each for *who*, *what*, *why*, *where*, *when*, and *how*).
5. Go over the questions as a class or collect them for grading later.

CAVEATS AND OPTIONS

1. Have students do this activity as individual or pair work. You can also assign it as homework.

2. Instead of asking students to write their own questions, provide a list of *wh–* questions. Students work individually or in pairs to find and underline the answers in the lyrics.

3. To extend the activity, in pairs, groups, or as a class, have students ask their fellow classmates the questions they wrote. For example, Student A can ask Student B one question he or she wrote. Student B would answer the question and then ask student C one of his or her own questions, and so on.

4. Discuss the song and fill in other details about the song that you know. Ask students to explain what they feel is going on in the song or how the song makes them feel, etc.

5. If using this as a writing activity, go over the grammar and writing rules for forming questions before doing it.

6. Ask students *yes/no* questions about the song. You can also ask students to identify where they found their answers (verse, line, etc.)

REFERENCES AND FURTHER READING

Aliakbari, M., & Mashhadialvar, J. (n.d.). Does it matter who makes comprehension questions? A comparison between the levels of comprehension obtained from author-generated questions and student generated questions. Retrieved from http://www.paaljapan.org/resources/proceedings/PAAL11/pdfs/01.pdf

Dorkchandra, D. (2013). The effects of question generating strategy instruction on EFL freshmen's reading comprehension and use of English tenses. *Journal of Liberal Arts, Prince of Songkla University, 5*(2).

Houston Independent School District. (2014). Student generated questions. *Effective Practices.* Retrieved from http://houstonisdpsd.org/images/pdfs/student-generated-questions.pdf

Pan, C. (2014). Effects of reciprocal peer-questioning instruction on EFL college students' English reading comprehension. *International Journal of English Language and Literature Studies, 3*(3), 190–209.

Question generation. (n.d.). Inquire. Retrieved from http://nycdoeit.airws.org/pdf/question_generation.pdf

Tanaka, M., & Sanchez, E. (2016). Students' perceptions of reading through peer questioning in cooperative. *TESL-EJ Teaching English as a Second or Foreign Language-Electronic Journal (19)*4, 1–16.

Wright, J. (n.d.). Question-generation. *The savvy teacher's guide: Reading interventions that work,* 44–45. Retrieved from http://www.jimwrightonline.com/pdfdocs/brouge/rdngManual.PDF

Storytelling Songs

Fergal Kavanagh

Levels	Low intermediate to advanced
Aims	Develop awareness of the chronological properties and development of a story
	Improve discourse competence
Class Time	≈ 40 minutes
Preparation Time	20 minutes
Resources	Audio recording of a storytelling song
	Handout of the song lyrics, cut up

Stories are a fundamental feature of students' first experiences of language, so learners are familiar with the basic narrative conventions of the format and can identify with the featured characters. Songs with stories, such as folk ballads or opera, exist in every culture. Such songs make the language more memorable and can help improve all four skills.

PROCEDURE

1. Select an audio recording of a song that tells a story chronologically. Prepare cut-up copies of the lyrics, divided verse by verse. Prepare a short written synopsis of the song, taking care to include information from each verse.
2. Distribute a copy of the synopsis to students in pairs or small groups and give them a minute to scan the text. Tell them that this is based on a song and ask if anyone can guess which one.
3. Play the song in class and discuss the story.
4. Give students a copy of the cut-up lyrics and ask them to put the verses in the correct order. To make this more challenging, suggest they do not initially refer to the written story.
5. Play the song again, allowing them to check.

CAVEATS AND OPTIONS

1. This activity can be reversed, by giving students the song lyrics and then the cut-up story or a description of each verse.
2. This activity can also be done as a jigsaw activity, in which students work in pairs and one reads the story aloud while the other orders the text.
3. Another option is to not prepare the story beforehand, allowing students to order the verses based purely on their content.

4. If you would like to incorporate more speaking and listening practice, or help students develop collaborative writing skills, students could then write the story in pairs or groups.

APPENDIX: *Example Worksheets and Songs*

The worksheets for "Bohemian Rhapsody" (Queen) and "The Foggy Dew" (Sinéad O'Connor and the Chieftains) on www.tuneintoenglish.com are based on this method.

Some good storytelling songs:
- "The River," Bruce Springsteen
- "A Boy Named Sue," Johnny Cash
- "Eleanor Rigby" or "Rocky Raccoon," The Beatles
- "Don't Stand So Close to Me," The Police
- "Stan," Eminem [Editor's note: Preview lyrics for appropriateness for your class.]
- "Hurricane," Bob Dylan

Speed Reading About Music

Jean L. Arnold

Levels	Intermediate to advanced
Aims	Increase reading speed, fluency, and accuracy
Class Time	8–10 minutes at the start of class, preferably daily
Preparation Time	2 hours (writing the text, questions, and answer key)
	5 minutes (copying text/questions, progress graph, and answer key)
Resources	Speed reading texts graded to your students' level (i.e., for which students already know all or almost all of the words)
	Progress graph
	Answer key
	Online stopwatch, mobile devices with stopwatch function, or clock with second hand

Tertiary students usually need to develop their reading speed to be able to cope with hefty reading assignments they will encounter as they progress through their university careers. Grabe (2010) found that better reading fluency equates to better comprehension, so training students in this skill is essential. When my students mention their favorite activities in the initial class icebreaker, listening to music or making music is often on the list. Using speed reading texts specifically written for the second language learner about a topic they enjoy, music, seems like an ideal way to engage students' interest. Millett (2014) states that "all fluency development work aims to increase confidence through enjoyment and success at the task" (p. 64). Having a stock of interesting speed reading texts at the appropriate level that can be used regularly will help your students achieve the goal of improving reading fluency.

Fluency development should comprise approximately one quarter of a student's English language program (Nation, 2007). Nation describes the necessary elements in a fluency development "strand" for reading: They involve texts with already-known language, a focus on meaning, an element of time pressure, and a lot of input (2007, p. 7).

At Victoria University in Wellington, English language classes often begin with "quick skills," where students put to use the knowledge they already have. Of course, one of the quick skills is speed reading, for which Millett (2005) has written a number of speed reading texts, most comprising twenty 400- to 550-word texts, geared to different levels. These books are freely available online (See Millett, 2005). The main criteria are that the activity be quick (finished in around 8–10 minutes), easy (not containing many/any unknown words), intensive (preferably done every day), isolated (not used for other activities), and motivating (students record their results on a graph and can see their progress; Millett, 2008).

I invite you to be a part of creating a set of speed reading texts about music available online to teachers who want to incorporate music in their classrooms. The subjects of the speed reading music texts are only limited by your imagination. They could relate to musicians, popular songs, genres of music, instruments of various countries, one-hit wonders, music used at different festivals or ceremonies (e.g., "Pomp and Circumstance" at graduations and the "Wedding March" at weddings), carols at Christmas, national anthems, and the list goes on.

I've written one about "The Stars and Stripes Forever" by John Philip Sousa. It has an interesting back story with a quirky fact that may pique students' curiosity, and it is written with vocabulary almost entirely within the first 2,000 words of English. The results of a study on improving reading rates and comprehension by Chang and Millett (2013, p. 142) "suggest that [second language] learners' reading rates can improve more with materials that are specially written for training reading fluency." I hope you'll consider checking this book's website for more speed reading texts and then composing and adding one or more of your own.

So that reading speed can be consistently calculated, the texts should be the same length: 400 words, or very close to it. The vocabulary level needs to be consistent and appropriate for your students. I have written this text at the 2,000 word level. (Calculate this using the instructions in Sundberg's, Cardoso's, and Bione's activity in Part VI of this book, on vocabulary). The vocabulary of the texts should be high frequency and familiar; you should avoid complicated sentences, complex noun groups, passives, and difficult time references, and there should be "nothing to stop readers in their tracks" (Chang & Millett, 2013; Millett, 2014). The comprehension questions need to be written with these constraints in mind, too. The multiple-choice questions should check for understanding of the passage rather than for overly detailed information (Chang & Millett, 2013).

If you like this idea and write a suitable speed reading text and comprehension questions on a music-related topic, please send it to newwaysmusic@yahoo.com for inclusion on this book's website.

PROCEDURE

1. Copy the speed reading text and comprehension questions, front to back, for each student. If you plan to do this on an ongoing basis, print the progress graph and the answer key. (See appendices online)
2. Tell students they will be practicing speed reading. Give tips such as:
   - Don't use a finger or pen to follow along.
   - Move eyes quickly across the page and try to chunk words in groups, not read them in isolation.
   - Don't try to sound words out.

   Students will read as quickly as possible and, when finished, will write down the time it took to read the text. They will then turn the text over and answer the 10 comprehension questions without looking back at the text. They should write their responses on another sheet of paper so that these reading texts can be reused. (It's useful to put them in a protective plastic sleeve to help remind students not to mark on the sheet itself). If you use this as an ongoing activity with a number of texts, make and give students an answer key so they can quickly check how many questions they got correct. They then record the number of questions answered correctly and plot their reading time on the graph.

3. Before giving the text and questions to the students, tell students the title of the reading and ask them to predict what the story will be about. If they don't mention some key vocabulary, ask some questions to try to elicit those words, or explain terms that are likely to be unfamiliar. Be sure all words in the title are known. In "The Stars and Stripes Forever," *stripe, forever, marine, march, nickname,* and *circus* are not in the first 2,000 English word list. Other than these words, the vocabulary is all from the first 2,000 words. Remember, the focus is speed and fluency, not learning new things, so be sure the text is pitched to your students' level.

4. Display the stopwatch function of online-stopwatch.com or have students time themselves with their mobile devices, and pass out the sheet with the reading text and questions. Tell students not to look at the text or begin until everyone is ready. Say "Begin reading" and start the stopwatch.

5. The first time you do this in class, keep an eye on the students and make sure they write down the time it took them to read the text. You may need to remind students not to look back at the text while they are answering the questions.

6. When everyone is done reading and answering questions, make sure they record their time and the number of questions answered correctly on the progress graph. Students should aim to get 70–80% correct; if they are getting all the answers correct, they are reading too slowly (Nation, 2009, p. 141). If they're getting six or more questions wrong consistently, they're perhaps reading too quickly or they have another problem with reading.

7. Collect the sheets with the text and questions and go on with the rest of your lesson. Students keep their progress graphs and answer key.

CAVEATS AND OPTIONS

1. Millett (2005) recommends that these texts not become the focus of other activities during the 20 days of the speed reading program. However, the texts may be revisited later. Chang and Millett (2013) report that there are benefits of repeated reading, so feel free to use them again or build on them once the initial speed reading program is over. Tell students about the positive results of rereading the same texts and have them reread the texts as homework.

2. If students are having trouble forcing themselves to read faster, a brilliant program called Spreeder (www.spreeder.com) can be used in class or as homework. After doing Spreeder's introductory sample speed reading, you can copy and paste any text into this speed reading program, set the pace to double your base rate of reading, and experiment with different chunk sizes. Make these texts on music available to students online. If students read at 400 words per minute on Spreeder, each reading would just take 1 minute.

3. Use as listening practice. If you make an audio recording of this text, you could have students answer the same questions after listening to the recording.

4. If you have more advanced students or teachers-in-training, have them research a music-related topic and write a text and questions. Have them grade the language on Vocab Profiler (www.lextutor.ca/vp/eng) to make sure it's at a suitable level.

5. Typically, the reading text is not focused on again until the end of the speed reading series, if ever. However, if students would like to hear the song or singer that the text spoke of, you could play it in class or during a break.

6. For "The Stars and Stripes Forever" text, you can have students watch a short talk by a U.S. Marine Band conductor introducing the song with historical facts and then leading the band in playing it (www.youtube.com/watch?v=a-7XWhyvIpE).

REFERENCES AND FURTHER READING

Chang, A. C-S., & Millett, S. (2013). Improving reading rates and comprehension through timed repeated reading. *Reading in a Foreign Language, 25*(2), 126–148. Retrieved from http://nflrc.hawaii.edu/rfl/October2013/articles/chang.pdf

Grabe, W. (2010). Fluency in reading—Thirty-five years later. *Reading in a Foreign Language, 22*(1), 71–83.

Library of Congress. (n.d.). The stars and stripes forever. Retrieved from http://www.americaslibrary.gov/aa/sousa/aa_sousa_forever_3.html

Millett, S. (2005). New Zealand speed readings for ESL learners, Book One. ELI Occasional Publication No 19. Wellington: SLALS Victoria University of Wellington. Retrieved from http://www.victoria.ac.nz/lals/about/staff/publications/Bookoneall.pdf

Millett, S. (2008). A daily fluency programme: The key to using what you know. *Modern English Teacher, 17*(2), 21–28.

Millett, S. (2014). Quicklistens: Using what they already know. *Modern English Teacher, 23*(4), 64–65.

Nation, P. (2007). The four strands. *Innovation in Language Learning and Teaching, 1*(1), 1–11.

Nation, P. (2009). Reading faster. *International Journal of English Studies, 9*(2), 131–144.

APPENDIX A: *Sample Speed Reading Text*

1. "The Stars and Stripes Forever," by John Philip Sousa

John Philip Sousa was the leader of the U.S. Marine Band in the late 1800s. Under his leadership, the band became more and more popular. People called him *The March King*, because he wrote 136 marches. (A *march* is a type of music with a strong beat—soldiers can easily keep in step and walk together, or *march*, when they hear this kind of song.) The most popular of the marches Sousa wrote is called "The Stars and Stripes Forever." He wrote this march several years after he had retired from being leader of the band.

Sousa and his wife were on a long holiday in Europe when they read some sad news in the newspaper. Sousa's band manager had died. The Sousas decided to travel back to the United States and, on the ship, John kept hearing the strong beat of a band playing in his head. It just wouldn't stop, so he put pen to paper. While he was writing the song, Sousa was missing his home, but he was happily remembering his time as U.S. Marine Band leader and thinking about the flag flying over the White House. A nickname for the American flag is *The Stars and Stripes* because these are on the flag. Sousa said that when he was in a foreign country, the sight of *The Stars and Stripes* was the best thing in the world to him.

In 1897, John Philip Sousa first played this song at a concert in Philadelphia. It was so popular with the crowd that he had to play it again to satisfy them, and even a third time! In 1987, "The Stars and Stripes Forever" became the national march of the USA. This quick, spirited march is often heard on the Fourth of July. It is also often played after the U.S. president gives a speech.

People usually love hearing this cheerful song, but there is one place where you would never want to hear it—at a circus. In show business, especially the circus and theater, another name for this song is *The Disaster March*. If circus workers hear it being played, they know something bad is happening. This is a signal for them to get all the people out of the circus tents or away from danger. The book and movie *Water for Elephants* has such a scene where the band plays "The Stars and Stripes Forever." (401 words)

Time _____   Score _____

APPENDIX B: *Sample Comprehension Questions*

1. "The Stars and Stripes Forever," by John Philip Sousa

1. John Philip Sousa led the
   a. U.S. Air Force Band
   b. U.S. Marine Band
   c. U.S. Army Band

2. He got his nickname for writing many
   a. marches
   b. waltzes
   c. concerts

3. Music to which soldiers can easily walk is called
   a. popular music
   b. a march
   c. progressive music

4. Sousa wrote "The Stars and Stripes Forever"
   a. the year he retired as band leader
   b. years after he retired
   c. in 1987
5. When he sat down to write the song,
   a. he already heard it in his head
   b. he had no idea what it would sound like
   c. he didn't want to stop
6. *The Stars and Stripes* is a nickname for
   a. John Philip Sousa
   b. disasters
   c. the American flag
7. This song is often played
   a. after the U.S. president makes a speech
   b. on New Year's Day
   c. on Christmas Day
8. The first time this song was performed in public, the band had to play it
   a. one time
   b. two times
   c. three times
9. The song's nickname among circus people is
   a. *The President's Song*
   b. *The Disaster March*
   c. *Water for Elephants March*
10. At the circus, this song is played when
    a. the show begins
    b. the elephants come in
    c. there is a problem

Go to www.tesol.org/teachingwithmusic to access progress graph, answer key and additional speed reading texts.

In Other Words

Tamara Guy

Levels	Intermediate to advanced
Aims	Practice paraphrasing
Class Time	≈ 1 hour
Preparation Time	15–30 minutes
Resources	Handout of the lyrics of multiple national anthems
	Audio recording of anthem

Using music is a soft introduction to paraphrasing because most people are comfortable working with music. National anthems are seen as sacred, so the ability to keep the meaning of the text will be very important. This is a great method to emphasize the importance of retaining the meaning of original text in paraphrasing.

PROCEDURE

1. Put students in groups of three or four. For fun, have them choose a team name and then write it on the board.
2. Draw columns to separate team names. In each team's column, label the parts of the song. For example: Section 1, Section 2, Chorus/Bridge.
3. Randomly give each team a copy of the English lyrics of a different national anthem. People on the same team will have the same song. Don't group nationalities together. You can use the song of a country not represented in your class.
4. Have students work together in their teams to paraphrase the anthem. Each person must write the paraphrase in his or her own book. Give them about 30 minutes to complete the activity. Be on hand to explain new words or idioms in the lyrics.
5. When time is up, have all teams stop writing.
6. Have teams exchange their paraphrased work and a copy of the original lyrics with a different team. The opposite team will grade the quality of each paraphrased stanza (A = excellent, B = good, C = okay, D = missed the meaning/too confusing). They will write the grade for the corresponding section on the board under the team's column.
7. After the grades are written on the board, each team will explain why it gave those grades. In looking at how to improve a paraphrase, they must read a particular line in the paraphrase they didn't like and offer a solution for improving it. You should give feedback as well.
8. If there is time, you can have the students improve their paraphrases. Any grade lower than an A should be edited. You can also give the editing as a homework assignment.

CAVEATS AND OPTIONS

1. For listening and speaking practice, have the students read aloud their original lyrics, then read their paraphrased work before passing it to another team to be graded.

2. Also for listening and speaking practice, play the same audio aloud for everyone and have students write down the lyrics. They can work together and you can help them with corrections. Then they paraphrase as a team and read aloud their paraphrase.

3. Another option is to use popular songs that students love instead of anthems.

Paraphrase Match Me Up

Tamara Guy

Levels	Intermediate to advanced
Aims	Practice paraphrasing
Class Time	≈ 1 hour
Preparation Time	15–30 minutes
Resources	Handout of song lyrics
	Scissors

Being true to the original meaning of a text is crucial in effective paraphrasing. Trying to find a match for each stanza requires attention to detail. Because some songs can be repetitive with their ideas, it will be necessary for the students to take the time to compare the original to its paraphrase. This activity also ensures that students must understand the text before they paraphrase. The activity of cutting and matching also appeals to kinesthetic learners who may need some form of physical action to help them learn.

PROCEDURE

1. Put students in teams of three or four.
2. For fun, have each group choose a team name.
3. Give each team a different song. People on the same team will have the same song.
4. Have students work together in their teams to paraphrase their song and write their team's paraphrase on one sheet of paper. Give them about 30 minutes to complete the activity.
5. When time is up, have all teams stop writing.
6. Ask one person on the team to cut up the paraphrased version by verse or section.
7. Have teams exchange their paraphrased work (now cut up in sections) and the copy of the original with a different team.
8. After receiving another team's paraphrased lyrics in strips, along with the original lyrics, team members must now put the paraphrased strips in the correct song order. They should match the song section by section. Tell students to carefully compare the original lyrics to the paraphrase.
9. Give them about 15 minutes to do this. After time is up, a teammate or you can check to see if the matching order is correct.
10. Students can share what they thought of the other team's paraphrasing. They can also share what key words helped them match the texts correctly. You should share feedback as well.

CAVEATS AND OPTIONS

One option is to write the team names on the board in two columns, print out the original texts in a large size font, and tape them to the board under the name of the team that has that song. Explain to the teams that they will have to rush to the board to match the strips of the paraphrased lyrics with the original lyrics of another team's song. They can affix the strips next to the original with tape or magnets.

Identifying POVs

Tamara Jones

Levels	Intermediate to advanced
Aims	Practice identifying bias and point of view in texts
	Develop summarizing skills
Class Time	≈ 30 minutes
Preparation Time	15 minutes
Resources	A song that has lyrics containing at least two differing points of view
	Audiovisual equipment (optional)

Detecting bias in a text is a challenging skill for English as a second language and English as a foreign language readers. Students may not have experience critically evaluating texts in their first language (Fand, 1989). Additionally, they may lack the linguistic knowledge to understand implied messages in a text. However, detecting bias is an essential skill: Students who can access a text more critically comprehend it more thoroughly (Fahim, Bagherkazemi, & Alemi, 2010). This activity can provide a nonthreatening way to introduce students to critical thinking skills such as identifying bias in a text.

PROCEDURE

1. Select a song that contains at least two points of view of an event.
2. Give the students context or a brief synopsis of the situation if necessary. For instance, if you are using "Somebody That I Used to Know" by Gotye, you could say that the song is about a break up.
3. Provide each student a copy of the lyrics. Play the song or video clip in class.
4. Divide the class into two groups or several small groups. Assign each group a point of view. For instance, if you are using "Somebody That I Used to Know," one group or half of the groups would be responsible for summarizing the man's perspective of the break up, while the other half of the class would be responsible for summarizing the woman's perspective of the same event.
5. Then, play the song again. Give students time to work in their groups to create a brief text summarizing the way their person perceived the event described in the song. Encourage the groups to engage with the text to explain how they reached their conclusion. For instance, if summarizing the man's perspective in "Somebody That I Used to Know," students might point to the line when he talks about becoming addicted to sadness as evidence that he was not very happy when they were together.

6. Have the groups share their summaries with the class orally or write them on the board.

CAVEATS AND OPTIONS

Some songs that work well with this activity include:
- "Summer Nights," John Travolta and Olivia Newton John
- "Somebody That I Used to Know," Gotye
- "Give Me a Reason," Pink
- "Life Effect," Stars
- "All I Have," Jennifer Lopez and LL Cool J
- "Secret Love Song," Little Mix, featuring Jason Derulo

REFERENCES AND FURTHER READING

Fahim, M., Bagherkazemi, M., & Alemi, M. (2010). The relationship between test takers' critical thinking ability and their performance on the reading section of TOEFL. *Journal of Language Teaching and Research, 1*(6), 830–837.

Fand, R. J. (1989). Detecting bias in newspapers: Implications for teaching ESL. *Reading in a Foreign Language, 6*(1), 315–322.

An Interview With a Songwriter

Elena Shvidko

Levels	Intermediate to advanced
Aims	Understand the text by identifying the main ideas and the most important details
	Develop a critical perspective on the text
	Apply the information from the text to relevant situations in real life
Class Time	≈ 1 hour
Preparation Time	20–30 minutes
Resources	Audio recording of a song (preferably ballads or songs that tell a story)
	Handout of song lyrics

The ability to question the text is essential for becoming a strategic reader (Anderson, 1999, 2008; Grabe, 2009). This interactive activity allows students to practice questioning the text by developing and responding to "thin" (factual) and "thick" (inference) questions (Schacter, 2006, pp. 5–7) based on the lyrics of a song.

PROCEDURE

Part 1: Introduction (Presentation)

1. Before class, select an audio recording of a song. (See recommendations for song selection in Caveats and Options.) Also make a copy of the song lyrics for each student.

2. Introduce the concepts of "thin" and "thick" questions.

    - Thin (factual) questions are questions whose answers can be found in the text and that can be answered with a few words, phrases, or short sentences.

    - Thick (inference) questions are questions that readers have to think about more fully or even critically because the answers do not come solely from the text but from one's own knowledge. Unlike thin questions, answers to thick questions are open to argument. Nevertheless, despite one's own reasoning, the text should support the reader's answer.

    Example:

    Sentence from text: *If your friend is going through a difficult time, show them support by spending more time with them, listening to them with genuine care, expressing empathy, and just being there for them when they need you.*

    Thin question: *How can you show support to your friend?*

    Thick question: *Why is it important to nurture relationships, including friendship?*

3. Briefly explain that as a critical reading strategy, asking thin and thick questions helps the reader understand the message conveyed in the text and develops critical thinking.
4. Play the song. If necessary, explain difficult words or phrases.

Part 2: Practice

1. Put students in pairs. Give each student the copy of the lyrics.
2. Give students about 10 minutes to become familiar with the lyrics.
3. Tell students to imagine that they will interview the writer of this song (their classmate), and in order to do that, they will have to prepare several questions about the song.
4. Ask students to draw a T-chart with the labels "Thin Questions" on the left and "Thick Questions" on the right. In the left column, students should write three thin (factual) questions about the song. These questions can start with the question words *who*, *when*, *what*, or *where*. In the right column, tell students to write three thick (inference) questions.

"Thin" questions	"Thick" questions

5. When students are done with their questions, ask them to role-play the interview. One person will be the interviewer and the other one the interviewee. Then they switch, and the activity repeats. The interviewer should take notes on the interviewee's responses.
6. Ask each pair to share some of their questions and answers with the class. Thin questions (and answers) might repeat across student pairs; however, thick questions might be unique. Bring this phenomenon to students' attention and explain that text interpretation may vary across readers because of the differences in background knowledge, life experience, and other factors.

CAVEATS AND OPTIONS

1. You can further develop this activity into a writing task by asking students to compose a short report on the interview. The target skills in this activity can be summarizing, paraphrasing, quoting, and using direct and indirect speech.
2. Some examples of good songs for this activity:
   - "Another Day in Paradise," Phil Collins
   - "Love Story," Taylor Swift
   - "A Day in the Life," the Beatles

REFERENCES AND FURTHER READING

Anderson, N. J. (1999). *Exploring second language reading: Issues and strategies*. Boston, MA: Heinle & Heinle.

Anderson, N. J. (2008). *Practical English language teaching: Reading*. New York, NY: McGraw-Hill ESL/ELT.

Grabe, W. (2009). *Reading in a second language: Moving from theory to practice*. New York, NY: Cambridge University Press.

Schacter, J. (2006). *The master teacher series: Reading comprehension*. Stanford, CA: Teaching Doctors.

Part II

Music for Writing

Part II: Music for Writing

In this chapter, you'll find activities that help students identify genres of music—and then transfer the concept to identifying and producing genres of writing. Elena Shvidko shows how you can make connections and get students thinking about characteristics of writing that enable them to identify different genres. Several activities use lyrics for analysis and as writing prompts, primarily with the rhetorical modes of description and narration, including contributions by Ann Bouma, Lilika Couri, Sally La Luzerne-Oi, Emily Herrick, Jovana Milosavljevic Ardeljan, and Patrick T. Randolph.

There are also activities offering practice with the tools needed in these types of writing: Ann Bouma has a clever activity on figurative language, as does Nadezda Pimenova. Some very practical activities work with brainstorming and developing grammatically correct sentences, such as those by Tamara Jones and Lilika Couri. Tamara Jones has another activity to practice paraphrasing, and Emily Becketti and Jessica Sarles make use of songs in musicals to teach summarizing.

Haley P. Vickers and Jace Vickers show how to use opera to get lower level students to compare and contrast in addition to describing and narrating, and Alan S. Weber and Vincent Corver illustrate how students can research the music industry and write a formal report.

These 16 activities cover the five competencies for writers in English: "organizational, accuracy, grammatical structures, technical vocabulary, and style" (Murray & Christison, p. 121). These competencies are critical for postsecondary second language writers and need to be considered in the language classroom. We're sure that as you look these activities over, you'll discover ways in which the needs of your students can be met through the power of music.

Music as background is another interesting use of music in the language classroom. When students are writing in their reflective journals, filling out their weekly study plan, or discussing, we often put on music to match the task. Colleagues who have come in while the music was playing commented on the nice atmosphere in the room, and students have asked for the links to the music. Brewer (2008) found that her students seemed more focused on writing when listening to background music, and she also reports that a college professor who did an informal experiment in two sections of a creative writing class he taught "found that the students who wrote with background music *consistently* wrote twice as much as those without it" (p. 182). Authors vary greatly on this subject—some must write in silence, but for many, it's a way to block out distractions and remain focused on writing (King, 2000, p. 159). If your students aren't writing as fluently or as much as they need, see if music can add interest, either in the foreground or background of a lesson.

REFERENCES

Brewer, C. B. (2008). *Soundtracks for learning: Using music in the classroom.* Bellingham, WA: LifeSounds Educational Services.

King, S. (2000). *On writing: A memoir of the craft.* New York, NY: Scribner.

Murray, D. E., & Christison, M. (2011). *What English language teachers need to know. II: Facilitating learning.* New York, NY: Routledge.

Collaborative Storytelling

Tamara Jones

Levels	Beginner to intermediate
Aims	Develop writing skills
	Provide students with guided practice of target grammar
Class Time	≈ 30 minutes
Preparation Time	15 minutes
Resources	Clip of a music video that tells a story
	Audiovisual equipment

Many researchers tout the benefits of using collaboration in the writing classroom. Duin (1991) argues that collaboration gives writers self-confidence because it puts a difficult task, such as retelling a story, within the reach of lower level learners. In addition, Storch (2005) found collaborative writing tasks resulted in better organization and grammatical accuracy. Though, admittedly, this kind of guided collaborative writing is somewhat uncommunicative, students really do take pride in producing a polished text as a class, and they benefit enormously from this kind of focused copying (Low, 2006).

PROCEDURE

1. Select a music video that tells a story.
2. Play the video in class.
3. Start playing the music video again. Pause after a few seconds. Call on a student to make a sentence containing the target grammar that describes what just happened in that part of the story. For instance, if you are using "Get Up," by Bingo Players, and you are working on time adverb connectors, after the first few scenes of the video, the student might say something like, "After the woman fed the ducks, they danced together."
4. Write the student's sentence on the board. If it is not grammatically accurate, elicit help from the other students to make it a correct sentence.
5. Have the students copy the correct sentence into their notebooks.
6. Continue playing the video and having students create and then copy sentences about the story until it has been retold. Then, read the story aloud as a class.

CAVEATS AND OPTIONS

Some music videos that work well with this activity include:
- "Goodbye Earl," The Dixie Chicks
- "Waiting All Night," Rudimental
- "Get Up," Bingo Players
- "Hall of Fame," The Script
- "My Heart Will Go on," Celine Dion
- "Roar," Katy Perry
- "Thriller," Michael Jackson
- "Telephone," Lady Gaga and Beyoncé

REFERENCES AND FURTHER READING

Duin, A. H. (1991). Computer-supported collaborative writing: The workplace and the writing classroom. *Journal of Business and Technical Communication, 5*(2) 123–150.

Low, G. (2006, April). *Intervening in "hopeless" writing.* Paper presented at the meeting of Teachers of English to Speakers of Other Languages, Tampa, FL.

Storch, N. (2005). Collaborative writing: Product, process, and students' reflections. *Journal of Second Language Writing, 14*(3), 153–173.

Opera for English

Haley P. Vickers and Jace Vickers

Levels	High beginner to high intermediate
Aims	Develop descriptive, compare-contrast, and narrative modes of writing
	Develop higher order thinking skills
	Develop descriptive vocabulary
Class Time	30–50 minutes (dependent on number of students)
Preparation Time	15–20 minutes
Resources	Operatic arias with plot and dialogue
	Audiovisual equipment
	Listening/speaking software (e.g., VoiceThread, Audacity)

By using one of the five senses (hearing), students can draw from their own background knowledge to create descriptors for operatic music. In so doing, students encounter descriptive words and want to create meaning in the target language firsthand, which helps them to remember and know how to use these words more forcefully. This activity also exposes students to a genre that they might not have otherwise come into contact with, and it provides speaking practice with a partner.

PROCEDURE

1. Choose a duet or trio opera aria not in the students' native languages or the target language. Preferably, choose duo and/or trio arias; a suggested aria is the Don Giovanni/Zerlina duet from *Don Giovanni* (see Appendix).
2. Students listen and write descriptive words that describe the piece.
3. With a partner, students use their word lists to create a story about what might be occurring in the piece.
4. Pairs orally share their stories with the class.
5. At the end, the teacher describes to students the actual situation of the opera (either visually by using images on slide software or by simply reading the plot and/or dialogue in English).
6. For reflection or as a homework assignment, students orally or in written form compare and contrast their stories with the actual story.

CAVEATS AND OPTIONS

1. Instead of creating a story, students could also develop conversations if they are learning dialogue.
2. Ask students to use a certain grammar structure when creating their stories or in their reflections.
3. For the homework assignment, have students record themselves using listening/speaking software to share with classmates.

APPENDIX: *Further Information*

Link to Don Giovanni/Zerlina duet: goo.gl/0tyFph

Story behind Don Giovanni/Zerlina duet: Don Giovanni (male singer) first meets Zerlina (female singer) and her husband-to-be, Masetto. Masetto leaves, and the aria consists of Don Giovanni attempting to seduce Zerlina. Don Giovanni invites Zerlina to his castle, but ultimately returns home alone (Cantoni & Schwarm, 2017)

Opera aria resource websites that can be used to find arias and plots/libretti:

Aria Database: www.aria-database.com

Aria Lyrics and Translations: classicalmusic.about.com/od/classicalmusictips/

VoiceThread.com is software that uses different forms of media (e.g., PowerPoint slides, pictures, videos) to provide communication among groups of people. It is often used in classroom settings, where a teacher can create a PowerPoint slide or picture and ask students to discuss remotely.

Reference

Cantoni, L., & Schwarm, B. (2017). Don Giovanni. In *Encyclopædia Britannica*. Retrieved from http://www.britannica.com/topic/Don-Giovanni-opera-by-Mozart

Emotional Involvement: Using Music as the Writing Muse

Patrick T. Randolph

Levels	High beginner to advanced
Aims	Develop descriptive and narrative writing proficiency
	Enhance creative and critical thinking skills
	Teach attentiveness to emotion and music as critically important tools in the writing process
Class Time	50 minutes–1 hour
Preparation Time	10–15 minutes
Resources	Instrumental music (see Caveats and Options) or any of the artists from the Windham Hill music label

Music is one of the most natural phenomena that inspires the brain and nervous system to feel, create, and move. In fact, "Musical instruments are among the oldest human-made artifacts we have found" (Levitin, 2007, p. 256). The human brain reacts to music in a positive and creative way; thus, it can help our students voice their inner feelings and responses, and organize these effectively in the written word. Moreover, instrumental music allows students to be more creative as they are responding only to the sounds of instruments. If students listen to music with lyrics, they might be influenced by the words and mimic the story in the song rather than creating their own story (Randolph, 2011).

This music-inspired writing activity commences with using music and emotion as its starting point in a very inspirational and natural way. Music and emotion are natural tools and attributes of the human brain and the human spirit (Levitin, 2007). Students react to these attributes positively and are less inhibited to write and create; they are consequently able to develop simple descriptions or narratives in a confident, clear, and controlled manner.

PROCEDURE

1. Choose a relatively short (2- to 4-minute) piece of instrumental music and play it for your students. Explain to them that they are not to write anything down; they only need to listen to the music, to let it "move" them. Ask them to visualize a scene in their minds as they listen to the music.

2. Next, after listening to the piece, have the students pair up and explain to their partner what they felt and saw while listening to the music. What scenes or stories played out in their mind's eye? It's important to note that having them orally discuss what images they see or what emotions they feel will help later in the actual writing process.

3. After the discussions, have the students open their notebooks.

4. Now, play the instrumental piece of music again, and have the students write down what they see in their imagination as the music plays. Play the piece a few more times as the students write their descriptions or personal narratives. Give the students 15–20 minutes to write. Of course, you can use more time if needed.

5. Next, play the piece at a very low volume and have the students read their written descriptions/narratives to their neighbors or the partner with whom they paired up for the discussion part of this activity.

6. As homework, have the students rewrite their work and add details so that it becomes a 300- to 400-word story about the music-inspired, imagined scenes. This will give them the opportunity to elaborate on their description or their personal narrative.

7. Collect these stories the next day and read two to three to the class. Reading these to the class legitimizes the students' writings and helps build a sense of student confidence and self-worth.

CAVEATS AND OPTIONS

1. When selecting music, typically the soundtracks from romantic comedies or dramas are very inspirational. For example, music from *Dan in Real Life* (2007), *About Time* (2013), *The Holiday* (2006), or *Love Actually* (2003).

2. Teach students how to write and use dialog so that they can add that element to their stories, especially if they are writing narratives.

3. Have students write narrative poems instead of narrative short stories.

REFERENCES AND FURTHER READING

Levitin, D. J. (2007). *This is your brain on music*. New York, NY: Plume.

Randolph, P. T. (2011). Using music and photos to jumpstart neuro-technology. *ITBE Newsletter 39*(3).

Music and Word-Go-Round

Lilika Couri

Levels	Low intermediate to advanced
Aims	Brainstorm and generate ideas for writing sentences that can develop into collective stories
Class Time	30–50 minutes
Preparation Time	≈ 10 minutes
Resources	Any piece of instrumental music that is not well known

Sentence writing and sentence structure are the basis of correct writing. Often, however, sentence writing becomes a boring activity for our students, especially for teenagers—and even adults. The use of music enables students to relax and forget they are doing a class chore, and thus, to brainstorm and complete their writing task.

PROCEDURE

1. Group students into fives, and have each group sit in a circle.
2. Have each student write his or her name at the top of a blank piece of paper.
3. Ask students to listen to the music you have selected and to write one word on the piece of paper. It can be a word expressing a feeling, thought, or reaction to the music.
4. Pause the music and ask your students to pass their paper to the person on their right.
5. Start the music again and students now write a new word on the piece of paper they have been given. Then they pass the paper to the person on their right. The words should be written as a list from top to bottom.
6. Continue this procedure five times, until each student has his or her original paper.
7. Listening to the same piece of music again, the students write as many sentences as they can with the words on their paper for 10–15 minutes.
8. Report back: Individual students read their sentences to the class or in small groups.

CAVEATS AND OPTIONS

1. In pairs or groups, students share and compare/contrast their words and sentences.
2. In pairs, students see if they can combine their sentences and create a dialogue or tell a story.

"Life's a Happy Song": Figurative Language

Ann Bouma

Levels	Intermediate to advanced
Aims	Expose students to similes, metaphors, and idioms
Class Time	50 minutes
Preparation Time	15 minutes
Resources	Video or audio recording of "Life's a Happy Song," by Bret McKenzie, from The Muppets movie
	Handout of song lyrics
	Information on or an introduction to figurative language
	Audiovisual equipment (optional)

Figurative language is often hard for students to use in their writing. Idioms are especially difficult because translations don't make sense in other languages. Exposure to figurative language gives students more confidence to use idioms.

PROCEDURE

1. Print a copy of the lyrics of "Life's a Happy Song" for each student. Find an audio or video recording to play for the students.
2. Discuss similes, metaphors, and idioms and how to identify them.
3. Play the song for the students and discuss the meaning of the lyrics. Talk about any vocabulary words that the students need defined.
4. Hand out the lyrics and ask the students to underline all of the metaphors and circle the similes.
5. Check to see if the students found and understood the difference.
6. Ask the students as a class to find all of the idioms.
7. Stop and discuss what each idiom might imply (e.g., "feel like you're three feet tall" or "catch your fall").
8. As a class, brainstorm a list of abstract ideas like "love" or "happiness" that could be explained using similes and metaphors.
9. Then put the following up on the board as an example. "Love is____" and "Love is like a _____." Use an example of both metaphor and simile to help students start to write their own. For instance, "Love is a warm blanket" or "Love is like a new pair of shoes."
10. Have students write a metaphor and simile about one of the abstract ideas that the class brainstormed, or another idea of their choosing.

CAVEATS AND OPTIONS

1. Let the students illustrate their figurative language and make a class book or display their illustrations.

2. If you or your students are musically inclined, the class can make its own song using figurative language and record it for other classes.

Getting to Know You

Lilika Couri

Levels	Intermediate to advanced
Aims	Brainstorm and generate ideas to motivate students to write a descriptive paragraph
	Interpret feelings and raise students' emotional quotient
	Analyze characters
Class Time	30–50 minutes
Preparation Time	≈ 10 minutes
Resources	Any piece of instrumental music that is not well known
	A small box (a shoe box will do)
	Blank flashcards

Most English language students find it difficult to express themselves in writing and to create ideas. The use of music can help them learn to brainstorm and generate ideas and thus overcome their difficulty and, often, fear of writing.

PROCEDURE

1. Give each student a blank flashcard. Ask your students to choose a pen name (a jungle animal, a flower) and to write it on the top left-hand corner of the flashcard.

2. Tell your students they are going to listen to a piece of music. While listening, they should write on the flashcard any words (at least five or six) that express the ideas and/or feelings elicited by the music. You should participate as well.

3. Collect the flashcards from the students and put all of them in the box; mix them up and ask your students to take one each. If they draw their own, have them choose a different one.

4. Then, ask students to start writing a paragraph in which they describe the type of person who would choose these words while listening to this specific piece of music. Remind students to be kind and considerate as they are writing about their classmates. The paragraph could be a brief character analysis (a description of what the student believes the person is like: his or her temperament, personality, emotions, etc.) based on the choice of the words written as well as on the type of music listened to earlier. For example, the paragraph could start as follows: "X seems to be a romantic person who looks for beauty in life and believes in people's goodness, etc."

Tell the students that they do not have to use all or any of the words written on the flashcard. These words take the place of an outline or guide, so they can see or feel for themselves the picture(s) created in the mind of their fellow student or the emotions felt. (While writing the paragraph, students should be listening to the same piece of music). Set a 10-minute time limit.

5. When time is up, ask students to stop and proofread their text.
6. Report back options:
   a. Ask individual students to read the pen name and the words on the flashcard, and then their paragraph. They would then invite the "real" person to comment on the personality description their fellow student has written.
   b. Ask individual students to read the paragraph they have written and then ask the rest of the class to guess the words on the flashcard that helped their fellow student write this specific paragraph.

CAVEATS AND OPTIONS

Depending on your students' needs and/or interests, you may choose to use this activity as a public speaking activity rather than a writing one. In this case, your students will need at least 7 minutes to look at the words written on the flashcard and to think of their outline.

The Back Story

Emily Herrick

Levels	Intermediate to advanced
Aims	Develop narrative writing and critical thinking skills
	Develop an understanding of contextualizing a piece of writing
Class Time	30 minutes–1 hour
Preparation Time	10–30 minutes
Resources	Audio recording of any song
	An example of a back story you wrote about the song (optional)
	Transcript of the lyrics (optional)

PROCEDURE

1. Select an audio recording of a popular song and, optionally, write a short back story about the song that you can share with the class.
2. Play the song in class and discuss the meaning of the lyrics. To ensure comprehension, students can read the lyrics along with the audio.
3. Provide students with an example of a short back story using the story you created. Explain that the back story could be something about the life of the songwriter, or it could be a story about the people mentioned in the song. For example, if you played Meghan Trainor's 2015 hit, "All About That Bass," students could write a story about the songwriter's experience with weight, write about why the mama in the song gave that advice to her daughter, or discuss issues related to obesity and self-image.
4. Give students 15–20 minutes to write their own back story.
5. Students can share their stories in small groups or with the class.

CAVEATS AND OPTIONS

1. Nearly any popular song can serve as a writing prompt for students to create a narrative back story. Variations on this activity are nearly limitless because the text they create can be used as a draft for further writing practice.
2. Instead of an example that you write, a class discussion can serve as an effective method of introducing the concept of a back story.
3. If you would like to incorporate more speaking and listening practice, or help students develop collaborative writing skills, have students write their back stories in pairs or groups.
4. If available, provide students with the real back story: an explanation from the songwriter about the origins of the song.

Musical Paraphrasing

Tamara Jones

Levels	Intermediate to advanced
Aims	*Provide students with guided practice paraphrasing targeted grammatical structures through restructuring*
Class Time	*≈ 30 minutes*
Preparation Time	*30 minutes*
Resources	*Song or music video (lyrics must contain several examples of the target structure)*
	Audiovisual equipment

Summarizing texts is a notoriously difficult, yet essential, skill for English learners. One important component of summarizing is paraphrasing. Students need to be adept with reformatting grammatical structures if they are to avoid plagiarizing the original text (Maxwell, Curtis, & Vardanega, 2008). Paraphrasing involves more than using synonyms for words in the text; students often need to transform the grammar of the text, changing the voice from active to passive, for instance. This "tax[es] their language proficiency and linguistic flexibility" (Leki & Carson, 1997, p. 59). Therefore, English learners need a lot of practice manipulating target grammar whenever they learn a new structure.

PROCEDURE

1. Select a song that contains several examples of the target structure. This activity works especially well if you use a clip of the song that contains the transcribed lyrics on the screen. If such a clip does not exist, or if you're using an audio file, prepare a handout with the song lyrics.

2. Play the song or video clip in class. If necessary, give each student a copy of the lyrics and write a bank of target grammar structure prompts on the board. For example, if you are reviewing the conditional, you might write prompts such as: *if*, *unless*, *provided that*, *as long as*, *whether*, and *otherwise*.

3. Play the song again. Pause once the target grammar occurs. For instance, if you are having students practice restructuring the conditional and you are using Passenger's song, "Let Her Go," you might pause after the line, "Well you only need the light when it's burning low."

4. Call on a student to restate the sentence using a different form of the conditional. For instance, the student might say, "If the light is burning low, you need it," or "When the light burns low, you need it."

5. Write the student's sentence on the board. If it is not grammatically correct, elicit help from the other students to make it an accurate sentence.

6. Continue playing the video and having students restructure the sentences that contain the target structures.

CAVEATS AND OPTIONS

1. Some songs that work well with this activity include:
   - "Let Her Go," Passenger (conditional)
   - "If I Were a Boy," Beyoncé (conditional)
   - "Moves Like Jagger," Maroon 5 (conditional)
   - "Parents Just Don't Understand," DJ Jazzy Jeff and the Fresh Prince (reported speech)
   - "Blow Me One Last Kiss," Pink (subjunctive)
2. Remind students that transposing clauses is only one step in the process of strong paraphrasing. If students become comfortable with this step, consider having them use synonyms as well.

REFERENCES AND FURTHER READING

Leki, I. & Carson, J. (1997). Completely different worlds: EAP and the writing experiences of ESL students in university courses. *TESOL Quarterly, 31*(1), 39–69.

Maxwell, A., Curtis, G. J., & Vardanega, L. (2008). Does culture influence understanding and perceived seriousness of plagiarism? *International Journal for Educational Integrity, 4*(2), 25–40.

A Special Place

Sally La Luzerne-Oi

Levels	Intermediate to advanced
Aims	Observe and reflect on surroundings
	Write about a location using the five senses
	Compose detailed descriptive sentences
Class Time	2 hours (minimum)
Preparation Time	20 minutes
Resources	Audio recording of "What a Wonderful World," by Louis Armstrong
	Handout of song lyrics (optional)

This well-known song provides the springboard for place-based writing. The activity encourages students to reflect on and explore their surroundings, focus on detail, and develop descriptive language and writing.

PROCEDURE

1. Play the song. Have students do a task, for example follow the lyrics while listening, do a cloze activity with the lyrics, or take notes on what they hear.

2. Discuss why, according to this song, it is a wonderful world. What does the singer see, hear, watch?

3. Tell students their assignment is to carefully observe an area on campus, a street, a park, or other special place in your town. As they observe, they should write down as many sentences as possible to illustrate the place and the thoughts or questions the scene evokes. Tell students to think about the following prompts as they write.

    I see . . .

    I hear . . .

    I feel . . .

    I smell . . .

    I think . . .

    I wonder . . .

4. Choose a word or phrase to describe the overall scene. In the song, "wonderful world" is used. Other examples might be "peaceful park" or "colorful street."

5. When students have completed the assignment, ask them to share their description with a partner and get feedback. For example, can the listener imagine

what this place looks/sounds/smells like, or are more details needed? Does the writer's full description illustrate the single word or phrase chosen to describe the overall scene?

6. Encourage students to revise their descriptions where needed and to put their sentences to the music of "What a Wonderful World" or another song and share their composition with several classmates.

CAVEATS AND OPTIONS

1. Have students work with a partner or in small groups. One suggestion is to have the group members write individually about the same place. Afterward, they can compare their observations and reflections. They may need to negotiate as they decide on one description and how to deliver it.

2. For this activity, "Penny Lane," by the Beatles, works well with advanced students.

Telling Images

Jovana Milosavljevic Ardeljan

Levels	Intermediate to advanced
Aims	*Develop writing skills*
	Create stories and images in response to a music video
	Approach writing with more creative thinking/impulse
	Work more autonomously
Class Time	30–45 minutes
Preparation Time	10–15 minutes
Resources	*Adele's music video for "Hello"*
	An example of narrated video (e.g., Sir David Attenborough narrating Adele's video)
	A computer with Internet access (or a downloaded video)
	Audiovisual equipment

Both practice and research have shown that incorporating music in teaching languages helps students with pronunciation, grammar, vocabulary, and listening. Therefore, it is not a surprise that many language exercises involve music (e.g., karaoke, filling in lyric gaps, rhymes). However, there has not been much research or many examples of exercises in which music is incorporated to help students write. As Newkirk (2014) says in his book *Minds Made for Stories,* students need to learn to turn everything into a story. Music, lyrics, and video can all inspire a story.

Having students watch a music video helps them to get ideas and use their imagination to build on what they saw. Furthermore, this activity gives students tools to overcome the issue of not knowing what to write about; at the same time, it provides space for them to create their own images through writing. The exercise is structured enough to provide students with guidelines and a model while allowing them to approach it in any way that they find to be best for them. The narrated video shows them how a music video can be turned into a story, but they have the freedom to explore different genres and create any kind of story they want.

PROCEDURE

1. Before you play the beginning of Adele's video, "Hello" (both the video and the narrated version can be found on YouTube), ask students to pay close attention to what is happening in the video, along with attention to details. Inform the students that you will ask them to talk about the video afterward. Play the first 2 minutes of the video.

2. Ask students to tell you what they recall seeing; and as they share, write down on the board as many ideas/images/explanations as you can.

3. Play the video of Sir David Attenborough narrating Adele's video. This will give students an opportunity to see and hear how someone narrated what they just watched.

4. Play it twice if necessary.

5. Point out the words/images/details that students shared and that were also used in the narrated video.

6. Ask students to continue narrating the video on their own. They can play it on their phones for themselves or you can continue playing it for the class.

CAVEATS AND OPTIONS

1. Students might dislike the activity if they do not like the song/video. Therefore, you may want to find out what songs and videos they are interested in.

2. Have students write a poem inspired by a video, instead.

REFERENCES AND FURTHER READING

Newkirk, T. (2014). *Minds made for stories.* Portsmouth, NH: Heinemann.

Want to Be a Songwriter?

Nadezda Pimenova

Levels	Intermediate to advanced
Aims	Help students develop an understanding of figurative language in songs
	Practice figurative writing
Class Time	45–50 minutes
Preparation Time	15–20 minutes
Resources	A classroom computer with Internet access
	Audiovisual equipment (optional) or handout of song lyrics

Songs are excellent resources in teaching English language students because songs provide examples of informal language (Schoepp, 2001) that has metaphors, similes, idioms, and other figures of speech. A number of English language instructors utilize activities involving rewriting lyrics and writing responses to songs.

PROCEDURE

1. Surf the Internet for a song whose lyrics contain figurative language. (For a list of suggested songs, see Appendix A.)
2. Play the selected song in class and ask students what they understood the song was about.
3. Project the song's lyrics on a screen, write them on the board, or give a copy of the lyrics to each student.
4. Discuss the meaning of the lyrics and draw students' attention to figurative language used in the song. Be sure to emphasize that figurative language creates powerful images. (For a list of examples of figurative language in songs, see Appendix B.)
5. Play the selected song in class again and ask students to sing or read along.
6. Ask students to think of any figurative language that can be used to express the same ideas in the song.
7. Model by writing a few lines. For example:
    a. "Angel in Blue Jeans," by Train: And though I rode a different road / And sang a different song / I'll love her till my last breath's gone.
    b. Your version: And though I rode a different road / And had different rules to live by / I'll love her till oceans go dry.

   Draw their attention to the fact that after you replaced a hyperbole, you changed the lyrics to rhyme.

8. Split students into groups of three, or ask them to work in pairs, and give them 10–15 minutes to write their own versions using at least one new expression.

CAVEATS AND OPTIONS

1. After students write their versions by replacing a simile, a metaphor, or another figurative expression from the original, they can share their work with the rest of the class.
2. Have students vote for the best lyrics.

REFERENCES AND FURTHER READING

Bjorklund, K. S. (2002). *Music application in the ESL classroom* (Master's thesis). Retrieved from ProQuest Dissertations and Theses. (Publication number EP24569)

Schoepp, K., (2001). Reasons for using songs in the ESL/EFL classroom. *The Internet TESL Journal*, 7(2). Retrieved from http://iteslj.org/Articles/Schoepp-Songs.html

APPENDIX A: *Recommended Songs*

- "Angel in Blue Jeans," Train
- "Drop in the Ocean," OMI featuring AronChupa
- "Fight Song," Rachel Platten
- "Firework," Katy Perry
- "Fuss About Nothin'," Ian Hunter
- "Glitterball," Sigma featuring Ella Henderson
- "History," One Direction
- "Little Liar," Paper Lions
- "Love the Way You Lie," Eminem [Editor's note: Preview lyrics for appropriateness for your class.]
- "Make a Wave," Demi Lovato and Joe Jonas
- "Nothing Can Stop Me Now," Mark Holman
- "Soft Touch / Raw Nerve," Depeche Mode
- "The Last Straw," Warrant
- "True Colors," Zedd and Kesha

APPENDIX B: *Figurative Language*

Metaphors

- Darling can't you see that *I'm your whole wide world* and *he's a drop in the ocean*? ("Drop in the Ocean")
- *This world is a ball with a map on* ("Fuss About Nothin'")

Similes

- *Like a small boat* / On the ocean / Sending big waves / Into motion ("Fight Song")
- Do you ever *feel like a plastic bag* / Drifting through the wind, wanting to start again? ("Firework")

Idioms

- I lost my patience in dealing with you / *That's the last straw* ("The Last Straw")
- You better run you little liar / If I get you, *we're even* ("Little Liar")

Personification

What we thought we knew has been *swallowed by the truth* ("True Colors")

Verbal Irony

Just gonna stand there and hear me cry / *But that's alright, because I love the way you lie* ("Love the Way You Lie")

Hyperbole

- *Nothing can stop me now* ("Nothing Can Stop Me Now")
- So don't let it go, we can make some more, *we can live forever* ("History")

Don't Mess With Genres!

Elena Shvidko

Levels	Intermediate to advanced
Aims	Raise awareness of genre conventions
	Understand the interconnectedness of genre with other writing components such as content, organization, language, and rhetorical strategies
Class Time	45 minutes–1 hour
Preparation Time	20–30 minutes
Resources	A few songs or pieces of music from several genres (at least 1 instrumental and 1 lyric song; see Caveats and Options for requirements and suggestions)

The concept of genre may be challenging for writers, particularly for language learners. Sometimes students struggle differentiating between various genres and find it difficult to appropriately follow genre conventions in their writing. By demonstrating the concept of genre through music, this activity raises students' awareness of genre requirements and helps students see the relationship between genre and other components of writing.

PROCEDURE

Part 1: Presentation

1. On the board, write the names of several music genres. Examples: country, pop, hip-hop, hard rock, love ballads, lullabies. For more examples of music genres, visit www.musicgenreslist.com or www.allmusic.com/genres.

2. Ask students to name some of the identifying characteristics of these music genres. To facilitate the brainstorming and to help students come up with the genre characteristics, ask them prompting questions:
    - What instruments are typical for this genre?
    - What emotional content is common in this genre?
    - What is the vocal style?
    - What kind of rhythm is common in this genre?
    - What kinds of lyrics are typical for the songs of this genre?

3. Write their responses on the board. For example:

Hard Rock	Love ballads	Pop	Lullabies
• aggressive vocals • loud volume and intensity • complex and fast rhythm • social, political, or violent lyrics	• soft and slow rhythm • romantic lyrics (love, feelings, and relationships) • appealing to audience's emotions	• catchy lyrics • simple themes • dance-oriented rhythm • appealing to a general audience	• soft, quiet, and mellow • slow tempo • melodious and harmonious • simple lyrics

4. For each of these genres, play a 10- to 15-second excerpt from the musical pieces you prepared.
5. Explain that each of these pieces has at least some characteristics typical for their genre and that, most of the time, an audience can identify the genre based on the underlying characteristics of a song. For example, when we hear the song "My Heart Will Go On" by Celine Dion, we know it's a love song because it has the features that are typical for this particular genre.

Part 2: Practice

1. Put students in small groups and ask them to briefly discuss the following questions (2–3 minutes): What would happen if the identifying characteristics in the chart above are not followed? For example, what happens if we switch the names of the first and the second genre categories in the chart? Allow students to share their thoughts.
2. Play the love song you selected. Give students a copy of the lyrics.
3. Tell students to think about what would happen if the same lyrics were used with different music. How effectively would the song fulfill its purpose? What would be the audience's reactions?
4. Play the instrumental piece you selected and ask students to think of/read the lyrics of the love song as you are playing the instrumental piece. For example, if the selected love song is "My Heart Will Go On" by Celine Dion and the instrumental piece is "To Live Is to Die" by Metallica, students will read the lyrics of the love song while you are playing Metallica for them.
5. Ask students to share their thoughts.

Part 3: Application

1. Explain that writing genres (e.g., grant proposals, emails, memoirs, business memos) have specific conventions that writers are expected to follow. For example, certain writing genres require formal language and objective information; in others, the writer is expected to use personal examples and informal word choice. If time allows, you can expand this part by explaining how particular components of writing are affected by the writer's choice of the genre.

Example

- Language (e.g., formal language used in business emails)
- Organization (e.g., proposals usually identify a problem and then offer a solution)
- Strategies (e.g., lab reports describe a process)
- Content (e.g., college papers commonly require the use of researched source material)

2. Reiterate the importance of following genre conventions in writing and discuss some of the consequences when the writer fails to observe the conventions.

CAVEATS AND OPTIONS

1. Song selection:

Requirements

- One piece of music for this activity should be instrumental (e.g., "Orion" or "To Live is to Die," by Metallica).
- One piece in your selection should be a song with relatively easy and straightforward lyrics. For the purpose of this activity, pop songs about love work best (e.g., "My Heart Will Go On," by Celine Dion; "I Will Always Love You," by Whitney Houston; "In this Life," by Collin Raye).
- The instrumental piece and the song should belong to separate genres.

Recommendations

- Select the pieces that best represent their particular genre. For example, "I Want to Hold Your Hand" by the Beatles is a classic example of a rock and roll song.

2. Select famous songs—the ones that your students would most likely be familiar with.
3. With more advanced learners, you can expand this activity by explaining how genre is interconnected with the other components of rhetorical situation: purpose, audience, tone, and medium.

REFERENCES AND FURTHER READING

Bullock, R. H. (2013). *The Norton field guide to writing (3rd ed.)*. New York, NY: W. W. Norton & Company.

Writing a Report: Music in Koolistan

Alan S. Weber and Vincent Corver

Levels	Intermediate to advanced
Aims	Develop report writing (formal discourse), public speaking, and critical/analytical skills
	Produce 2–3 pages of revised formal writing
Class Time	≈ two 45- to 60-minute class periods
Preparation Time	1 hour
Resources	Background information on the music industry (see References and Further Reading)

This activity requires the following skills: oral discussion, critical thinking, group collaboration (brainstorming), multiple-draft writing, and public speaking. Students are encouraged to explore the political, social, economic, and cultural dimensions of music, as well as the role of governments in music education and development (censorship, market regulation, preserving traditional music, encouraging national content). The class may additionally debate different national economic models, such as free markets, socialism, and mixed and planned economies.

PROCEDURE

Class 1

1. Explain to students that they will write a short report called *The National Music Vision of Koolistan* on a hypothetical scenario: They have been appointed Minister of Music of Koolistan and their task is to develop and regulate the music industry to satisfy the citizens, musicians, and music companies. Students can invent the musical, political, and social history of the country.

2. Lead a 15-minute combined lecture/discussion on how music is currently created, distributed, and sold, and the role of government support of the arts (heritage preservation, music education, etc.).

3. In small groups, students discuss the elements of their national music plan for 15 minutes and write down their ideas in bullet-point form. Although collaborative work is encouraged at all stages, each student is responsible for writing an individual report in his or her own words.

4. Students write a draft of their report for 15 minutes.

5. Students may continue to work on their report outside of class with peer tutors or peer reviewers or in consultation with the instructor during office hours.

Class 2

1. Students engage in one-on-one or small-group peer review for 15 minutes by exchanging papers and discussing them. After peer review, students revise silently in class for 15 minutes while preparing notes for a 5-minute oral presentation of their ideas.

2. Randomly choose three students to give 5-minute presentations their individual music plans (suggested 3 minutes speaking time and 2 minutes Q&A).

3. Outside of class, students revise their papers based on peer feedback and then submit the final assignment.

CAVEATS AND OPTIONS

1. You should do 1 hour of background reading on the music industry and be familiar with basic concepts, such as music education, royalties, music copyright, and streaming audio revenues. These resources may be distributed to students as well.

2. You may also wish to provide a brief government report as a template.

3. The activity can be shortened to a one-class discussion and in-class writing exercise.

4. The project can also be extended to a 2- to 3-week multisource guided research paper in which you gather background reading materials on the music industry and students additionally search for reliable Internet sources (2–3 sources recommended). Instruction in proper citation, revision strategies, peer reviewing, and the multiple draft process should be incorporated into the longer assignment.

REFERENCES AND FURTHER READING

Gray, J. (2013). How does the music industry make money? *The New Economy*. Retrieved from http://www.theneweconomy.com/business/how-does-the-music-industry-make-money

Knopper, S. (2011). The new economics of the music industry: How artists really make money in the cloud—or don't. *Rolling Stone Magazine*. Retrieved from http://www.rollingstone.com/music/news/the-new-economics-of-the-music-industry-20111025

Australian Ministry for the Arts (2016). Music. Retrieved from http://arts.gov.au/music

Schneider, N. (2016). Getting played: The false promise of music opportunity sites. *The Bay Bridged*. Retrieved from http://thebaybridged.com/2015/04/28/getting-played-false-promise-music-opportunity-sites/

Woodworth, M., & Grossan, A. J. (Eds.). (2015). *How to write about music*. New York, NY: Bloomsbury.

Every Song Tells the Story: Using Musicals to Practice Summarizing

Emily Becketti and Jessica Sarles

Levels	High intermediate to advanced
Aims	Develop summarizing skills
Class Time	≈ 3 hours if video of musical is viewed outside of class; 5 hours if the musical is viewed during class.
Preparation Time	≈ 2 hours
Resources	Audio and video recording of a musical
	Visuals from selected musical
	Audiovisual equipment for each group, or student personal devices
	A/B cloze activities for each of four to five songs (teacher created)
	Graphic organizer of the timeline of the selected musical (teacher created)
	Large pieces of paper and the means to post them

Summarizing is a difficult skill to develop. One of the principal challenges is learning how to use one's own words and not copy from the text. Summarizing a song, rather than a reading passage, requires students to search for new language to describe the main point. The challenge of summarizing a long narrative is further scaffolded by practice summarizing shorter song narratives. Additionally, using musicals creates a high-interest task that stimulates student engagement. This activity can be split over multiple class sessions.

PROCEDURE

1. Select a musical with a straightforward, linear narrative; examples include *The Music Man*, *Oklahoma!*, *Oliver!*, and *The Little Mermaid*. Choose four or five songs from the musical that move the story forward. Using the song lyrics, create two different versions of a cloze (A and B) for each song, with key vocabulary indicated. [Working with two copies of the full lyrics side by side on the computer screen makes this a simple task]. Also create a graphic organizer that includes the show timeline. The timeline should include spaces for each song with prompts for students to fill in the following information:
    i. Who sings the song?
    ii. What does he or she want, or what do they want?
    iii. What happens?

2. Make enough copies of the timeline for each student and enough copies of the cloze so that half of the students get cloze A and half receive cloze B.

3. Introduce the activity to the students and provide background information on the show by presenting photographs of the sets and characters. Play the overture. Talk about mood. Ask students to make predictions about what might happen in the story. During this presentation, draw a timeline of the narrative arc on the board. Mark the inciting incident of the story, but don't fill in the events in detail. (25 minutes)

4. Divide the class into small groups. Assign each group one song. Tell the students which characters are singing. Each group will listen to their assigned song and complete the following activities:

   a. Listening and Cloze Completion. Students listen and complete the cloze, then compare with each other to check their work and come up with the complete song lyrics. (20 minutes)

   b. Vocabulary Work. On the cloze worksheets, identify and mark key vocabulary from the song. Groups will discuss and make sure they understand the meaning of the key words. (20 minutes)

   c. Comprehension Focus. Students answer the following questions to help them identify the main idea and key points of the song.

      i. Who are the main characters?

      ii. What do the characters want?

      iii. Is there a problem or a decision that needs to be made?

      iv. Is the problem resolved or the decision made? What is the resolution? (10–15 minutes)

5. Students then use the answers to the questions to write a one- to three-sentence summary of the song. Example:

   > In "Food, Glorious Food" from *Oliver!*, Oliver Twist and other orphans want to have something delicious to eat. They decide to make Oliver ask for more food. When he asks for more, the caretakers of the workhouse become angry and make him leave.

   Have students write their summary on a large piece of paper that can be attached to the board. (30 minutes)

6. Give each student a graphic organizer that has the same timeline you put on the board.

7. Each group presents its song by posting its summary in the correct spot on the timeline drawn on the board and reading it to the class. During each of these presentations, the rest of the class actively listens and fills in the information under each song on their copies of the timeline graphic organizer. After presenting their group's summary, they preteach the key vocabulary and play their song for the class. (1 hour)

8. Once all the groups have made their presentations, students can use the graphic organizer to draft a summary paragraph of the entire show. This can be done individually or as a whole class. It can also be done as homework if time is an issue. (30 minutes)

9. The class watches a recording of the musical and fills in any missing information on their timeline graphic organizer. Using their draft and the updated graphic organizer, students write a final summary paragraph of the show. Viewing the musical and writing a final summary can be completed in class, if time allows, or can be assigned as homework. (2.5 hours)

CAVEATS AND OPTIONS

1. Address multilevel needs by assigning students to groups based on the listening difficulty of the song (vocabulary, speed, length).
2. In small classes, assign songs to individual students rather than groups.
3. When selecting a musical, be aware of the variety of cultural expectations and sensitivities your students bring to the classroom. Knowing your students well will help you select a musical they will enjoy and that will be appropriate for the class.

Elements of a Narrative

Ann Bouma

Levels	Advanced
Aims	Develop an understanding of the elements found in a good narrative
	Use narrative elements in the writing of a personal narrative
Class Time	2–5 hours
Preparation Time	30 Minutes
Resources	Video of "Goodbye Earl" or another song illustrating a story
	Handout of song lyrics
	Audiovisual equipment
	Worksheets and graphic organizers for each student (see Appendices)

Writing narration requires students to understand that the purpose of narration is to illustrate how a character solves a problem and learns a lesson. The thesis of a narrative is the lesson that the protagonist learns. The rising action to the climax lends excitement to the narrative. These elements are often forgotten when attempting to write in a new language. Reminding the students of these elements helps them create a richer narrative. Additionally, learning that the thesis or theme of the narration is often given at the end of a piece of writing rather than in the introduction is also a skill that will help the students become more effective readers of narratives and short stories. Having the students record their narrative with music and pictures reinforces these skills and offers an alternative method of assessment.

PROCEDURE

1. Make copies of the handouts for your class. Make sure a video of the song is available (on YouTube or other media that you can use in class).

2. Go over the vocabulary used to discuss a narrative. As a peer dictation, have the students define the terms on the "Elements of Narrative: Vocabulary" worksheet (Appendix A) or give as a handout with terms already defined. (20 minutes)

3. Give students a copy of the "Elements of Narrative: Graphic Organizer" (Appendix B). Go over the parts: lead, background, rising action, climax, falling action, and resolution. Make sure the students understand the vocabulary. (20 minutes)

4. Watch the video in class. Hand out the lyrics and discuss the meaning of any lyrics that the students have questions about. Watch the video again. (10 minutes)

5. Have the students fill in the information that illustrates each of the elements of the story. This can be done with partners or as a whole class. Check to see that the students understand the elements illustrated. (15 minutes)

6. Watch the video again; discuss the vocabulary; and identify the setting, characters (antagonist/protagonist), background, conflict, climax, resolution, and theme/thesis.

7. Brainstorm ideas for a personal narrative (30 minutes). Using the "Elements of a Narrative: Outline" worksheet (Appendix C), have the students outline their personal narration, making sure it contains all the elements of a good narrative. (1 hour)

8. Have the students write and submit the narration. (Optional: 1 hour in class, or assign as homework)

9. The students can do a peer-review of the narratives, or the instructor can mark their narratives and meet with the students to help them improve their writing. (optional; 1 hour)

10. After writing the final draft of the narration, have the students use a storytelling app (e.g., Toontastics, Adobe Voice, TouchCast, etc.) to record the story with music. (optional; 1 hour)

CAVEATS AND OPTIONS

1. This activity mainly features the elements found in a narrative. Depending on the level of the students and time constraints, you should spend several lessons on time order, figurative language, development of setting, writing of dialogue, punctuation of dialogue, and character development as the students are writing their narratives.

2. For higher level students, more work can be done analyzing story elements in other writings.

Part III

Music for Listening

Part III: Music for Listening

Do you like listening to music? Do your students like it? These questions are perhaps too broad, because there are hundreds of types of music. No matter what types of music you and your students tune in to, there's sure to be an activity in this chapter to please them. When thoughtfully chosen, music adds a positive dimension to a listening lesson.

Listening to music and listening to language go hand in hand. Neuroscientists Strait and Kraus (2011, p. 139) report that "cross-cultural study of the rhythmic structures of language and music suggests that the rhythm of a culture's music is reflected in the rhythm of native-language prosody." If we want students to learn the rhythms of English, why restrict them to spoken English? Combining language with rhythm and melody encourages rehearsal and boosts long-term retention (Lake, 2003; Engh 2013). Murphey (1992) studied pop songs in particular and found that they are "conversation-like, repetitive and occur at roughly half the speed of spoken discourse." These characteristics provide ideal conditions for enabling students to work on breaking down the stream of language into understandable bits without the ennui induced by repetitive language drills.

The majority of activities in this chapter on listening relate to noticing the phonological properties of language in songs—a bottom-up listening strategy. Schön et al. (2008) mention several ways that songs assist language acquisition, including that "the presence of pitch contours may enhance phonological discrimination, since syllable change is often accompanied by a change in pitch" (p. 982). The contributions by Jacob Huckle; Paul Keyworth; Rebecca Palmer; Timothy R. Janda; Vander Viana and Sonia Zyngier; Jean L. Arnold; Walcir Cardoso, Ross Sundberg, and Tiago Bione; Jon Noble; Christopher Pond and Sean H. Toland; Mohamed A. Yacoub; Jim Cracraft; and Chris Walklett all work on differentiating phonological items, whether they be discrete phonemes or suprasegmentals, aspects of connected speech or rhymes.

Furthermore, many of the activities attend to different learning preferences: visual, auditory, reading/writing, or kinesthetic. Presenting information in more than one modality "selectively recruits attention and facilitates perceptual differentiation more effectively than does the same information presented unimodally" (Schön et al., 2008). The activities contributed by Arlyn Mañebo-Baron, Joseph V. Dias, Nathan Galster, and Stacie A. Swinehart draw on art or visuals to connect to music. Requiring some type of creative output is an aspect of many of these activities, too. Teaching using "intersensory redundancy" has been in vogue for the past few decades, but Schön and her colleagues (2008) believe that using music and language in song go beyond that and "may be more efficient than a combination across sensory modalities" (p. 982). Music appears to be a very important learning strategy that we should exploit.

Education is a process in which we restructure our knowledge and how we think. One study by Malyarenko, Kuraev, Malyarenko, and Khatova (1996) "suggests that listening to music even one hour per day changes brain reorganization" (as cited in Jensen 2000, p. 32). Music has been found to "have a biological basis, and . . . the brain has a functional organization for music" (Weinberger, 2004). We do better when we can "retune our brains" and learn to focus on sounds that are important to us. In this chapter, you'll see how Walcir Cardoso's, Ross Sundberg's, and Tiago Bione's "Sound Scavenger Hunt" enables students to do just this. You'll read how Mohamed A. Yacoub uses music to develop listening skills while at the same time helping Muslim students feel more comfortable with the activity. Lisa Leopold's activity helps students get a feel for cultural differences in the context of apologizing, in which they can use top-down listening strategies, and Rita M. Van Dyke-Kao focuses on affixes to make students more aware of word boundaries, a bottom-up listening strategy.

Another way to restructure knowledge is to use humor. When students hear language used in novel ways that do not match their previous experience, their curiosity is piqued. Jensen (1988, p. 122) reports on studies in two different countries that both found using humor can increase retention of information and raise attention levels. Jim Cracraft, Timothy R. Janda, and Chris Walklett have engaging contributions combining music and rhythm with humor.

We hope you'll peruse these ideas and find at least one that you'll try the next time you're teaching.

REFERENCES

Engh, D. (2013). Why use music in English language learning? A survey of the literature. *English Language Teaching, 6*(2), 113–127. doi: 10.5539/elt.v6n2p113

Jensen, E. (1988). *Superteaching: Master strategies for building student success.* Del Mar, CA: Turning Point.

Jensen, E. (2000). *Music with the brain in mind: Enhance learning with music.* San Diego, CA: Corwin Press.

Lake, R. (2003). Enhancing acquisition through music. *The Journal of the Imagination in Language Learning and Teaching, 7,* 98–106.

Murphey, T. (1992). The discourse of pop songs. *TESOL Quarterly, 26,* 770–774. doi: 10.2307/3586887

Schön, D., Boyer, M., Moreno, S., Besson, M., Peretz, I., & Kolinsky, R. (2008). Songs as an aid for language acquisition. *Cognition, 106*(2), 975–983.

Strait, D., & Kraus, N. (2011). Playing music for a smarter ear: Cognitive, perceptual and neurobiological evidence. *Music Perception: An Interdisciplinary Journal 29*(2), 133–146.

Weinberger, N. M. (2004, September). Music and the brain. *Scientific American Special Edition, 16*(3), 36–43.

Chorus Reconstruction

Jacob Huckle

Levels	All
Aims	Develop skills in listening for detail, with a focus on accuracy of word recognition
	Collaborate to practice reconstructing the meaning of listening texts
Class Time	10 minutes–1 hour (≈ 10 minutes for the listening activity; up to 1 hour for the follow-up activities)
Preparation Time	15 minutes
Resources	Large pieces of paper for groups (or mini-whiteboards)
	Audio recording of a song with a chorus

This kind of group reconstruction task can be used successfully with any short (one- to several-sentence) listening text: Listen to the short extract a number of times, write down what you hear individually, work as a group to come to a final decision, compare the group's final product to the transcript. During the process of reconstructing the chorus, students practice subskills such as guessing the meaning of words that were not clearly heard, or using logic or common sense to reconcile various students' different ideas about what they heard.

Applying this method to songs is interesting for a number of reasons. Firstly, the fact that the chorus of a song is, by definition, repeated numerous times allows students to listen again and again without losing interest. Secondly, songs can be chosen to target specific listening needs of the students. For example, you might choose a song with strong elements of connected speech if this is where students struggle. Songs can also be chosen to suit the topic of the lesson or series of lessons (e.g., ABBA's "Money, Money, Money" if the topic is about finances) or to introduce a grammar point (e.g., Simply Red's "If You Don't Know Me by Now" for introducing first conditional). This activity works best with songs that have a chorus that repeats at least three times. If the song does not have a chorus, or it is only repeated twice, the song—or parts of it—can be replayed a number of times.

PROCEDURE

1. Explain to students that they should listen carefully to the song and try to write down every word they hear in the chorus. Each student should write on his or her piece of lined paper. If necessary, the first time, you might need to indicate to students where the chorus starts and ends (e.g., "You should start/stop writing now").

2. Allow students to listen to the whole song, and thus listen to the chorus a few times, each time adding to their notes.

3. Once the song has finished and students have had at least three opportunities to listen to the target language, students should work in pairs or groups of no more than four students. They should compare to see whether they missed anything in their notes or made any other errors.

4. Students should compare their notes and come up with a group decision as to the content of the chorus, writing this final version onto the larger piece of paper or whiteboards.

5. Ask each group to read their group chorus aloud and lead the students in making comparisons between them. Ask the class to choose the chorus they believe is correct, or closest to the actual chorus. With some classes, it might also be appropriate to ask students to sing the chorus aloud as groups or as a whole class.

6. Finally, reveal the lyrics to the students, compare their versions to the real one, and elicit any possible reasons for the differences.

CAVEATS AND OPTIONS

1. The listening task can be followed up with comprehension questions or, for more advanced students, questions focused on the songwriter's creative decisions. To improve students' creative writing skills, you could ask them to rewrite the chorus in a different way. For example, in a song written from a male's perspective, students might be asked to write it from a female one. These rewriting tasks can develop students' understanding of perspective and lead to more advanced discussions about opinions and bias.

2. It is important to make students aware that songs do not always represent authentic speech patterns (in terms of pronunciation and, sometimes, grammar) and, for this reason, it is strongly recommended to use the group reconstruction method with other kinds of listening texts as well. The activity's basic procedure of listening, individual note-taking, and group reconstruction could be repeated when listening to short announcements, short extracts from longer texts or lectures, or children's stories, for example.

Dueling Kazoos

Paul Keyworth

Levels	All (song dependent)
Aims	Develop listening skills
Class Time	≈ 1 hour
Preparation Time	20 minutes
Resources	Audio recording of any duet
	Handout of song lyrics
	Copy of Gilbert's (2008) Prosody Pyramid diagram
	A kazoo for each student

This fun activity is a logical extension to the type of listen-and-repeat activities that Gilbert (2008) advocates in her seminal work. She strongly recommends using the Prosody Pyramid and kazoos to prosodically train language learners "to understand how rhythmic and melodic cues are used to organize information and guide the listener" (p. 6). Many researchers in the related fields of psycholinguistics and neurolinguistics have discovered that the brain processes musical melody and speech prosody in similar ways. In many instances, songs simply exaggerate the prosody that is inherent in everyday speech. The advantage of using songs in the language classroom is that they are undeniably more engaging than listening to bland dialogues.

Moreover, as Palmer and Hutchins (2006) found, "music training is associated with increased sensitivity to pitch processing in language tasks" (p. 245). The "Dueling Kazoos" activity is not only fun and effective, but it also takes pressure off students who are too shy to sing in front of the class. Finally, the metacognitive discussion exercise at the end is important for helping students to appreciate the relationship between prosody and meaning.

PROCEDURE

1. Introduce Gilbert's (2008) Prosody Pyramid to the class on the board or screen if your students are not already familiar with it from previous lessons. A copy is available online at www.tesol.org/docs/default-source/new-resource-library/teaching-pronunciation-using-the-prosody-pyramid.pdf?sfvrsn=0 Have students jot down a copy of the pyramid diagram in their notebooks. Iterate that the primary-stressed syllable is very important because it represents the "peak of information" (Gilbert, 2008, p. 10) within a thought group.

2. Find a definition of the word *duet* in a dictionary and write it on the board. Try to elicit the word *duet* from the students or tell them if they do not know, perhaps elaborating on other words in the family such as *duo, dual, duel,* etc.

3. Tell the class that they are going to listen to a duet. Show them the lyrics for the first or select verse of your chosen song on the board/screen, preferably containing lines for two singers. Play the verse and have students listen, especially for the stressed words and syllables. Model the activity together with the class by eliciting the thought groups (circle them) and their respective focus words (underline them) and peak syllables (draw a square above). For example, if using the 1920s duet, "That Old Gang of Mine," by Henderson, Rose, and Dixon, you would elicit the following:

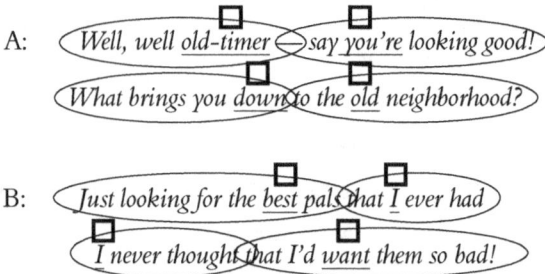

4. Hand a kazoo to each student. Then hum the lines of the verse using the kazoo and have your students repeat back, emphasizing the peak vowels in each thought group. Have fun by switching the roles according to the duet. Optionally, you can then have students repeat and practice singing the lines as a class.

5. Pass a copy of the complete lyrics to each pair of students. Tell them to imagine that it is a dialogue between two people and to circle the thought groups, underline the focus words, and draw a square above the peak syllables. Then play the recording of the entire duet a couple of times so the students can check their answers and learn the song, hopefully singing along as they go.

6. Play the song back to the class while eliciting where the peak syllable is, line by line.

7. Dueling Kazoos: Pairs can then practice humming into their kazoos and/or singing the duet. It can be truly entertaining (sometimes hilarious!) to watch and hear the duets that the students perform. Monitor and give feedback on their prosodic productions as needed. Willing students can then perform their duets for the class.

8. Put pairs into small groups and ask students to discuss why they think certain words in the song are stressed more than others. What is the significance of the peak vowel?

9. Provide feedback to the whole class.

CAVEATS AND OPTIONS

As an extension activity, more advanced learners can prepare lyrics to a duet of their choice (perhaps a favorite song) by marking the focus words and peak syllables and then practicing it with a partner (by singing and/or playing kazoo). Volunteers can perform their duet at the start of the next class with kazoos, and the other students can guess the tune.

REFERENCES AND FURTHER READING

Caulfield, B., Tye Comer, M., Concepcion, M., Letkemann, J., Lipshutz, J., Mapes, J., & Trust, G. (2011, February 14). *The 40 biggest duets of all time*. Retrieved from http://www.billboard.com/articles/list/473075/the-40-biggest-duets-of-all-time

Gilbert, J. B. (2008). *Teaching pronunciation: Using the Prosody Pyramid*. Cambridge, United Kingdom: Cambridge University Press.

Gilbert, J. B. (2013). Teaching pronunciation using the Prosody Pyramid. *TESOL Resource Center.* Retrieved from http://www.tesol.org/connect/tesol-resource-center/search-details/teaching-tips/2013/11/06/teaching-pronunciation-using-the-prosody-pyramid

Hausen, M., Torppa, R., Salmela, V. R., Vainio, M., & Sarkamao, T. (2013). Music and speech prosody: A common rhythm. *Frontiers in Psychology, 4*, 566. doi: 10.3389/fpsyg.2013.00566

Henderson, R., Rose, B., & Dixon, M. (1923). "That old gang of mine." *Vocal Popular Sheet Music Collection.* Book 5235. Retrieved from http://digitalcommons.library.umaine.edu/mmb-vp/5235

Palmer, C., & Hutchins, S. (2006). What is musical prosody? *Psychology of Learning and Motivation, 46*, 245–278.

Listen for Your Line

Rebecca Palmer

Levels	All
Aims	Negotiate the sequence of lines in a text
	Notice rhythm, rhymes, and repetition
Class Time	15–20 minutes
Preparation Time	20–30 minutes (students may help prepare the materials)
Resources	Music and lyrics for 2–3 songs related to current topic in class
	Cut-up copies of the lyrics for each song
	At least one mobile device per group

Students who are taught how to use a text's structure have better comprehension skills (Sanders & Spooren, 2010; Taylor, 1992). In this kinesthetic text mapping activity, students use a song's structure to arrange the lyrics in the right sequence.

PROCEDURE

1. Select two or three songs that you will ask the class to sing. The songs should contain vocabulary or cover themes related to course material.

2. Break the class into two or three large groups. Give each student in a group a section from a song assigned to their group. (To determine the number of lines in a section, divide the number of lines in each song by the number of students in the group.) On their own, students listen to the song and sort their bodies in the order that the sections are sung without showing each other their sections.

3. After the groups have their sections in the right order, the groups should practice performing the song, with each person holding up the lines in their section and walking across a pretend stage as their lines are played. It may be necessary for two or three people to walk across at the same time or for two people to sing to each other, as the song dictates. Have students be creative as they prepare their performance.

4. Set the class up so there is an audience and a stage. Have each group perform their song by walking across as they have practiced.

5. When the groups are finished, discuss what patterns and repetitions in each song helped students put the sections in order. Discuss whether there were any elements of a beginning, middle, and end to help guide the students.

CAVEATS AND OPTIONS

Students may sing along or mime the words as the music plays. It would also be fun to make a video of students' final performances.

REFERENCES AND FURTHER READING

Sanders, T. J. M., & Spooren, W. (2010). Discourse and text structure. In D. Geeaerts & H. Cuyckens (Eds.), *Handbook of cognitive linguistics* (pp. 917–937). Oxford, England: Oxford University Press.

Taylor, B. (1992). Text structure, comprehension and recall. In S. J. Samuels & A. E. Farstrup (Eds.), *What research has to say about reading instruction* (2nd ed.; pp. 220–235). Newark, DE: International Reading Association.

Aural to Visual: Turning Songs Into Tableau Vivant

Joseph V. Dias

Levels	Beginner to high intermediate
Aims	Confirm understanding of lyrics by collectively creating a tableau vivant *that represents them*
	Break the ice and facilitate bonding
	Develop group discussion and negotiation skills
Class Time	≈ 1 hour
Preparation Time	30 minutes–1 hour
Resources	Audio recording of a song that is rich in visual imagery (see Caveats and Options)
	Handout of lyrics as a cloze activity (optional)

Young learners in particular respond well to converting what they are learning to action and movement. This activity fits under the total physical response (TPR) framework, emphasizing comprehension and having students coordinate physical movements with the language they are learning. There are ample opportunities for genuine communication to take place among group members as they must negotiate their roles in the tableau and direct each other to create a visually attractive and intelligible scene. As students cooperate to form the tableau, they must confirm their understandings of what the song means to them and resolve or incorporate alternative interpretations.

PROCEDURE

1. Tell the students that they will listen to a song and they should write down as many key words and images from it as they can. In the case of lower level students, the printed lyrics may be provided with blanks for the vocabulary or constructions that the teacher wishes to highlight.

2. Group students into fours or fives, allocate verses for them to work on, and play the song again, asking each group to pay particular attention to its assigned verse. Explain that a *tableau vivant* is a group of immobile people visually representing a moment frozen in time, and that they will be portraying characters or objects in the verse that was assigned to them.

3. In their groups, students share interpretations of their assigned verse with each other. Prioritize getting students to the point where they can turn their interpretations into a tableau, rather than aiming at perfect comprehension.

4. Tell the groups that they must cooperate to create a *tableau vivant*, with every member of the same team representing a different aspect of an action, object, or interaction described in the verse. The members may produce scenes in which the actors interact with each other to tell a story or illustrate the verse through independent characterizations. Give groups up to 10 minutes to discuss what the verse means to them, conceptualize their tableau, and practice it. Circulate, giving guidance and encouragement to each group and feedback about how the tableaux look from a distance.

5. Students present their *tableaux vivants* sequentially to the rest of the class as the song is played and paused during the transitions between tableaux. Provide students with the complete lyrics only after all the tableaux have been presented to classmates. For classes in which the lyrics were previously given out as a cloze activity, do not reveal the answers until after the tableaux have been performed.

CAVEATS AND OPTIONS

1. Two good songs for this activity are the folk favorite "Froggie Went A Courtin'" and Pearl Jam's "Last Kiss."

2. Photograph the *tableaux vivants* and then present them to students through a slideshow after they have all been completed. Slideshows can easily be prepared with photos taken by most smart phones and, if a phone is connected to a classroom's AV system through an HDMI adaptor, the slideshow can be shown with little advance preparation. As the slides are displayed, call upon each group to narrate the action taking place or recite the corresponding verse.

3. Have students write a synopsis for each of the tableaux, giving their interpretations of what is being represented; these can later be compared with what the performing groups had intended.

4. If you wish to emphasize spoken language, highlight and practice expressions from songs that illustrate phonetic features, particularly such suprasegmentals as stress, tone, and word juncture.

Find and Fix the Mistakes!

Timothy R. Janda

Levels	*High beginner to intermediate*
Aims	*Develop the ability to make phonological distinctions between select vocabulary items while reading a text*
Class Time	*10–15 minutes*
Preparation Time	*20–30 minutes*
Resources	*A transcript of any song that can be manipulated using a word processer*
	Handout of the altered document
	Audio recording of a song

Reading while listening has long been accepted as a pedagogically sound practice for helping students decode a text. In this activity, students are required to listen carefully while reading a text to hear the mistakes in the transcript and substitute corrections. Because reading involves phonological processing, this activity allows students to capitalize on this aspect of message decoding, testing their ability to see beyond the distractors in the text.

PROCEDURE

1. Select an audio recording of any song and a corresponding transcript of the lyrics.

2. Using a word processor, manipulate the document by changing select words, as many as one every other line, substituting an alternative vocabulary item. Double or triple space between lines so students have room to write in corrections. Substituted words can be as odd or funny as the teacher sees fit. For example, in a love song, you might substitute the word *hate* for *love*. Alternatively, to make the exercise a bit more challenging, words could be closer in sound; for example, *worry* could be substituted for *sorry*.

3. Distribute copies of the altered transcript to students, telling them that some of the words are wrong, and they will have to listen closely, cross out wrong words, and write in corrections.

4. Play the song several times, giving ample opportunity for students to hear the mistakes and correct them. If preferred, students can compare and share answers with one another.

5. Review the corrections with students. Play the song again if desired.

CAVEATS AND OPTIONS

1. As noted above, this exercise can be made as easy or challenging as you deem appropriate. Altering a text by substituting a minimal pair, for example, even with the context of the text as a secondary resource for identifying the distractor, creates a subtle change that can be quite challenging.

2. On the other hand, making extreme changes creates a potentially less challenging exercise, with the absurdity of the change adding the element of humor to the activity.

Rhyming Words in Lyrics: Exploring Student Creativity in TESOL

Vander Viana and Sonia Zyngier

Levels	Intermediate
Aims	Raise sensitivity to and understanding of rhymes
	Increase awareness of the importance of rhyming in lyrics
	Exercise rhyming skills
Class Time	50 minutes
Preparation Time	10 minutes
Resources	Audio recording of "The Power of Love," by Huey Lewis
	Handout (see Appendix online)

Patterns regulate the way we see and understand the world, organizing order out of chaos. They are also responsible for the way we respond to art and beauty (Zyngier, van Peer, & Hakemulder, 2007). One way of acquiring and consolidating new vocabulary is by spotting patterns. In songs, rhyming patterns establish regularity of sound and contribute to meaning creation. Thus, songs provide necessary and authentic material for the teaching of English to speakers of other languages (ESOL).

Using rhyming lyrics in the ESOL classroom may foster students' personal involvement and motivation. Rhyming may also help students develop language awareness and acquire vocabulary in an effortless and enjoyable way. The benefits of using songs and rhymes in ESOL education are to make learning relevant to students; create a context in which students can express their feelings and opinions; encourage imagination, creativity, and playfulness; foster students' experimentation with, exploration of, and innovativeness through language; and make students aware of personal and cultural multiplicity and difference.

PROCEDURE

1. Write these words on the board and ask students to arrange them in rhyming groups: *shoe, no, he, wine, contain, snow, true, shine, see, me, go, pain, who, combine,* and *remain*.

2. Check if the students have categorized the words as follows:
    - *shoe, true, who*
    - *no, snow, go*
    - *he, see, me*
    - *wine, shine, combine*
    - *contain, pain, remain*

3. In pairs, ask students to add at least one word to each of the groups above and check their answers as a class.

4. As a class, encourage students to discuss where they think rhyming would be appreciated. They might refer to poems, advertisements, and songs.

5. Ask students why rhymes are common in songs. They could answer, for instance, that rhyming is fun, that it makes songs memorable (thus contributing to their popularity), and that rhymes establish symmetrical sound patterns.

6. Explain to students that they will work with the lyrics of a song in which some of the words have been omitted (See Appendix), and ask them to individually complete the lyrics with rhyming words (line 1a should rhyme with line 1b, 2a should rhyme with 2b, etc.).

7. Ask students to compare their answers in pairs, ensuring that the words chosen by their peers rhyme with the underlined and italicized words in the lyrics.

8. Play the song "The Power of Love" so that students can identify the original words. Check the students' answers.

9. In trios, ask students to compare their suggestions with the artist's word choices, decide which they think works best in terms of both rhyme and meaning, and report their opinions to the class.

CAVEATS AND OPTIONS

1. Should students be unfamiliar with rhyming, ask them to do Steps 1 and 6 in pairs. If Step 6 is completed in pairs, Step 7 will need to be conducted in groups of four.

2. The answers provided in Step 2 are a guide. If students propose a different categorization, ask them to justify their groupings and show how they think the words would actually rhyme.

3. For homework, students choose a song they like and identify its rhyming words. They can present their songs and the rhyming words in the following class. If time is limited, this can be scheduled as a warm-up or final activity for the remaining classes in the term.

REFERENCES AND FURTHER READING

Fergusson, R. (1985). *The Penguin rhyming dictionary.* London, England: Penguin Group.

Maley, A., & Moulding, S. (1985). *Poem into poem: Reading and writing poems with students of English.* Cambridge, England: Cambridge University Press.

Zyngier, S., van Peer, W., & Hakemulder, J. (2007). Complexity and foregrounding: In the eye of the beholder? *Poetics Today, 28*(4), 653–682.

Close Listening: What'd He Say?

Jean L. Arnold

Levels	Intermediate to advanced
Aims	Improve close listening skills
Class Time	15–20 minutes
Preparation Time	30 minutes
Resources	Two varying renditions of a song
	Handout of lyrics worksheet (teacher created)

This activity emphasizes attention to detail. It also demonstrates that there is scope for variation in the way we express ourselves: The use of grammar, word order, word choice, and other linguistic features may be a matter of stylistic preference and may affect how our message is received.

PROCEDURE

1. Find a song that is covered by two different artists and that have some lyrical variations. Pete Seeger and John Denver's versions of "The Garden Song," and Pete Seeger and Simon and Garfunkel's renditions of "Last Night I Had the Strangest Dream" work well.

2. To prepare a worksheet, find the lyrics online and cut and paste them into a word document. Listen to one artist's version of the song and check for accuracy; make any corrections needed. Then listen to the other version. On the worksheet, whenever there is a difference in the lyrics between the versions, include both choices with a slash between them, randomizing in which order the choices appear. This way, students have to listen carefully to decide which of the two alternatives are being sung. Mark the words that differ with bold font. For example: "Last night I had the strangest dream **"I'd ever / I ever"** dreamed before."

3. In class, play one version of the song and have students listen and underline which of the two variants is used. After listening, they can compare answers with a classmate.

4. Next, play the other version of the song. They should circle the wording used in the second version of the song. The second listening serves to check the answers of the first listening, too.

5. Take a vote to see which version students prefer and play that version again, having students sing along using the lyrics that that artist used.

6. Discuss the differences in wording used by the artists. Is the meaning in both versions the same? Is the grammar the same? Is the word order the same? What effect do the differences have, if any? Which way of expressing the ideas sounds more natural to students? Do they have a preference for one set of lyrics over the other?

CAVEATS AND OPTIONS

If you teach English learners who share a common native language, and a cover version of a song exists in that language, it may be interesting to explore variations between the versions of the song. For example, "Where Have All the Flowers Gone?," by Pete Seeger, is also sung by Joan Baez in German: "Sagt Mir Wo die Blumen Sind," which translates literally to "tell me where the flowers are." Variations in word choice and composition can be explored: Are they only linguistic or does the different way of conveying the idea say something about the people or culture who use the other language?

Irony

Arlyn Mañebo-Baron

Levels	Intermediate to advanced
Aims	Recognize and use irony in speech and in writing
Class Time	1 hour–80 minutes
Preparation Time	15–30 minutes
Resources	*Audio recording of the song "Ironic," by Alanis Morissette*
	Audiovisual equipment
	Lyrics to be posted or projected
	Pictures that show examples of irony

"I hear and I forget. I see and I remember. I do and I understand." These three phrases are very important when considering the value of experiential learning for students. Using a song to help them understand the concept of irony provides them with examples of how irony is applied in the real world. Providing visual examples along with the song "Ironic" is more powerful than just reading about the idea of irony or hearing the teacher talk about it.

PROCEDURE

1. Show the students pictures of some ironic situation; for example, a picture of a stop sign next to a sign that says "keep moving," a T-shirt with the slogan: "I hate T-shirts," or some other funny example of your own or from online. Have students discuss what they see and how they understand it.

2. Show students examples of verbal irony, for example, someone saying, "Thanks for the ticket, officer—you just made my day," or "I can't wait to read this 700-page report." Ask the students if they know what this kind of humorous statement is called. One possible answer is sarcasm, which is a form of irony.

3. Discuss irony as one type of figurative language and its use in stories and/or poetry (verbal, situational, and dramatic). Limit your discussion to 5–8 minutes.

4. Post or project the lyrics on the board, play the song "Ironic" by Alanis Morissette, and ask students to listen carefully and jot down all the ironies that they hear in the song.

5. Let volunteers in the class recite what they have written down and explain what it means to them.

6. Divide the students into three groups and ask them to do the following within 15 minutes:

    a. Group 1: Create a skit that shows situational irony

    b. Group 2: Compose a poem or a song using verbal irony

    c. Group 3: Write a short play of an ironic situation from a classical play they know, for example, *Romeo and Juliet*

7. Let the students present what they have prepared.

CAVEATS AND OPTIONS

Ask the students to research examples of situational, verbal, and dramatic irony as an advanced assignment so that they will have something to use in their activity. You can also provide students in advance with examples of different kinds of irony for them to classify and later use in their group activity.

Sound Scavenger Hunt

Walcir Cardoso, Ross Sundberg, and Tiago Bione

Levels	Intermediate to advanced
Aims	Develop phonological awareness
Class Time	30–45 minutes
Preparation Time	10–20 minutes, depending on the amount of students' involvement
Resources	Audio recording of any song
	Handout of song lyrics
	Printed or electronic copies of the handout (See Appendix)

Some of the problems in listening comprehension and, consequently, speaking (pronunciation) can be attributed to how students segment the sounds they hear in natural speech (e.g., the words "born in" may be incorrectly perceived as a single, nonexistent word due to the resyllabification of the two words as "bor-nin"). English learners need to become aware of these phonetic processes (e.g., via noticing activities). The combination of sound (music) and orthography (lyrics) reinforces noticing and helps students become aware of certain English spelling-to-pronunciation rules such as those that characterize linking and assimilation phenomena. For more information about developing listening skills through pronunciation awareness, see Celce-Murcia, Brinton and Goodwin (2010) and Wilson (2008).

PROCEDURE

1. Make a list of songs and copies of their lyrics, unless you have students use their own songs.
2. As recommended by Celce-Murcia, Brinton, and Goodwin (2010, p. 370), explain the importance of recognizing connected speech processes such as linking and contraction for the purpose of understanding "fast, messy, authentic speech," not necessarily to produce them. In addition, highlight that some of these processes are features of normal, everyday speech (Kelly, 2001).
3. Divide the class into small groups of three to four students or allow students to work individually, depending on learner/class needs.
4. Distribute a printed or electronic copy of the handout (Appendix) and explain the activity: Students listen to songs in order to identify the connected speech phenomena listed and exemplified in the handout.
5. Provide a list of preselected songs accompanied by their lyrics, or ask your students to search for their favorite songs and related lyrics.

6. Using available audio playback devices (computers, mobile devices, electronic media players or CD/DVD players), students listen to a variety of songs accompanied by their lyrics and identify the specified phonetic processes. Ask them to provide the name of the song, the singer, and examples of each target phonetic process.

7. Students share their findings in group or individual presentations, emphasizing what they have learned and the importance of connected speech processes for listening comprehension and speaking.

CAVEATS AND OPTIONS

1. The main anticipated problem involves the students' selection of songs containing inappropriate subject matter or language. To ensure that songs are learner- and age-appropriate, preselect the music genre and/or the songs to be used.

2. To vary and expand the proposed activity, there are many options. If you would like to increase your students' motivation and encourage higher levels of collaboration and participation, you could gamify the activity by assigning points to each phonetic process based on its frequency in English and its ease of identification. For example, while the use of linking is widespread (and in most cases obligatory) in English, assimilation phenomena such as the one found in "good boy" (pronounced "goo[b b]oy") are variable and not easily identifiable. Accordingly, the identification of the latter phenomena should be rewarded more points in a gamified version of the Sound Scavenger Hunt.

REFERENCES AND FURTHER READING

Celce-Murcia, M., Brinton, D., & Goodwin, J. (2010). *Teaching pronunciation: A course book and reference guide*. Cambridge, England: Cambridge University Press.

Kelly, G. (2001). *How to teach pronunciation*. Essex, United Kingdom: Pearson Longman.

Wilson, J. J. (2008). *How to teach listening*. Essex, United Kingdom: Pearson Longman.

APPENDIX: *Sound Scavenger Hunt*

You are on a sound scavenger hunt to find songs that contain the following connected speech processes found in English (note that some won't be easy to find). Your findings can come from as many songs as you want.

	Connected Speech Processes	Song, Artist & Example/s
Examples	**Linking** (e.g., "left arm" pronounced "lef-tarm")	"All By Myself" by Irving Berlin; I am all by myself
	Sound change: Word-final /t/ sounds like another consonant	"Oh, Susanna!" by Stephen C. Foster; Susannah, don't you cry
Your Findings		
Linking (e.g., "left arm" pronounced "lef-tarm")		
Consonant deletion (e.g., "last night" pronounced "las-night")		
Vowel reduction (e.g., "o" in "tonight" does not sound like "o" in "go"; it sounds like "a" in "ago")		
Contraction (reduced version of some words) (e.g., "want to" and "is not" pronounced "wanna" and "isn't")		
Sound change 1: Word-final /d/ sounds like another consonant		
Sound change 2: Word-final /t/ sounds like another consonant		
Sound change 3: Word-final /s/ sounds like another consonant		
The song with the greatest number of connected speech processes:		

Lyrical Visualization and Interpretation

Nathan Galster

Levels	Intermediate to advanced
Aims	Develop creative thinking, discussion, and listening skills
	Interpret music lyrics using artistic creativity
Class Time	50 minutes
Preparation Time	10 minutes
Resources	Computer with audiovisual equipment
	Downloaded copy of song or Internet access
	Cut-up copies of lyrics
	Drawing materials

Music often tells a story and seems to have a specific and set meaning. However, there are often multiple interpretations of a song. This activity allows learners to use their own ideas and creativity to interpret part of the lyrics and caters to multiple learning styles by allowing students to work through various tasks in groups. Some students may be stronger in reading and comprehending the lyrics, while others may excel at using their imagination to interpret them. Hands-on learners might enjoy drawing, while others can use their speaking skills to share and present their group's work to the class. This activity also incorporates listening practice when students put the verses in order and discuss them.

PROCEDURE

1. This activity could be done with any song that tells a story or has multiple verses. Some good examples are Billy Joel's "The Piano Man," America's "A Horse with No Name," Johnny Cash's "A Boy Named Sue," or Adele's "Someone Like You." Print the lyrics to a song and cut into strips. Each strip should contain one verse or section of the song.

2. Divide students into groups to work on the chosen song. Give one verse or section to each group.

3. Ask each group to read their section of the song together and discuss their interpretations of the meaning. Stress to students that there is no "correct" answer and it is not essential that they understand all of the words. They should then draw a picture that represents the group's understanding of the section.

4. After all groups have completed their picture, have the groups read the lyrics from their section of the song and share their picture with the class. They can explain their interpretation of the lyrics and their drawing.

5. Listen to the song (it can be helpful to use YouTube and show the music video, which could lead to more interpretation, discussion, and comparison) and ask all the groups to work together to put the pictures/verses in order.
6. Students engage in a class discussion on the overall meaning of the song, as an entire class or in groups.

CAVEATS AND OPTIONS

1. Lyrically abstract songs could be more enjoyable for creative or higher level students.
2. Adjust into a writing activity by having students write about their interpretation along with the drawing rather than sharing it orally with the class.

REFERENCES AND FURTHER READING

Galster, N. (2016). Media for task-based language learning. Retrieved from http://nathangalster.wix.com/medialanguage

Galster, N. (2014). An educator's C.R.E.A.T.I.V.E. approach to learning. Retrieved from http://nathangalster.wix.com/creatinglearning

Lyrics: Dictation and Note-Taking

Jon Noble

Levels	Intermediate to advanced
Aims	Understand the difference between note-taking and dictation
	Develop note-taking skills
Class Time	≈ 1 hour
Preparation Time	15–30 minutes
Resources	Audio recording of song with clearly audible lyrics (especially one with a narrative or story)
	Handout of song lyrics (or a projector)

Note-taking involves both accuracy of word transcription and paraphrase. Raising awareness of these two different skills should help students understand ways of listening. By using a song with a narrative, a context is provided that helps the students use top-down strategies of inference to fill in the blanks.

PROCEDURE

1. Select an audio recording of a narrative song and print out or project the lyrics. A short song such as Elton John's "Rocket Man" or a long one such as Johnny Cash's "A Boy Named Sue" are good examples of clear narration.

2. Play the song in class and discuss the meaning.

3. Demonstrate the difference between taking dictation versus taking notes. Dictation is a word-for-word transcription without necessarily understanding the meaning. Notes, on the other hand, are paraphrase resulting from some reflection of meaning. Notes may also be abbreviated. Write examples on the board:
   - Dictation: "I miss the Earth so much; I miss my wife."
   - Notes: "misses home/family bc he is far away."

4. Play the song again and give students 20 minutes to check their dictation/notes with a partner or small group depending on length or difficulty of the song. Suggestion: Collect mobile phones or ask students to turn them off so students don't look up the lyrics!

5. Finally, review the entire song with the class as a whole. Distribute or project the lyrics and check for accuracy. Discuss notes about the narrative (story) of the song in terms of meaning. If all goes well, sing the entire song together either with or without audio.

CAVEATS AND OPTIONS

1. Instruct the class to draw a line down the center of the page and tell them to take dictation on the left side and notes on the right side. You may want to play only a portion of the song and repeat it a couple of times until the students get accustomed to this task. After checking that they are on task, finish the song.

2. Cloze exercises can be provided for songs that have difficult passages, or for lower level classes.

3. Select songs with a good story or strong context for discussion of meaning. Some songs may be supplemented with stories from another genre, such as Elton John's "Rocket Man" and Ray Bradbury's short story "The Rocket Man," which share a common theme of a man missing his family when he's in space. Yet another example of this loneliness theme is David Bowie's "Space Oddity."

Taylor Swift Lyrics Gap Fill

Christopher Pond and Sean H. Toland

Levels	Intermediate to advanced
Aims	Become familiar with the notion of rhyme and meter
	Deepen understanding of idiomatic language
	Build vocabulary
	Develop prediction skills
Class Time	60–90 minutes
Preparation Time	30 minutes
Resources	Handout (teacher created; see Appendix)
	Internet-connected computer
	Audiovisual equipment
	A music video
	Handout of song lyrics (or a projector)

This activity introduces colloquial language through a gap-fill activity. A focused listening task along with lyrics interpretation helps to improve prediction and comprehension skills. The focus on rhyme along with cadence aids memorization. The repetitive pattern of lyrics helps to reinforce language.

PROCEDURE

1. Prepare gap-fill activity and Speculation Questions handouts (see Appendix) before class. This example uses the lyrics to Taylor Swift's "Blank Space" song. Print out the lyrics and white out key vocabulary for the gap-fill handout. Create questions based on the song and provide multiple-choice answers. For example:

   "I can read you like a _____"

   a) magazine   b) book   c) novel   d) newspaper

   Focus on colloquial language and idiomatic phrases. (This example is a surprise because the expected idiom with "book" is not used in the song).

2. Divide the class into pairs. Ask students to brainstorm their favorite music artists. Students then share their partner's responses with the class.

3. Tell the students they are going to watch and speculate on a music video from a famous American artist. First watch the video without sound. Hand out the speculation questions and have students work in pairs to answer them. Once they have completed the activity, elicit responses from the students.

4. Pass out the gap-fill activity. Tell students these are the lyrics to the song with words missing. Before listening to the song, students should fill in the missing words in pairs. Encourage them to first think about the type of word that is missing (i.e., part of speech). Additionally, tell them to use rhyme to help them fill in the gaps.

5. After the activity has been completed, elicit responses.

6. Play the video again, this time with sound. In pairs, students listen and check their answers. Elicit responses and give feedback. Provide each group with the lyrics to check their answers, or project the lyrics on the board.

7. Draw attention to the use of metaphors and idiomatic expressions (in this case, "read you like a magazine," "rumors fly," "go down in flames," "perfect storm," and "get drunk on jealousy"). Ask the students why they think the singer used the title "Blank Space." (She is likening her love life to a series of romantic stories, and all she needs is a man's name for her next chapter).

8. Draw attention to the rhymes. Ask students to highlight the rhyming words. What do they notice? (e.g., they occur at the end of phrases; they vary between adjoining sentences and alternate sentences; they are not always perfect rhymes, which are a common feature in music).

9. Tell the students they will rewrite the prechorus to the song with their own ideas. Provide a copy of the chorus with one half of the rhyming pairs whited out.

10. Ask them to highlight the rhyming word and then speculate on possible rhyming sounds. Remind them that it doesn't have to rhyme perfectly. Also point out that to fit with the cadence of the sentence, they will need to consider the number of syllables.

11. Students read out their examples to the class.

CAVEATS AND OPTIONS

As a follow-up task, ask students more about their interpretation of the song. What was Taylor Swift trying to say? Is there a message? (It has been interpreted as Swift's response to criticism over her personal life). If they were to write about themselves, what would the title and theme of the song be? Students rewrite a verse of the song to reflect their own life. This activity can be done as a gap-fill only activity without the multiple-choice aspect. In this case, prior to the listening activity, ask the students to speculate on the missing words. Get the students to first focus on the type of word, number of syllables, and possible rhymes that would be appropriate. Although this example uses Taylor Swift's lyrics, this activity can be done with any song.

APPENDIX: *Speculation Questions (for Taylor Swift's "Blank Space")*

1. Who is the artist?
2. What is the title of the song?
3. When was it released?
4. How many characters are there in the video?
5. Who are they?
6. Where are they?
7. What is the story about?

Answers: (1) Taylor Swift   (2) "Blank Space"   (3) 2014   (4) Two—a man and woman   (5) A new couple   (6) In a country estate   (7) A couple whose romance turns sour.

A Musical Tribute to Vincent Van Gogh

Stacie A. Swinehart

Levels	Intermediate to advanced
Aims	Listen for specific vocabulary words
	Learn new vocabulary
	Discuss and make connections between lyrics in a song and images in artwork
Class Time	30–45 minutes
Preparation Time	15 minutes
Resources	Audio recording of "Vincent," by Don McLean or Josh Groban
	Cloze exercise of "Vincent" (teacher created)
	Video of "Vincent" with art images of Vincent Van Gogh

Music can be a helpful tool to aid in language learning classrooms and language acquisition (Engh, 2013). This activity allows students the opportunity to acquire new vocabulary as well as strengthen listening and speaking skills in a creative environment beyond the textbook.

PROCEDURE

1. Prepare the students to listen to and watch the audio recording and video of "Vincent" by presenting a brief introduction of Vincent Van Gogh and the background of the song.

2. Have the students research both artists, the singer and Van Gogh, in small groups. Afterward, have each group write a sentence about what they learned to share with the class. For example, "Vincent Van Gogh is a 19th century Dutch artist who is considered to be one of the greatest Post-Impressionist painters of all time," and "Don McLean is an American singer-songwriter who was inspired to write 'Vincent' after reading a book about the artist Vincent Van Gogh."

3. Play the audio recording of the song two times and have the students fill in the missing vocabulary words as a cloze exercise. Discuss the meaning of the lyrics with the class and have students speculate about who "they" is from the context provided.

4. Play the YouTube video with the art of Vincent Van Gogh (see www.youtube.com/watch?v=dipFMJckZOM). Ask the students to explain how the images in the video relate to the song lyrics and key vocabulary words in the song. Also, students might identify which Van Gogh paintings are referenced in the music, such as "Sunflowers," "The Potato Eaters," and "Starry Night."

5. For further discussion, allow the students to express their own interests in music and art. Students will then be able to apply the new vocabulary they have learned.

6. For homework, have students choose a song they like and talk about the meaning of the lyrics the following day in short presentations.

CAVEATS AND OPTIONS

1. This activity could be adapted to other songs for further listening practice. Instead of using an art video, the music video for a song could be played and discussed.

2. If you would like to add further practice in writing, students could listen to a song and write about their interpretation of the song lyrics. This writing could later serve as a small-group discussion activity.

3. A tour of a local museum would allow students to expand upon and use new vocabulary in a real-life setting. If an art tour of a local museum is arranged, students could each choose one painting that interests them, do some research on the artist and painting, and give a presentation in class discussing the images that are represented in the art. Students may also try to write some lyrics that would represent the images in the painting to share with the class.

REFERENCES AND FURTHER READING

Engh, D. (2013). Why use music in English language learning? A survey of the literature. *English Language Teaching*, *6*(2), 113–127.

Affix Awareness

Rita M. Van Dyke-Kao

Levels	Intermediate to advanced
Aims	Develop listening strategies
	Decode connected speech by locating word boundaries
	Develop awareness of lexical segmentation
Class Time	≈ 45 minutes
Preparation Time	15–20 minutes
Resources	Audio recording of any song that contains words with prefixes and suffixes (see Caveats and Options for suggestions)
	Handout of song lyrics (or projector)

Listening is a complex skill that requires the listener to determine where in a continuous stream of speech one word ends and the next begins. Locating word boundaries can be difficult for L2 learners because they lack the strategies necessary for segmenting speech. However, familiar suffixes and prefixes can help learners decode connected speech. By using song lyrics that include numerous words with various affixes, students learn to notice and credit affixes as clear markers of word boundaries.

PROCEDURE

1. Ask students to define the terms *prefix* and *suffix*. Solicit examples of each type of affix and write the words on the board.
2. Play a section of a song that contains several words that use affixes. Ask students to listen carefully and write down any words they hear that begin with prefixes or end with suffixes.
3. Replay the same section of the song several times. Ask students what words they wrote down.
4. Give students a copy of the lyrics or display them for the class. Point out the words in the song that contain affixes. Emphasize the value of affixes in aiding listening comprehension.
5. Play the song one more time as the students read the transcript of the lyrics.

CAVEATS AND OPTIONS

1. Suggested songs:
   - "Dog Days Are Over," by Florence + the Machine
   - "Un-thinkable (I'm Ready)," by Alicia Keys
   - "Killing the Blues," by Alison Krauss and Robert Plant
   - "Belief," by John Mayer
   - "Beautiful," by Christina Aguilera

2. Don't worry if students spell words incorrectly, because the important thing is for students to demonstrate their ability to hear and recognize words.

3. If you would like to incorporate speaking practice into the activity, ask students to read the lyrics aloud in pairs or small groups. Encourage students to link the affixes to the preceding and following words.

Islamic Songs and the Mastery of Listening Skills

Mohamed A. Yacoub

Levels	Intermediate to advanced
Aims	Develop a sensitive ear to intonation and stressed and unstressed syllables (weak forms)
	Increase vocabulary
	Expand cultural knowledge
	Promote concepts of equality, love, and peace
Class Time	≈ 1 hour
Preparation Time	15–30 minutes
Resources	Audio recording of any song by Islamic singers (See Appendix)

Western music is controversial in Muslim societies; many Muslims believe it is *haram* (religiously prohibited) because the songs usually express *haram* male-female relationships and do not urge people to strengthen their relation with God. Thus, many Muslim students feel uncomfortable learning English with this music, but feel shy to express their opinions. However, it is important to find alternatives. There are what are called "Islamic songs," which have become well known and have been welcomed by a large majority of Muslims. These songs can be used to scaffold students when teaching listening skills.

PROCEDURE

1. Choose an audio recording of an Islamic song.
2. Introduce the singer to the students if they do not already know about him or her.
3. Play the song in class and ask students to write what they hear. Replay the song or parts of the song as needed.
4. Let students compare what they wrote and see where they meet and where they differ.
5. When students come up with wrong words, discuss possibilities of why they heard them incorrectly.
6. Discuss the intonation, stressed, and unstressed (weak forms) syllables. Pinpoint the patterns you have identified, or ask students to identify patterns that they have studied and are practicing.

CAVEATS AND OPTIONS

1. Instead of having students write the full lyrics, you can give them the lyrics as a gap-fill activity. To work on intonation, leave unstressed syllables as gaps in the given lyrics.//
2. There is no limit to variations and options in this activity; however, be careful to choose songs that convey general messages of equality, nondiscrimination, love, peace, and so on, so that these songs can also be appreciated by students of other religions.

APPENDIX

The following is a list of artists that sing Islamic songs, with suggested songs.*

- "Forgotten Promises," "Hasbi Rabbi," "Mother," "I Am Your Hope," and "Never Forget," by Sami Yusuf
- "Open Your Eyes," "One Big Family," "Forgive Me," "Hold My Hand," and "Awaken," by Maher Zain
- "Peace Train," "I Look, I See," "God Is the Light," and "Father and Son," by Yusuf Islam (born Cat Stevens)
- "Our Creation," "The Mountain," "My Hero," and "Your Beauty," by Hamza Robertson (born Tom Robertson)
- "Zamilooni," "First We Need the Love," "Slowly Slow," and "Mum & Dad," by Zain Bhikha
- "Children of the World" and "Color of Islam," by Dawud Wharnsby Ali (born David Howard Wharnsby)
- "I Believe," "I Am So Sorry," "You and I," "Mamma," and "Waiting for the Call," by Irfan Makki
- "I Am Near," "Our Earth," "Rain Song," "Intentions," and "Still Strong," by Native Deen (a band)
- "Wedding Nasheed," "The Greatest Gift," "Imagine a Day," and "Ask Him," by Labbayk Group (a band)
- "The Full Moon," "Mother," "Wake Up," "Hold on," and "Hypocritical," by No Beats Necessary (a band)

*The best website from which to get the songs is YouTube.

Listening for and Noting Large Numbers: "The Galaxy Song"

Jean L. Arnold

Levels	High intermediate to advanced
Aims	Improve note-taking skills, particularly related to recording large numbers in English
Class Time	20–30 minutes
Preparation Time	15 minutes
Resources	Computer with Internet access and speakers (or recorded version of the "Galaxy Song")
	Gap-fill handout (teacher created)

Students from different cultures do not all record numbers in the same way. This creates difficulty when quickly noting large numbers, such as in a lecture situation. For example, in Chinese, large numbers are broken down into units of ten thousands, not thousands, leading to confusion. Additionally, not all language learners' system of noting numbers uses the same punctuation, and there is often confusion with using periods and commas. Students need to be able to quickly and accurately note large numbers during lectures, and this activity provides a fun practice of this skill.

PROCEDURE

1. Prepare enough copies of a gap-fill handout for each student. Also, find a copy of the song that you can play (see www.youtube.com/watch?v=buqtdpuZxvk).

2. Begin the activity by asking how large numbers are written in English. Do we use periods or commas to separate units? Do we use different punctuation marks when writing other types of numbers, such as percentages? Where do we separate numbers—between hundreds or thousands?

3. Elicit a few large numbers from students and write them on the board. Then ask for a volunteer to come up, dictate a few large numbers to him or her, and have the volunteer write them on the board.

4. Introduce the name of the song that will be played, the "Galaxy Song" by the comedy group Monty Python, and ensure that everyone knows what a galaxy is.

5. Pass out the gap-fill handout and give the instruction to listen and fill in the numbers that are mentioned.

6. Play the song once for students to fill in the gaps.

7. Have students check what they heard with their peers and then play a second time to verify the numbers.

8. Have students tell you the numbers they heard and write them on the board, spelling them out. Then ask for a volunteer to come write the numbers in Arabic numerals beside the spelled-out form. Be sure that the commas are put in the right place.

9. After discussing anything the students have questions about, play the song again and have them sing along.

CAVEATS AND OPTIONS

1. Although a video accompanies the song on YouTube, it may distract or be offensive to some students, so I do not show the video and only play the audio.

2. For grammar input, you may want to take time to discuss lexical features of the song, such as the use of –ing. In this song, it is used both as a verb in the present progressive ("you're standing," "that's evolving and revolving," "that's orbiting," "are moving") and also as an adjective ("amazing and expanding universe"). After analyzing these parts of speech, you could also get students to identify the parts of speech of the words *galaxy/galactic* and *amazing/amazingly*.

This Is an Important Announcement!

Jim Cracraft

Levels	High intermediate to advanced
Aims	Practice listening with authentic material
	Practice pronunciation by developing a better understanding of the suprasegmental features of English
Class Time	≈ 1 hour–90 minutes
Preparation Time	45 minutes–1 hour
Resources	Computer with Internet access
	Projector
	Gap-fill exercise (Online Resource)

Rap music is not only becoming more mainstream, it is also becoming more international, with many countries now boasting their own homegrown rap artists. Using authentic materials in the classroom—in this case a routine airline safety message delivered as a rap—can motivate students. Incorporating rap songs can add variety to existing pronunciation lessons and can highlight suprasegmental features (rhythm, stress, thought groups, intonation, etc.) of the language in a meaningful way.

PROCEDURE

1. After discussing elements of rap music/songs, especially rhythm and rhyme, play the video of the Southwest Airline rap which is about 2:30 in length (www.youtube.com/watch?v=DYA_ivyj3kE). Ask students how well they understood the message.

2. Play the video again and this time have students write down rhyming words they hear.

3. Pass out the gap-fill activity (Appendix) and play the recording a third time so that students can fill in the rhyming words. Go over the correct answers.

4. Have students practice reading (rapping) in pairs, alternating every four lines. Direct them to note the rhythm, sentence stress, and thought groups. The student not reading can try to (softly) keep the STOMP-CLAP-STOMP-CLAP beat by tapping the desk.

5. In pairs or small groups, have students brainstorm situations in which they typically hear safety information, procedures, or other step-by-step instructions. Alternatively, this step could be done at the very beginning of the activity.

6. Give students 25–30 minutes to write their own important announcement, safety, or instructions rap.

7. Students can share/perform their rap in small groups or for the class.

CAVEATS AND OPTIONS

1. This activity is flexible and could be easily adapted for different groups. For example, international teaching assistants could be encouraged to use field-specific vocabulary to write a rap about lab safety or about how to do an experiment. Others might create a rap about tornado safety or another topic important for their community. Because writing a rap is very challenging, offer support for students who have trouble with rhyming, rhythm, and so on. For some groups, coming up with a just few lines of a rap might be sufficient.

2. Take care when playing examples of rap music in class, as songs in this genre often come with "explicit content" warnings and can deal with controversial themes. See References and Further Reading for a few examples of "clean" rap songs.

REFERENCES AND FURTHER READING

A Sampling of Rap Artists with Mostly Clean Lyrics

- "The Fresh Prince of Bel Air Theme Song," by Will Smith
- "Rapper's Delight." by the Sugar Hill Gang
- Much of Run D.M.C.'s music

Pronunciation Resources

Exercises and resources on using public service announcements to practice listening and pronunciation skills can be found in *Targeting Pronunciation* by Sue F. Miller. Materials in this text can serve as a useful lead-in or extension to this activity.

Miller, S. F. (2006). *Targeting pronunciation: Communicating clearly in English*. Boston, MA: Houghton Mifflin.

For Practice With Rhythm (Especially With Younger Learners)

Graham, C. (1978). *Jazz chants: Rhythms of American English for students of English as a second language.* New York, NY: Oxford University Press.

APPENDIX: *Southwest Airlines Safety Rap Gap-Fill Worksheet*

Put one of the following in a numbered gap.

aboard	advice is	back	can	devices	dollars	exit
expect it	fantastic	feet	first	holler	ignored	places
plan	plastic	raise	rhyme	seat	suitcases	SWA
that	thirst	time	today	trays		

This is Flight 3-7-2 on _____(1)

The flight attendants on board servin' you _____ (2)

Teresa in the middle, David in the _____ (3)

My name is David and I'm here to tell you _____ (4)

Shortly after takeoff, first things _____ (5)

There's soft drinks and coffee to quench your _____ (6)

But if you want another kind of drink, then just _____ (7)

Alcoholic beverages will be four _____ (8)

If a Monster Energy Drink is your _____ (9)

That'll be three dollars and you get the whole _____ (10)

We won't take your cash; you gotta pay with _____ (11)

If you have a coupon, then that's _____ (12)

We know you're ready to get to new _____ (13)

Open up the bins, put away your _____ (14)

Carry-on items go under the _____ (15)

In front of you, so none of you have things by your _____ (16)

If you have a seat on a row with an _____ (17)

We're gonna talk to you, so you might as well _____ (18)

You gotta help evacuate in case we need you

If you don't wanna, then we're gonna reseat you

Before we leave, our _____ (19)

Put away your electronic _____ (20)

Fasten your seatbelt, then put your _____ (21) up

Press the button to make the seat-back _____ (22) up

Sit back, relax, have a good _____ (23)

It's almost time to go, so I'm done with the _____ (24)

Thank you for the fact that I wasn't _____ (25)

This is Southwest Airlines, welcome _____ (26)

Polite Apologies in American English

Lisa Leopold

Levels	High intermediate to advanced
Aims	Acquire pragmatic strategies for apologizing in American English
Class Time	1 hour
Preparation Time	30 minutes
Resources	Audio recording of "Sorry," by Justin Bieber
	Handout of song lyrics

An extensive body of research suggests there are cross-cultural differences in apologies (Blum-Kulka, House, & Kasper, 1989; Wei, 2008). Yet learners may have difficulty adopting pragmatically appropriate strategies for apologizing in different cultural contexts. This activity incorporates popular song lyrics to engage learners and helps learners adopt pragmatically appropriate strategies for apologizing in American English.

PROCEDURE

1. Ask learners what they would say to apologize for a mistake and record their ideas. Options might include "Sorry," "I apologize," "This is my fault," or "This won't happen again."

2. Introduce learners to the following research-based strategies for apologies from Cohen and Olshtain (1981):

    - An expression of apology (e.g., "I'm really sorry for not calling").
    - Responsibility or acknowledgement of the blame (e.g., "I know my actions were wrong").
    - Explanation or account for why the situation occurred (e.g., "The phone was down").
    - Offer of repair to carry out some action or provide payment for some kind of damage (e.g., "If there is any way to make it up to you, please let me know").
    - Promise of nonrecurrence (e.g., "This will not happen again").

3. Ask learners to classify each of their ideas from Step 1 as one of the categories from Step 2.

4. Ask learners which strategies they think might be used more or less frequently in their cultures to formulate polite apologies and present research findings relevant to learners' cultural and linguistic backgrounds (Blum-Kulka, House, & Kasper, 1989). For example, whether in their native language of Hebrew or in their second language of English, Israeli participants in one study were less

likely than native English speakers from the United States to include an expression of apology (when forgetting to take one's son shopping), to acknowledge the blame (when bumping into a lady), and to offer repair (when forgetting a meeting with one's boss) (Cohen & Olshtain, 1981). Because there have been numerous studies on the apology speech act, you should selectively present research relevant to your learners' cultural and linguistic backgrounds, and, if appropriate, engage your learners in a discussion in which they hypothesize what might account for the cultural variation.

5. Invite learners to listen to Justin Bieber's song "Sorry" while labeling the apology strategies as they follow along with a transcript. Here is the number of occurrences of each apology strategy in the song:
   - An expression of apology: 1
   - Responsibility or acknowledgement of the blame: 3
   - Offer of repair: 1

6. Invite learners to brainstorm modifications to the apology strategies to make the apology more sincere. For example, instead of him saying "I'm sorry," learners could intensify that with the words *extremely*, *so*, *very*, *terribly*, or *awfully*.

7. Discuss the differences between the songwriter's lyrics and students' revisions and highlight the importance of admitting fault, accepting blame, and expressing regret when apologizing.

8. In the song, "Sorry," there is one strategy that is missing from his apology. Ask learners what they might add to strengthen the apology. One option might be a promise of nonrecurrence (e.g., "I promise this will not happen again.")

9. In class or for homework, ask learners to craft an (oral or written) apology for a scenario in their daily or professional life using the strategies learned.

CAVEATS AND OPTIONS

1. After crafting an apology in Step 9, have learners seek feedback from native English speakers about the appropriateness of their apology and report their findings to the class.

2. Have learners compare apology strategies from a variety of song lyrics, such as "The Apology Song," by The Decemberists; "Hard to Say I'm Sorry," by Chicago; "Forgive Me," by Evanescence; or "Apologize," by Chris Brown.

REFERENCES AND FURTHER READING

Blum-Kulka, S., House, J., & Kasper, G. (1989). *Cross-cultural pragmatics: Requests and apologies.* Norwood, NJ: Ablex.

Cohen, A. D., & Olshtain, E. (1981). Developing a measure of sociocultural competence: The case of apology. *Language Learning, 31*(1), 113–134.

Wei, H. (2008). Effects of cultural background of college students on apology strategies. *International Journal of the Sociology of Language, 189,* 149–163.

Lady Mondegreen Rides Again!: How to Use Mondegreens (Misheard Song Lyrics) to Further Listening Skills and Understand Phonetic Features

Chris Walklett

Levels	High intermediate to advanced
Aims	Understand the usefulness of songs and their lyrics for listening practice and pronunciation awareness
	Practice close listening and phonetic transcription
	Become aware of similar phonetic utterances
	Explore syllable stress and other areas of connected speech
Preparation Time	15 minutes
Class Time	20 minutes, plus 10–15 minutes for each student presentation
Resources	Appropriate examples of misheard lyrics

Misunderstanding speech is common. This miscommunication is because of a variety of factors, including unknown vocabulary (e.g., slang), accent, or speed of delivery. Miscommunication may also arise because English is a stress-timed as opposed to syllable-timed language and because of connected speech, including assimilation, epenthesis, and elision. There's a special word for misheard or misunderstood music lyrics—mondegreens—and they're more common than you might think.

PROCEDURE

1. Give students an example to show how words/phrases from songs can be misunderstood.
2. Play a part of a song, picking one where the lyrics are perhaps ambiguous or difficult to figure out. Adapt to your students' level (see Caveats and Options).
3. The students should write down what they hear, regardless of whether they think it is right or not.
4. After a second listen, students compare answers with each other.
5. The students should then share their responses while you write them on the board.
6. Compare the answers using a phonetic chart. Discuss why those different answers might have come about (e.g., issues of connected speech).

7. Have students try to decide through discussion (based on logic and context) what the actual lyrics are.

8. Write these up and transcribe them phonetically, discussing any issues of phonetic similarities or connected speech.

9. Schedule a future lesson in which the students bring in their own song and "take the stage," playing a selected part of the song as the other students follow the steps above to try to work out what the lyrics are. This could be done as a student presentation.

CAVEATS AND OPTIONS

1. You should explain the relevance of song lyrics to difficulties in understanding spoken language.

2. There can occasionally be cultural resistance to the use of songs. If this is the case, videos and CD recordings of speech may have a similar outcome with a slight variance in procedure.

3. These ideas can be adapted to suit differing levels. Mostly, this will come down to difficulty of vocabulary, as clearly both the actual word and mondegreen need to be known by students.

REFERENCES AND FURTHER READING

Find an archive of misheard song lyrics at www.kissthisguy.com/

Keddie, J. (2012). Lessonstream. Retrieved from http://lessonstream.org/topic/music-music-videos/

Smith, G. P. (2003). Music and mondegreens: Extracting meaning from noise. *ELT Journal, 57*(2), 113–121. doi:10.1093/elt/57.2.113

Part IV

Music for Speaking

Part IV: Music for Speaking

Pitch. Rhythm. Melody. Phrasing. Contour. Tempo. Tone. Pausing. Beat. Though no language teacher would argue that speech and song should be presented as phonologically or prosodically identical, the parallels are undeniable. In fact, speech and music are so similar that the scientific community has debated whether music evolved from speech, or speech from music, and even if music, like language, is an evolutionary adaptation (Levitin, 2007; Patel, 2008).

These similarities between speech and song provide the creative teacher with a fertile source of classroom material. The rhythms of music, from a traditional folk song in Marsha J. Chan's activity, to everything from nursery rhymes to R.E.M in Ildiko Porter-Szucs's activity, to the beats of rap in Tom Lackaff's, can provide a platform for speaking practice. Mike de Jong, who shares an original composition, and Marie Webb focus on song lyrics to explore rhyme and vowel sounds respectively, and Benjamin J. White brings together multiple characteristics of spoken English to show students that they can speak faster than they ever thought possible.

The richest use of music in a spoken language classroom, however, may not depend on any scientifically explored relationship. It is simply music as the basis for discussion. What student has never thoroughly enjoyed a conversation about music, and what teacher has never discovered students sharing music with each other before class? Social issues as presented in popular songs are discussed in activities by James Broadbridge and Lauren Lesce, while activities by Nathan Galster and Peter McDonald use songs as a basis for discussion of more personal topics, such as past experiences and likes and dislikes. Students discuss movie theme songs in Islam M. Farag's activity, character in Matthew Kobialka's activity, and musical instruments in Christopher Stillwell's. Students simulate the complex task of putting together a music festival in Simon Thomas's and Sean H. Toland's activity, and in Meaghan Harding's activity, students create a karaoke presentation through which they can review for their classmates anything from grammar and figurative language to reductions, linking, and assimilation.

Regardless of which came first, their similarities or differences, or their classification as an evolutionary adaptation, music and spoken language go together in comfortably complimentary harmony in a language classroom.

REFERENCES

Levitin, D. (2007). *This is your brain on music: The science of a human obsession.* New York, NY: The Penguin Group.

Patel, A. (2008). *Music, language and the brain.* New York, NY: Oxford University Press.

Singing to Develop Rhythm and Linking

Marsha J. Chan

Levels	All
Aims	Focus on rhythm, linking, and emotional expression
Class Time	30–50 minutes
Preparation Time	15–20 minutes
Resources	Recording of a song with a regular rhythm, repeated occurrences of linking, and a story to tell (see Appendix A)

This step-by-step procedure provides the scaffolding that can help learners understand a song from various perspectives, with the focus of listening and singing moving from one element to another. Eventually, learners will be able to incorporate rhyme, rhythm, linking, and expression as they sing the song with expression.

PROCEDURE

1. Preteach key vocabulary or grammar points.
2. Play or sing the song; students listen one or more times.
3. Discuss the meaning of the song lyrics. Elicit from students as much as possible; fill in with explanations of literal meaning, vocabulary, grammar, and cultural viewpoints.
4. If the lyrics have rhyming words, have students identify them.
5. Play or sing the song again; ask students to listen for strong beats (stressed syllables). Have them do one of the following:
   - Clap their hands together on the strong beats.
   - While holding up one hand, open the hand with fingers extended on the strong beats, and close the hand into a fist on the weaker beats.
   - Tap their fingers on their desks on the strong beats.
6. Have students sing the song, focusing on rhythm and rhyme, making stressed syllables clearer and louder than the others.
7. Listen for difficulties students are having, for example mispronouncing *bonnie* as boney, and model the correct pronunciation.
8. Play or sing the song again; ask students to listen for linking between words. At each instance they hear, have them raise their hands quickly and bring them down. Have students sing the song, paying attention to linking.

9. Ask students to consider the mood of each verse, prompting with questions, as needed: Is the singer happy? Sad? Grieving? Worried? Excited? How can you indicate the feeling with your tone, facial expression, gestures?
10. Have students sing the song, keeping the rhythm and linking, and incorporating the emotional expression into the lyrics.

CAVEATS AND OPTIONS

1. If you are a musician, perform the song live.
2. Listen to the song that you plan to use and write down the lyrics, or find the lyrics online and check them with the selected version of the song. Include the names of the lyricist and song writer, if available.

Desert Island Songs

Peter McDonald

Levels	All
Aims	Give personal information
	Express opinions, feelings, and emotions
	Talk about likes and dislikes
	Converse about past experiences
	Discuss personal relationships
Class Time	≈ 1 hour
Preparation Time	1 hour
Resources	Audio recording of songs or access to YouTube

Songs support fluency because music provides a stimulus that can unlock memories, feelings, emotions, and so on that may not appear under normal classroom settings. This activity is based on the popular British radio program *Desert Island Discs*, in which prominent people (movie stars, musicians, business people, etc.) talk about the songs they would choose if they were cast away on a desert island. Through context and structure, this activity gives students a clear communicative function.

PROCEDURE

1. Select four songs that you would take to a deserted island. Prepare an explanation for each song using the following questions as guidelines.
   - Why did you choose this particular song to be included in your castaway disc?
   - What does the song mean to you?
   - Which stage in your life (early childhood, teenage years, etc.) does the song represent?
   - Which memories of people, places, and other things does the song evoke in you?
2. Play/sing the songs or part of the songs to the students and explain why you selected them. Encourage the students to ask questions to initiate a discussion about music and what music means in your life.
3. Have the students create their own desert island song list based on your model.
4. Ask the students to share their songs and experiences with their classmates.

CAVEATS AND OPTIONS

1. It is important to inform the students that any song that represents things that are meaningful to them is acceptable. The song does not have to be one that they like or that is critically important.

2. You can easily adapt this activity to different levels; you can provide elementary classes with teacher-centered models and advanced classes with more autonomy.

3. The activity also provides a good foundation for follow-up activities. For example, students can make their own listening comprehension tasks based on the songs and explanations of why they selected the songs, and use these to test their classmates. Students may also search for a famous person on the BBC website (www.bbc.co.uk/programmes/b006qnmr) and discuss what they have found in class.

Learning to the Beat: Improving Speaking Fluency and Pronunciation With a Metronome

Ildiko Porter-Szucs

Levels	All
Aims	Practice pronunciation, particularly rhythm
	Increase spoken fluency
Class Time	30 minutes
Preparation Time	10 minutes
Resources	Online metronome (see Caveats and Options)
	Audio or video recording of selected songs (see Caveats and Options and the Appendix)
	Handout of song lyrics

Every language teacher knows intuitively that music can be used both as a powerful facilitator of learning and the subject matter of instruction. Research findings support this common practice. Schön and her colleagues, for instance, found that when speech is delivered as a song, learning is enhanced considerably (2008). Though music can be used to teach a variety of language skills, it perhaps lends itself best to the teaching of oral skills.

According to Pike (1972), English stress-timed rhythm can be challenging for learners from syllable-timed language backgrounds (e.g., Hungarian). These learners tend to pronounce each syllable with approximately equal length instead of compressing the unstressed syllables and elongating the stressed ones. The present activity is aimed at improving students' rhythm and fluency. It utilizes a metronome (or hand clapping) to tap the beat and the lyrics to a song with a strong regular beat.

PROCEDURE

1. If the students are unfamiliar with the concept of syllables, preteach it now.
2. Elicit from students any simple songs they may have learned as young children. Introduce an English nursery song (such as "Row, Row, Row Your Boat" from the Appendix).
3. As a class, count the number of syllables per beat in the first line of the nursery rhyme as 1, 1, 1, and 2.
4. Have students in pairs count the number of syllables per beat with the rest of the song.
5. Set metronome to 50 beats per minute (bpm). Have students clap to the metronome.

6. Sing the song to the beat of the metronome. (In the Appendix, the beats have been marked with a vertical line.)

7. Elicit how many syllables fit between two vertical lines, or between two beats of the metronome. Students are likely to discover for themselves that the number of syllables in one beat ranges from one to three in the song.

8. Elicit guesses how this is possible. Introduce the concepts of stressed versus unstressed syllables and content versus function words. Introduce the importance of accentuating only the prominent, or stressed, syllables in content words rather than all syllables. Draw students' attention to the fact that this prominence in each beat may occur inside a word (such as the first syllable of *merrily*) or across words (such as the noun in *life is*).

9. Practice singing the song to the metronome, monitoring students' pronunciation. [Note: These rules of pronunciation are occasionally violated in songs.]

10. Once students feel comfortable singing the song to 50 bpm, turn up the metronome to 60. Repeat at this pace for increased fluency.

CAVEATS AND OPTIONS

1. Free online metronomes are available (e.g., Metronome Online, www.metronomeonline.com)

2. I recommend starting with a nursery rhyme, regardless of age group and instructional setting. Once the students feel comfortable with the concepts, more age-appropriate songs can be found on YouTube. Here are some good options for different levels.

    - **Young learners:** "The Itsy Bitsy Spider," "Twinkle, Twinkle, Little Star," "The Wheels on the Bus Go Round and Round," "Rain, Rain, Go Away," "Five Little Monkeys"
    - **Preteens/Teens:** "Oompa Loompa," from the film *Willy Wonka and the Chocolate Factory*; "Stereo Hearts," by Gym Class Heroes; "Try," by Colbie Caillat; "Happy," by Pharrell Williams (disregard the drummer's off beat and focus on the singer's down beat)
    - **Adults:** "My Bonnie Lies Over the Ocean," a Scottish folk song; "Let It Be," by The Beatles; "The Boxer," by Simon & Garfunkel; "Losing My Religion," by R.E.M.

3. For more good song options, go to the Public Domain Information Project (www.pdinfo.com) or see McCormick (2016) for a list of the "100 Greatest Songs of All Time."

REFERENCES AND FURTHER READING

McCormick, N. (2016, May 30). 100 greatest songs of all time. *The Telegraph*. Retrieved from http://www.telegraph.co.uk/culture/music/11621427/best-songs-of-all-time.html

Pike, K. L. (1972). The intonation of American English. In D. Bolinger (Ed.), *Intonation: Selected readings* (pp. 53–83). Harmondsworth, United Kingdom: Penguin.

Schön, D., Boyer, M., Moreno, S., Besson, M., Peretz, I., & Kolinsky, R. (2008). Songs as an aid for language acquisition. *Cognition, 106*(2). 975–983.

APPENDIX: *Row, Row, Row Your Boat*

The beats have been marked with a vertical line.

Row | row | row | your boat,
Gently | down the | stream. |*pause*|
Merrily | merrily | merrily | merrily,
Life is | but a | dream.

Do You Hear What I Hear? Discussing the Pieces in a Musical Ensemble

Christopher Stillwell

Levels	All
Aims	Gain appreciation for a common but infrequently considered listening ability
	Practice describing musical sounds
	Use persuasive language
Class Time	10–15 minutes
Preparation Time	10–15 minutes
Resources	Audio recording of a song
	Copy of a picture-dictionary page of musical instruments with the labels removed

The best conversation practice happens when students fully understand the topic and have something they want to say. Identifying the sounds of instruments in a song is an engaging activity that does not require language skill, thus putting learners of all proficiency levels on equal footing in terms of the content to be discussed. As students compare notes regarding what instruments they think they hear, they are naturally drawn into a debate.

PROCEDURE

1. Provide students with a copy of a picture-dictionary page of musical instruments with the names removed. Have students work with partners to label the instruments.

2. Tell students that you will play a snippet of an instrumental piece of music and that they will be asked to count the number of different instruments they hear. (I recommend using a 20- to 40-second clip, with no more than six instruments. One option is the first 41 seconds of "Blue Drag" as performed by the New Orleans Jazz Vipers; tinyurl.com/newobdrag)

3. After playing the music, have students compare their answers in small groups. If the answers are not too obvious, this simple discussion is likely to yield a surprisingly engaged debate.

4. Without telling students if their guesses are right or wrong, write all the instruments they think they heard on the board. Then have them listen again to see if they can hear any of the instruments on the list that they had not heard previously. (There is a good chance that they will). After listening, revisit the discussion of which instruments were really in the song, and guide the class to a consensus. If you have a way of verifying the answers, now is a good time

to reveal the truth (and if you don't actually have a way of proving the correct answers, then it's a good idea to warn the class in advance that you don't really know, and you are hoping they can help you figure it out). (For "Blue Drag," the instruments appear to be acoustic guitar, bass, saxophone, and trombone).

5. Ask students to consider how the skill of singling out individual instruments to listen to might be similar to listening to conversations. Possible answers include conversations that take place in noisy environments, and even some circumstances of eavesdropping. Also draw attention to the fact that it is easier to understand what we hear when we have been primed to hear it—we may notice more instruments in the song after our peers point them out, and we might understand a conversation better if we first know what the topic is. You may invite students to try this out by playing conversation clips with and without having been given the topics first.

CAVEATS AND OPTIONS

1. Depending on students' cultural backgrounds, some kinds of music might sound especially foreign to their ears, which will bring added challenge to the task of picking out different musical instruments. Western teachers may test this idea out on themselves by playing a clip of Chinese opera and trying to identify the instruments. For this reason, it is useful to begin this activity by going over the vocabulary for different musical instruments (adding snippets of audio examples of each instrument may help as well. See References and Further Reading).

2. One fun way of extending the activity is to inform your class that we have a capacity to pick out specific things to listen to, when we set our minds to it. Challenge them to listen to the snippet of music again and tap their fingers along to the bass line, then to the strumming of the guitar, and then to the melody played by the saxophone.

REFERENCES AND FURTHER READING

Bardi, J. (2012). How selective hearing works in the brain. *UCSF News Center*. Retrieved from https://www.ucsf.edu/news/2012/04/11868/how-selective-hearing-works-brain

Kids Learning Videos. (2013 January 20). Musical instruments sounds [*Video file*]. Retrieved from https://www.youtube.com/watch?v=17V-bP1XEao

Let's Make Rhymes

Mike de Jong

Levels	*Beginner to low intermediate*
Aims	*Develop speaking skills*
	Expand vocabulary
Class Time	*≈ 1 hour*
Preparation Time	*15–30 minutes*
Resources	*Audio recording of original song "Let's Make Rhymes" (see References and Further Reading)*
	Audio recordings of select songs
	Lyrics from popular songs with strong internal rhymes

Rhymes and repetition are a foundation of popular music and are helpful in developing language skills. Learning to recognize rhyming schemes also helps students interpret song concepts and ideas. By listening to and analyzing song lyrics, students develop speaking skills and vocabulary and better understand song narratives and the songwriting process. Developing an understanding of lyrical complexity allows students to expand their own vocabularies.

PROCEDURE

1. Divide the class into groups and discuss the concept of rhymes in popular music. Instruct students to find new rhyming words to share with the class.

2. Play the original song "Let's Make Rhymes" and stop the song at various intervals. Have student group leaders make whiteboard lists of rhymes relating to particular words from the tune. Continue with rhymes from other recordings.

3. Provide students with examples of lyrics from other popular songs with strong internal rhymes. Explain how a songwriter conveys meaning through rhyme and repetition, starting with simple nursery rhymes before moving to more complex rhyming schemes from popular pop, hip hop, and funk recordings.

4. Give students 15–20 minutes to come up with their own rhymes and song verses.

5. Students share their own lyrics and song verses with the class.

CAVEATS AND OPTIONS

1. Use other lyrical devices, such as antonyms. For example, another original song, "Opposites Attract" (soundcloud.com/user-899196356), could be used to help students develop words and concepts that are opposite in meaning. It helps

students understand that words have numerous antonyms and by finding them, they can expand the breadth of their own communication skills.

2. Students further develop speaking and listening skills by discussing words and their meanings.

REFERENCES AND FURTHER READING

A free audio recording of the original song "Let's Make Rhymes" is available on this book's companion website, www.tesol.org/newwaysmucic, or at soundcloud.com/user-899196356/lets-make-rhymes.

Rap 101: Keeping It Real

Tom Lackaff

Levels	Beginner to intermediate
Aims	Share different aspects of your life orally
	Write about yourself in a musical fashion
Class Time	20–30 minutes
Preparation Time	15 minutes
Resources	Handouts (see Appendix)
	Recording of an instrumental 4/4 beat, no more than 80 beats per minute (optional)
	Access to an online metronome (optional)

This activity is designed to activate students' multiple intelligences (Gardner, 1983) by drawing their attention to the inherent musicality of language. By scaffolding reading, writing, and speaking skills, you will teach students an invaluable language-based life skill: introducing oneself. This form of introduction is also a classical trope of hip-hop music, and thus students will learn more about the cultural traditions of this global art form with American roots.

By approaching hip-hop in a step-by-step fashion, students will be empowered to learn that they have the same abilities as any of the seemingly larger-than-life rappers they may have seen, thereby promoting an enhanced appreciation of the value of writing and speaking skills. This activity also allows students to learn more about each other by sharing details of their lives in a fun, supportive environment, with the added benefits of lowering affective filters and promoting class cohesion and camaraderie.

PROCEDURE

1. Make copies of the handout (Appendix) that is appropriate to your students' level.
2. Ask students what they know about rap/hip-hop music. Ask if anyone in the class can rap.
3. Explain that everyone in the class will learn to rap. If there are any doubters, a friendly wager may be placed with the nonbelievers (e.g., "loser" has to tell a joke or do a dance).
4. Distribute handouts. Demonstrate how to fill them out with authentic, preferably humorous details from your own life.
5. Students fill in their own sheets. Answer questions and help as necessary.

6. Students reconvene in a circle and take turns sharing their self-descriptions. This may be greatly augmented by the addition of an instrumental beat or online metronome (www.metronomeonline.com). Students may also clap their hands, stomp their feet, snap their fingers, or "beatbox" (i.e., create rhythm vocally) to support their classmates.

7. Ask students to share reflections on what they have learned about themselves and each other. You may give a prize to whoever remembers the most details about other students. If any wagers were made (See Step 3), they may be decided by a class vote and settled immediately (i.e., with the putatively punitive public performance of puns or performance pieces).

CAVEATS AND OPTIONS

1. Many students, especially shy ones, may be hesitant to share their self-laudatory odes with the class. You may mitigate students' performance anxiety by first demonstrating the activity with relatable aspects of your own life. Encourage the use of hyperbole, as students will enjoy the humorous exaggeration of authentic personal details. By demonstrating a range of lighthearted possibilities, you can model how students need not necessarily emphasize the most impressive or intimidating aspect of themselves in order to gain acceptance from their peers. Here's my example:

    My name is Tom and I'm here to say:

    I'm the silliest teacher in the USA!

    I know I'm silly 'cause when I dance

    I can hear people laughing from here to France!

2. One way to adapt this for lower level learners is to provide illustrated word lists with popular choices for students to write about (e.g., games/sports, favorite foods, hobbies/pastimes). This will allow students with low literacy and/or vocabulary skills to follow a template for this writing activity, while still exercising creative choices for self-expression.

3. As seen in the Appendix, this activity may also be adapted for higher level learners by asking students to generate more complex grammatical structures, as well as by providing open space for additional self-description.

4. The challenge for students of all levels will be to balance the semantic content of their writing (emphasizing authentic self-expression) with their growing appreciation of rhythm and rhyme.

REFERENCES AND FURTHER READING

Gardner, H. (1983). *Frames of mind: The idea of multiple intelligences.* New York, NY: Basic Books.

APPENDIX: *Sample Handouts*

RAP 101

My name is _____ and I'm here to **say**:

I _____ in a major **way**!
    (something you like to do)

RAP 201

My name is _____ and I'm here to **say**:

I'm the _____ _____ in the **USA**!
    (superlative adjective)   *(noun)*

RAP 301

_____
(something else about you)

_____
(something that rhymes with the last line)

Rocking out for Better Pronunciation and Spelling

Marie Webb

Levels	Beginner to intermediate
Aims	Develop pronunciation and orthography skills
	Acquire an understanding of the rules and identification of long and short vowel phonemes
Class Time	≈ 75 minutes
Preparation Time	30–45 minutes
Resources	Any audio recording of a song with much repetition of long and short vowel words
	Cut-up strips of paper with vowel rules and examples
	Projector

Regardless of student proficiency in English, research shows that Arabic speakers in particular struggle with orthographic features of English because of the absence of short vowels in Arabic writing (Deacon, 2015). This activity uses music to demonstrate the differences in short and long vowel pronunciation and contributes to raising awareness of spelling norms and nuances. Such explicit teaching of phonological rules to students provides them with the comprehensible input they need to help improve their speaking and listening abilities, not to mention reading fluency. Many adults remain unaware of the strategies practiced in this activity; thus, researchers urge teachers to give their students such analytical strategies (Whitten & Mohan, 2008). Likewise, this activity uses the analytical skill of identifying phonemes (Florida Institute of Education, 2010).

PROCEDURE

1. Introduce common vowel pronunciation rules such as: when there is the letter *e* on the end of the word, the vowel that precedes the *e* makes a long vowel sound such as in the words *blame*, *time*, and *tale*. For more common vowel rules, see "More Vowel Rules" (Moore, 2009) and "7 Secret Pronunciation Rules Your Teachers Never Taught You" (Verner, n.d.) in References and Further Reading. Distribute the cut-up strips of vowel rules and examples and have students match the rule with the appropriate word to demonstrate understanding. You can have students do this in groups, pairs, or individually, and have them teach their rule to the class. This can take between 10 and 15 minutes.

2. Create a chart on the board in which students match a list of words from a song to a corresponding short or long vowel sound. For example, the words *waves* and *planes* would go under the long *A* vowel descriptor, and the words *shadow*

and *plans* would belong under the short *A* vowel descriptor. When you give directions to the students, make sure to remind them to use the vowel rules previously learned in Step 1 to help make informed decisions about placing words accurately on the chart. A good song to use is Jack Johnson's "Traffic in the Sky" because of its steady, slow rhythm and simple vocabulary. Students may do this activity with a partner and then the teacher may go over the answers with the entire class by projecting the chart and having student volunteers fill in the blanks. This will take about 20 minutes of class time. Any word from a song that includes long and short vowel phoneme practice is acceptable.

3. Play the song for the students. Provide the students with the lyrics, but leave blanks for all of the words that you used in the matching activity for Step 2. Have the students try to fill in the blanks by listening for the long and short vowel words in their chart.

4. Have students discuss their answers in groups and play the song again for students to confirm their answers. This, along with Step 3, will take roughly 15–20 minutes.

5. Students can further practice listening and speaking with long and short vowel words by identifying and repeating lyric segments, which should be cut up and distributed to each student on a small strip of paper. First, play the song one time and have students line up in the classroom when they hear their segment. When the song is finished, check to make sure the students are lined up in the correct order. This may take 10–15 minutes. Play the song a second time, but more quietly. Have the students step forward out of the line and speak or sing their song segment along with the music. To make this more challenging, have students emphasize the underlined/missing long or short vowel word from the gap-fill exercise in Step 3.

CAVEATS AND OPTIONS

1. To help students with other phonemes with which they are struggling, simply find a new song featuring such sounds and use the same activity.

2. You may also assign students the task of presenting a song with specific phonemic awareness goals to the class.

3. Have students reflect on their pronunciation issues before embarking on any kind of phonemic or semantic activity through spoken discussion and writing.

REFERENCES AND FURTHER READING

Deacon, R. (2015). Arabic ESL orthographic errors in English: Production difficulty in comparison to Korean ESL performance. *International Journal of Language and Applied Linguistics, 1*(2), 42–48.

Florida Institute of Education. (2010). Families learning together training session four: Phonological awareness. Retrieved from https://www.unf.edu/uploadedFiles/aa/fie/S-4-Phonological%20Awareness%20article.pdf

Moore, C. (2009, October). More vowel rules. *ABC Fast Phonics*. Retrieved from http://www.abcfastphonics.com/vowel-rules.html

Verner, S. (n.d.). 7 Secret pronunciation rules your teachers never taught you (but you should teach your ESL students). *Busy Teacher*. Retrieved from http://busyteacher.org/21353-7-secret-pronunciation-rules.html

Whitten, M., & Mohan, N. (2008, October). *Decoding: Teaching phonics to adults*. Presentation at the meeting of the Australian Council for Adult Literacy.

Character in Music

Matthew Kobialka

Levels	Intermediate
Aims	Make inferences from song lyrics
	Develop authentic listening skills
	Paraphrase and summarize materials
Class Time	80 minutes
Preparation Time	1 hour
Resources	Audio and lyrics for three or four songs that focus on a character (See Caveats and Options for examples)
	Handout of song lyrics
	Character worksheet (Online Resource)
	Cloze lyrics worksheet

Literary analysis, such as character analysis, does not need to be limited to traditional forms of literature, and using music provides students with an alternative approach to analyzing stories and character. Students can use the clues in the song lyrics to create a more detailed character profile. By engaging in this activity, students become experts on their song and must rely on each other to complete all the activities.

PROCEDURE

1. Divide the class into small groups and give each student a packet including
   a. a copy of the complete lyrics to the song assigned to the group (each group receives the complete lyrics to one of the songs and the cloze lyrics to the other songs);
   b. the character worksheet (Appendix A; categories can be explicit, e.g., age and gender, or implicit, e.g., interests and favorite movies); and
   c. a cloze worksheet from each of the other songs being used in the class.
2. Give the students 5–10 minutes to read the lyrics of their song and ask questions about vocabulary.
3. In their groups, have the students complete the character worksheet for the character in their song. Encourage students to make inferences about the characters and go into as much detail as possible. For example, what does the character look like, what are their characters' interests, and what kinds of movies might this character like?

4. Rearrange the student groups so that at least one student from each of the previous groups is included in a new group. In the new groups, have the students explain their character and the story in their song. Students should summarize the story and the character. Do not have the students share lyrics yet.

5. Listen to each of the songs. For each song, students should attempt to fill in the missing words on the cloze for that song. Play each song as many times as is needed. After each song has been played, allow the students to compare their answers on the cloze to the real lyrics, provided by the student in the group with the lyrics handout.

CAVEATS AND OPTIONS

1. Examples of good songs for this activity include
   - "A Boy Named Sue," by Johnny Cash
   - "The Jack of Hearts," by Bob Dylan
   - "Johnny B. Goode," by Chuck Berry
   - "Billie Jean," by Michael Jackson
   - "Bad Bad Leroy Brown," by Jim Croce
   - "El Paso," Marty Robin
   - "The Mariner's Revenge Song," by The Decemberists

   Most songs are available on sites such as YouTube.com, and song lyrics can be found online.

2. This activity emphasizes character, but it can also focus on plot. If you emphasize plot, have students complete a plot diagram (See Appendix B) in addition to, or in lieu of, a character worksheet.

3. You can use any song with narrative structure, depending on the students' level of English and musical interests. The cloze activity can focus on developing listening skills by having the students listen for the missing words in the song, or it can focus on new vocabulary words if you wish develop vocabulary.

Battle of the Planets

James Broadbridge

Levels	Intermediate to advanced
Aims	Work collaboratively to create a utopian fantasy world
	Compete with each other to create the most perfect and imaginative world
	Consider and discuss problems of the world we live in
Class Time	90 minutes
Preparation Time	10–15 minutes
Resources	Audio recording of "Saturn," by Stevie Wonder
	Planet Comparison handout (Appendix)

In the song "Saturn," Stevie Wonder describes a fantastical world on the planet Saturn, where people live to be 205, smile, and can fly, and where people look after the environment around them and the people living in it. It is written in a way that highlights much of what was wrong with the world in 1976, but it is still very relevant today. This song creates an opportunity for students to address what they believe is wrong with their world and to try to create a better world to live in. The activity pits teams of students against each other as they present an alternative version of life.

PROCEDURE

1. Draw a quick sketch of the solar system on the board and ask students to name the planets.
2. Highlight Earth. Ask students to form groups and make a list of problems the Earth is facing. Write them on the board.
3. Introduce the song "Saturn." Distribute the Planet Comparison handout (Appendix). Tell students they will listen to a song about life on the planet Saturn. They must fill in the table on the handout and find the differences between Saturn, as portrayed in the song, and Earth.
4. Students work in groups to complete the table and report their findings to the class.
5. Compare the list on the board created in Step 2 with the list from the song to see which problems are missing from either list.
6. Introduce the main task. Assign each group one of the remaining planets in the solar system. Students will work in groups to create a new world. They can create whatever kind of world they wish. They are not held by the laws of science and are free to be as creative as they wish. Groups must describe how

their planet will deal with many of the problems described in Steps 2 and 5 so that the world they live in is perfect.

7. Ask groups to present their findings to the class.
8. Students vote to choose the world they would most like to live in. They are not allowed to choose their own world.

APPENDIX A: *Planet Comparison Chart*

Listen to the song and note as many of the differences between the singer's world, Saturn, and our world, Earth, as you can.

Saturn	Earth
The air is clean on Saturn	Earth's air is polluted

Movie Theme Songs

Islam M. Farag

Levels	Intermediate to advanced
Aims	Focus on listening and speaking skills
	Think critically while listening to a theme song
	Analyze the relationship between a movie and a theme song
Class Time	45–50 minutes
Preparation Time	10–15 minutes
Resources	A video recording of a movie theme song
	Transcript of the song lyrics, optional
	Audiovisual equipment

Theme songs may urge students to speak and take a stand for or against an issue that the song deals with. Students will be passionate and engaged in the analysis and discussion of a theme song and a movie. This activity provides an opportunity for students to write an essay in which they express their opinions about the movie.

PROCEDURE

1. Choose a popular movie that has a popular theme song (e.g., "Let It Go," from *Frozen*; "My Heart Will Go On," from *Titanic*; "I Want to Spend My Lifetime With You," from *Mask of Zorro*, or "Eye of the Tiger," from *Rocky III*).
2. At the point in which the theme song is played, play the video two times.
3. Ask students to prepare oral and/or written answers to the following questions (you can create different questions):
    a. What is the main theme of the song?
    b. Describe the scenes of the song.
    c. Does the video of the theme song reinforce the message of the movie or not? Why?
    d. Do the lyrics of the theme song reinforce the message of the movie or not? Why?
    e. In most cases, theme songs are considered part of the movie. Do you think the theme song of this movie is displayed at the right moment during the movie? Why?
4. Play the video again or distribute lyrics if needed.
5. Divide students into groups and have groups present their answers to the class.

CAVEATS AND OPTIONS

1. It is better to use the most popular movies and their theme songs to ensure that students are familiar with the movie.
2. If students have not seen the movie, provide a synopsis of the movie or play a trailer or clip of it.
3. Require students to write a reflection on the theme song and its connection to the movie.

My Musical Autobiography

Nathan Galster

Levels	Intermediate to advanced
Aims	Develop creative thinking, speaking, and presentation skills
	Think creatively about your life story
	Make meaningful connections to English through music
	Prepare to write an autobiography or biodata
Class Time	50 minutes–2 hours (depends on class size and time limits for presentations)
Preparation Time	30 minutes
Resources	Computer(s) with audio/sound capabilities
	Microsoft PowerPoint or comparable program for each student

Music has powerful connections to memory and life experiences. People often associate songs with important events in life. Capitalizing on this phenomenon can give students a chance to make deeper connections to English and utilize it as a tool for discussion and presentation. By relating personal experiences and selecting songs of interest and personal value, you can make learning more meaningful and students can achieve greater retention.

PROCEDURE

1. Tell students to outline the important events in their lives and/or consider songs (in English) that have been important in their lives, or have a special connection to an event or time period in their lives. They should create a musical timeline of their lives. They can determine the number of songs they'll use. Around five songs would be appropriate. Brainstorming and planning stages could be conducted in groups to promote idea generation.

2. Students create a PowerPoint presentation that presents their musical timeline in sequential order. Include links (e.g., YouTube videos) to the songs in the slides. Include song titles, headings, and/or brief explanations of life events/song connections in slides.

3. Students give their PowerPoint presentations. They share their biography in music, progressing through the main/important events in their lives, sharing the music they chose and explaining the significance or connection to their lives.

CAVEATS AND OPTIONS

1. Students will need 30 minutes–2 hours to prepare their presentations, depending on student level and ability. They can prepare primarily at home, but you can give time in class for brainstorming and outlining.

2. If the classroom has numerous computers or students bring their own PCs to class, students can give presentations simultaneously in small groups. In this case, less class time would be needed.

3. It might be beneficial for you to prepare an example PowerPoint presentation. A sample musical autobiography is available on this book's companion website, www.tesol.org/newwaysmusic.

4. Employ this activity in the classroom more simply as a group discussion topic. Ask students to prepare for a class discussion by listening to music in English at home or choosing their favorite music that relates to their lives. Any number of songs could be selected at your or your students' discretion. As an example, one song for one important event in each student's life could lead to a 10–15 minute discussion in a small group of four or five students.

5. Adjust this activity into a writing activity in which students write about the songs and why they chose them (this might be done in place of a presentation).

RESOURCES AND FURTHER READING

Galster, N. (2014). *An educator's C.R.E.A.T.I.V.E. approach to learning.* Retrieved from http://nathangalster.wix.com/creatinglearning

Galster, N. (2016). *Media for task-based language learning.* Retrieved from http://nathangalster.wix.com/medialanguage

Karaoke Presentations

Meaghan Harding

Levels	Intermediate to advanced
Aims	Gain comfort and familiarity with participating in a group presentation
	Demonstrate mastery of previously-studied grammatical structures, vocabulary items, figurative language, and elements of spoken English
	Gain awareness of English-language songs through peer recommendations
Class Time	≈ 30 minutes plus 15–20 minutes per group for presentations
Preparation Time	30 minutes–1 hour
Resources	Assignment Description (Online Resource)
	Screen and projector
	Cloze handouts
	Video recordings of select songs
	Internet and printer access for students

PROCEDURE

1. Select a song to present as an example. Locate the original recording as well as a karaoke video with lyrics, a complete copy of the lyrics, and a cloze activity using the song's lyrics. (See References and Further Reading for sites with karaoke videos and premade cloze activities.)

2. Distribute the cloze and direct students to fill in the blanks while listening to the original version of the song once or twice.

3. After they've done the cloze, play the song and show the complete lyrics for students to read and check their own answers.

4. Point out two to three examples of previously studied language functions in the song. These could be grammatical items, contractions, reductions (e.g., gonna, wanna), linking (e.g., thisafternoon, howbout), assimilation (e.g., didja, wouldja), vocabulary items, figurative language, or any combination of these. Discuss with the students how these elements contribute to the song, what the song is about and what the lyrics mean, and why you chose this song.

5. Play the karaoke video of the song. If you are very brave you can perform it yourself or (more comfortable for most teachers) encourage the students to sing it all together. If your example presentation included features of spoken English (such as contractions, reductions, linking, or assimilation), encourage students to imitate the original singer's utterance of these features.

6. Divide students into groups of three or four and instruct them to prepare a similar presentation using a song of their choice (see Appendix for assignment description).
7. Students should submit their presentation materials to you ahead of time to check for any potential problems.
8. During a later class, groups can present their songs to classmates.

CAVEATS AND OPTIONS

1. Here are some examples of songs that would be appropriate for this assignment and some language examples that students might choose:
   - "Call Me Maybe," by Carly Rae Jepsen (simple past, assimilation, metaphor)
   - "Across the Universe," by The Beatles (U.K. accent) or Fiona Apple (U.S. accent; metaphor, linking, simple present)
   - "As Long as You Love Me," by The Backstreet Boys (contractions, conditionals)
   - "Roar," by Katy Perry (simile, contractions, reductions)
   - "Over the Rainbow," by Judy Garland (simile, metaphor, simple future, relative clauses, contractions, assimilation)
   - "Chandelier," by Sia (simple future, reductions, simile)
   - "Goodbye," by Who Is Fancy (simple past, metaphor, reductions)
2. College-level and adult learners are often nervous about singing in class, so your leading by cheerful example is crucial. Older students tend to be more comfortable with a group singalong rather than a prepared musical performance, but individual group dynamics will vary.
3. To adapt this activity for younger students or in a context where homework cannot be assigned, students could spend a period in a computer lab (or in their classroom using phones or laptops) preparing for their presentations.
4. Streamline the activity by preselecting a list of song options or narrowing the scope of features to discuss.
5. For college students needing exposure to Western norms of academic honesty, instead of creating their own cloze activity, task students with finding a cloze worksheet online and citing it correctly.
6. Rather than dedicating one or more whole periods to the activity, spread song presentations over multiple classes with only one or two groups presenting each day.

REFERENCES AND FURTHER READING

Good cloze worksheets can be found here:
- www.newtongue.com/lyrics-worksheets
- www.isabelperez.com/songs
- www.qualitytime-esl.com/spip.php?article322

Karaoke videos can often be found by typing "song title + lyrics," "song title + karaoke," or "song title + backing track" into a search engine. There are also many YouTube channels that specialize in sharing karaoke videos such as The KARAOKE Channel, Sing King Karaoke, Karafun, and You Sing the Hits. These channels feature videos that are free to view and do not require a subscription.

Impromptu Speaking

Lauren Lesce

Levels	Intermediate to advanced
Aims	Develop ability to think critically and express ideas orally "on the spot" about a topic from a song
Class Time	30 minutes
Preparation Time	15 minutes
Resources	Audio recording or music video of a song with a social message Handout of the song lyrics

Impromptu speeches develop speaking fluency and "on the spot" critical thinking skills, both of which are essential for participation in group discussions common in American classrooms. Connecting an impromptu speech topic to a song contextualizes the speech, and discussion of the song establishes a cursory understanding of the social issue before students have to form an opinion about it. This is also an opportunity for students to gain greater cultural knowledge about current issues discussed in popular culture.

PROCEDURE

1. Find the video or audio of a song with a social or debatable message. Prepare a transcript of the lyrics to hand out or display.
2. Play the song or video in class. As a class, have students discuss the social issue described in the song, the message of the song, and important vocabulary.
3. Introduce an impromptu speech topic that is related to the message of the song. For example, if you use the song "Where Is the Love?" by the Black Eyed Peas, you could have students give an impromptu speech about which social issue needs the most attention and why the world needs more love and compassion. Give students 1–2 minutes to prepare and outline their impromptu speech.
4. Give each student 3–5 minutes to deliver their impromptu speech in groups of three or four.

CAVEATS AND OPTIONS

1. If time allows, students can deliver their impromptu speech individually to the whole class. This will allow students to develop confidence speaking in front of a larger group.

2. To add an extra challenge, require students to incorporate a certain number of new words or phrases from the song into their speech. Classmates can monitor each other for the number of vocabulary words used in their speeches.

3. In a conversation or public speaking class, use this activity as a way to introduce a debate, presentation, or larger speaking project, or as assessment of the social issue presented in the song.

Music Festival: Looking for a Headliner and Opening Act!

Simon Thomas and Sean H. Toland

Levels	Intermediate to advanced
Aims	Develop research and reading skills
	Expand music-related vocabulary to improve communicative competencies
Class Time	90 minutes (minimum)
Preparation Time	15–30 minutes
Resources	Images of music festivals
	Method for showing images
	Smart phones/tablets
	Handouts (Appendices A–D, Online Resources)
	Stopwatch/timer

nabling students to take on the persona of their favorite music idol or performer can increase motivation and encourage increased communication abilities. In this activity, students play the dual roles of a music pop star and music festival promoter looking for acts. They use Internet research skills to investigate a musician, complete a profile card, and discuss this information in a speed interview session. This activity gives learners opportunities to enhance research and reading skills, develop vocabulary, and expand communicative competencies.

PROCEDURE

1. Print out Appendices A–D for each student.
2. Divide students into small groups. Write the following words on the board: *venue, headliner, featured performer, opening act, music festival, concert promoter,* and *speed interview*.
3. Give groups 5 minutes to discuss the words' meanings, then elicit students' ideas, providing feedback where necessary.
4. Provide students with a copy of the Lady Gaga Profile Card (Appendix A). Discuss the profile points and vocabulary.
5. Show preselected images of music festivals and discuss musicians students would like to see opening and headlining.
6. Distribute the Musician Profile Card handout (Appendix B). Using mobile devices, students research an individual musician or one member of a group and complete the profile with specific details or their own ideas. The activity works best if students all select different musicians.

7. Ask students to imagine they are a festival promoter looking for musicians. Groups brainstorm questions that a promoter might ask a musician (e.g., What style of music will you play? Which songs will you perform? How long will your show last? Do you have any special requirements?).
8. Each group writes several questions on the board; provide corrective feedback.
9. Students prepare answers that their profile musician would give to these questions.
10. Students select five questions from the board and write them on the speed interview handout (Appendix C).
11. Explain how the speed interview activity works.
    - The class is divided into two groups: musicians and promoters.
    - Tables in the classroom are reconfigured to allow festival promoters to sit on one side and musicians on the other.
    - You model the two roles with a student volunteer, emphasizing that this a communicative role-play activity and not a reading exercise.
    - The musicians have 4 minutes to meet, greet, and introduce themselves to the promoters, and answer questions.
    - After 4 minutes of the interview activity, the musicians use their mobile devices to show a clip from a song or music video.
    - Thirty seconds later, you signal it's time for the next interview. The musicians rotate to the next promoter while the promoters make brief notes on the Speed Interview Chart (Appendix D).
12. After six interviews, the promoters and musicians change roles. Repeat the speed interview process.
13. Upon completion, promoters have a short time to decide which musicians will be the opening act and headline their music festival.
14. The students get in small groups to discuss their choices and their reasons. They decide on one opening act and headliner and present their ideas to the class.

CAVEATS AND OPTIONS

1. Throughout the activity, you can make adjustments to suit the learners. For example, introduce the profile card (Appendix A) as a gap-fill research activity with model questions to elicit the profile information or by tasking students with making questions to quiz their classmates about the profile.
2. Modify the Musician Profile Card (Appendix B) information and questions to focus on musical styles, influences, or inspirations.
3. Teach advanced Internet search techniques.
4. Ask learners to produce their own gap-fill listening activities with lyrics.
5. Practice communicative aspects needed in the final interviews, such as listener clarification of questions asked.
6. In the role-play activity, ask promoters to find musicians for specific styles of festival.
7. Task students with writing concert reviews or fan letters to musicians.

Fast Song Sing-Along

Benjamin J. White

Levels	Intermediate to advanced
Aims	Raise awareness of rhythm in connected speech
	Promote abilities to reduce vowels in unstressed syllables and to link words
Class Time	≈ 1 hour
Preparation Time	15–45 minutes
Resources	Audio recording of a song with a fast chorus
	Handout of song (chorus) lyrics
	English dictionaries
	Online metronome (optional)

Natural spoken English is sometimes difficult for learners to understand. There can be significant differences between the way connected English speech sounds when spoken (or sung) and the way learners anticipate words will sound when seen on paper. This is an engaging activity that uses music to illustrate some of the phenomena of connected speech in English.

PROCEDURE

1. Create a worksheet with the lyrics of a song's chorus.
2. Play a song and ask students if the song is difficult to understand and why.
3. Tell students to focus on the chorus. Ask them to write down as many words in the chorus as they can. Signal each time the chorus starts and ends when the song is playing.
4. Ask students to compare their notes. Tell students that, by the end of the activity, they are going to sing the chorus just like the singer(s). This usually generates a mix of laughter and incredulity.
5. Hand out the lyrics worksheet. Ask students how close their notes are to the actual words in the chorus. Lead the students in a choral reading of the chorus lyrics. Read at a relatively slow pace.
6. Nominate individual students to read the lyrics aloud as fast as they can. Make sure everyone gets a turn.
7. Ask students how they think they sound and why it is difficult to read the chorus aloud quickly.
8. Ask students to do the following:
    a. Underline content words (e.g., nouns, verbs, adjectives, adverbs) in the chorus.

b. Circle primary and secondary stressed syllables in the content words. Encourage students to use dictionaries. It helps to model for the students how to use a dictionary to find stress patterns in words. Do the first few content words in the chorus as a group.

c. Still focusing on the content words, cross out vowels in unstressed syllables and write the schwa /ə/ over the top of the cross out. Make sure students know how to make this important sound. Have them relax their mouths and then make a sound without moving their tongues or lips.

d. Cross out vowel letters in the single-syllable prepositions *at*, *for*, *in*, *of*, *on*, *to*, and *with* if these words appear in the lyrics. Students replace the crossed-out letters with schwa. They should also change *f* to *v* in *of*. This results in *ət*, *fər*, *ən*, *əv*, *ən*, and *tə*. (Note: Do not do this for prepositions *by*, *near*, *off*, *past*.)

e. Cross out vowels in conjunctions *and*, *but*, and *or* and replace with schwa. For the word *and* have students cross out the final *d*.

f. Cross out vowels in *is*, *are*, and *will* and turn remaining letters into a contraction with the preceding word (e.g., *song will* → *song'll*).

g. If *he*, *him*, *his*, *her*, or *hers* are not at the start of a new line or sentence, ask students to cross out *h* at the start of the words.

h. For all words that end in consonants and are followed by a word that begins with a vowel, draw a line making a connection between the two words (e.g., *found out* → *found‿out*, *out* should now sound like *dout*).

9. Read the chorus out loud, modeling the notations made to the lyrics worksheet.

10. Do choral reading with students. Read at a slower pace to make sure students are reducing unstressed syllables and linking words. Then read at increasingly faster paces. An online metronome can be used to keep time.

11. Students take turns reading lyrics as fast as they can.

12. Ask students to reflect on any differences they notice between Steps 11 and 6. Was it easier to read quickly this last time? Have they noticed linking and vowel reduction in everyday speech in the past?

13. Play the song again. Students sing along during the chorus.

CAVEATS AND OPTIONS

1. Possible songs for the activity include:
   - "All the Single Ladies," by Beyoncé
   - "American Kids," by Kenny Chesney
   - "Happy," by Pharrell Williams
   - "Honey, I'm Good," by Andy Grammer (Editor's note: This song contains language and content that may be offensive to some listeners.)
   - "Pinch Me," by Barenaked Ladies
   - "We Can Work It Out," by the Beatles

2. Be careful of using songs with much slang and new vocabulary in the lyrics. Students' natural curiosity to understand all the lyrics can sidetrack a lesson.

3. It should also be noted that not all natural spoken English makes all of these connected speech changes all the time. There can be idiosyncratic speech patterns in both songs and spoken language.

REFERENCES AND FURTHER READING

Celce-Murcia, M., Brinton, D. M., & Goodwin, J. M. (2010). *Teaching pronunciation: A course book and reference guide* (2nd ed.). New York, NY: Cambridge University Press.

Part V

Music for Grammar

Part V: Music for Grammar

What do an improvisational jazz musician performing in a club and an ESL/EFL student studying a grammar lesson have in common? According to a study at the Johns Hopkins University, they may be using the same parts of their brains, those usually associated with syntax and spoken language. Whether communicating verbally in speech or musically with instruments, functional magnetic resonance imaging tests demonstrated that two parts of the brain—the inferior frontal gyrus and the posterior superior temporal gyrus—are hard at work (Johns Hopkins Medicine, 2014). Evidence is mounting that the brain processes both musical and linguistic syntax in a similar manner (Fiveash & Pammer, 2014; Engh, 2013).

Although the differences between musical and linguistic syntax are clear, so are several parallels (Patel, 2008). Both musical and grammatical skills include recognizing patterns and understanding and applying rules, whether deliberately or spontaneously; both are generative in that an infinite number of new patterns can be created by recombining elements (Levitin, 2007). Additional research has shown a possible link between children's skill at perceiving musical rhythms and their grammatical abilities (Gordon et al., 2015). Combining music and grammar instruction has long seemed to make sense pedagogically, and now also, quite possibly, neurologically. The contributors to this section, therefore, just might be on to something in providing a musical context for grammar instruction.

The variety of ideas in this section includes musical activities for instruction in grammatical topics from verb forms and tenses (Ann Bouma, Jacqueline Foster, Jolene Jaquays, Juan Manuel Rivas, Josefina C. Santana) to clause and sentence structure (Carrie K. Bach; Eman Elturki; Diana Hemmelgarn; and Sara Okello, Allison Piippo, and Wendy Wang), using everything from musical parodies to Elvis Presley, and Anne Murray to Sia to an original musical score. Perhaps the creation of musical grammar lessons is as generative as language and music are!

REFERENCES

Engh, D. (2013). Why use music in English language learning? A survey of the literature. *English Language Teaching, 6*(2), 113–127.

Fiveash, A., & Pammer, K. (2014). Music and language: Do they draw on similar syntactic working memory resources? *Psychology of Music, 42*(2), 190–209.

Gordon, R. L., Shivers, C. M., Wieland, E. A., Kotz, S. A., Yoder, P. J., & McAuley, J. D. (2015). Musical rhythm discrimination explains individual differences in grammar skills in children. *Developmental Science, 18*(4), 635–644.

Johns Hopkins Medicine. (2014, February 19). The musical brain: Novel study of jazz players shows common brain circuitry processes both music, language. *ScienceDaily*. Retreived from https://www.sciencedaily.com/releases/2014/02/140219173136.htm

Levitin, D. (2007). *This is your brain on music: The science of a human obsession.* New York, NY: Penguin.

Patel, A. (2008). *Music, language and the brain.* New York, NY: Oxford University Press.

What About Me? Pronouns

Ann Bouma

Levels	All
Aims	Learn the different types of pronouns used in English
Class Time	50 minutes
Preparation Time	15 minutes
Resources	Video or audio recording of "I Wanna Talk About Me," by Toby Keith
	Handout of song lyrics
	Audiovisual equipment (optional)
	Grammar lesson on types and usage of pronouns

Grammar can be an unexciting topic for students. When grammar rules are illustrated in music, students can have better retention. Using "I Wanna Talk About Me," by Toby Keith, is a good way to help students learn the English pronoun rule of using an object pronoun after a preposition.

PROCEDURE

1. Play the song for the students.
2. Hand out the lyrics and ask the students to underline all of the pronouns.
3. Introduce or review information on types of pronouns.
4. Ask the students to make a chart of all the types of pronouns used in the song.
5. Remind them about the differences between subject and object pronouns.
6. Ask them to find the one error in pronoun use in the song. Discuss why this is an error. Discuss the fact that this error was made for the sake of rhyme rather than to illustrate correct English usage.
7. Ask them to write about what they would talk about. Prompt:

    "I would rather talk about my _____ than your _____. I want to talk about me. I would rather talk about our _____ than their _____. I want to talk about us."

    Have your students write as many sentences or sentence variations as their level permits.

8. Students share sentences with a partner.

CAVEATS AND OPTIONS

Have the students write their own verses and perform them as a rap for the class.

My Daily Routine

Juan Manuel Rivas

Levels	Beginner to high beginner
Aims	Improve comprehension of the simple present
	Learn some common daily routine phrases
	Produce original sentences using the simple present
Class Time	≈ 30 minutes
Preparation Time	20–25 minutes
Resources	Audio recording of "Daily Routines" song
	Audio recording with karaoke version of "Daily Routines"
	Handout (see Appendix A)
	Handout of song lyrics (see Appendix B)

PROCEDURE

1. Provide students with handout (Appendix A).
2. Ask learners to describe, in pairs, what they see in each picture.
3. Explain that three short songs about three of the five pictures will be played ("Daily Routines" audio recording, available on *New Ways in Teaching with Music* companion website, www.tesol.org/newwaysmusic) and that they should identify the picture described in the song.
4. Students self-check their answers using the lyrics handout (Appendix B). Optionally, check with the whole group to make sure learners got all the answers right.
5. Play "Daily Routines" karaoke version (available on *New Ways in Teaching with Music* companion website) and ask learners to sing the songs using the lyrics handout.
6. Students use sentences from the lyrics handout as a model to write about their own daily routines.

CAVEATS AND OPTIONS

1. Instead of writing their sentences, students can just talk about their daily routines using language models from the song.
2. Use a score of the "Daily Routines" song (Appendix C) if you are interested in using musical rhythms to teach pronunciation.
3. Use the karaoke version of the song to boost learners' creativity. For example, instead of asking learners to write or talk about their daily routines, invite them to write short songs describing their daily routines and use the karaoke version of the song to sing their original lyrics.

And His Momma Cries: Present Tense

Ann Bouma

Levels	Beginner to intermediate
Aims	Develop and reinforce the usage rule of using a final –s on regular verbs when used with a third-person singular subject in the present tense
Class Time	50 minutes
Preparation Time	15 minutes
Resources	Video or audio recording of "In the Ghetto," by Elvis Presley Handout of song lyrics

The adding of a final –s to third person singular verbs is a rule that is often very hard for students to remember to apply. With this song, the students discover and make their own rules; usage rules are easier for students to internalize when the rules have been created in the students' own words first.

PROCEDURE

1. Discuss the vocabulary word *ghetto*.
2. Play the song for the students and discuss the meaning of the lyrics. Talk about any vocabulary words that the students need defined.
3. Hand out the lyrics and ask the students to underline all of the subject-verb combinations.
4. Ask the students to make a generalization of what is done with the verbs (how each verb is conjugated) in each subject-verb combination. Identify whether each subject is singular or plural and first, second, or third person. With higher level students, ask the students if they recognize the imperative in "Take a look at you and me," and why the subject is missing.
5. Point out the words *cries* and *tries*. Discuss what generalization can be made for adding the –s to verbs originally ending in –y.
6. Discuss the noncount words *snow* and *hunger*. Discuss what generalization can be made for verb agreement in the present tense for noncount nouns.
7. In higher level classes, point out the word *crowd*. Discuss the verb agreement rule for collective nouns.
8. Look at the questions in the song. Analyze how a question is formed in the present tense.
9. Give a lesson on present tense rules and verify or change and add to the generalizations the class made from the song for present tense usage.

CAVEATS AND OPTIONS

1. This song leads to great discussions of what is being done to reduce poverty around the world.
2. Many related issues such as gun or gang violence, world hunger, or single parenting may generate writing assignments or serve as short debate topics.
3. This song is also good practice for the pronunciation of the final –*s*.
4. I don't discuss the rules for negative forms during this activity because the grammar in the song is incorrect when negative forms are used.

"You Needed Me": The Simple Past Tense in Action

Jacqueline Foster

Levels	Low intermediate to intermediate
Aims	Review the simple past tense
Class Time	25–30 minutes
Preparation Time	10 minutes
Resources	Audio and video recording of "You Needed Me," by Anne Murray
	Handout with song lyrics (Online Resource)

he use of "You Needed Me," by Anne Murray, in a culminating activity can be very motivating and appealing to learners because "singing, performing, and listening to music are often associated with play, happiness, and relaxation" (Abbott, 2002, p. 10). The song can inject a feeling of fun and enjoyment into the study of the simple past tense while helping students stay engaged and interested.

In addition, using this song provides an opportunity for students to experience authentic language. This can be very pleasing, especially for EFL students who may not have had opportunities to listen to a song in English. "You Needed Me" introduces students to genuine music and extends learning beyond the classroom to real language contexts.

PROCEDURE

1. Have students share their favorite songs.
2. Introduce Anne Murray (see Appendix) and have them discuss the title of the song, "You Needed Me."
3. Tell students that they are going to listen to the song and circle the simple past tense verbs. Provide the lyrics handout. Review the verbs.
4. Play the first verse and then check the circled verbs as a class.
5. Play the rest of the song twice. Students continue circling the verbs.
6. Have students share answers with partners and then check the circled verbs as a class.
7. As a review, students can divide the circled verbs into "be" verbs, regular verbs, and irregular verbs. The regular verbs can be divided further by orthographic endings (–ed, –d and –ied).
8. Play the song again, so students can just listen to it. They can also watch an older YouTube version and sing along as a culminating activity.

CAVEATS AND OPTIONS

1. This activity can be modified in a variety of ways. The past tense verbs can be deleted, so the students must write the entire past tense verb themselves.

2. Another option is to delete only the endings of the past tense verbs. For example, the verb *cried* can be typed as "cr _ _ _" on the handouts. Students must listen and write the ending.

REFERENCES AND FURTHER READING

Abbott, M. (2002). Using music to promote L2 learning among adult learners. *TESOL Journal, 11*, 10–17.

What Would You Do if You Had $1,000,000?

Eman Elturki

Levels	Intermediate to advanced
Aims	Construct conditional statements to talk about hypothetical situations
Class Time	≈ 1 hour
Preparation Time	25 minutes
Resources	Audio recording of "If I Had $1000000," by Barenaked Ladies
	Transcript of lyrics for projection
	Projector

This inductive teaching approach makes use of student noticing. It supports students being active participants in the learning process by analyzing and noticing what specific examples have in common.

PROCEDURE

1. Begin by reviewing the three types of real conditionals, which students should have already been introduced to. Ask students to write two sentences for each type on the board, circle the verb forms in each sentence, and explain what they want to convey through the use of each conditional statement. For example:

    Present Real Conditionals

    If you heat water to 100 degrees, it evaporates. [Fact]

    I take a walk if I feel bored. [Habit]

    Past Real Conditionals [Habits in the past]

    If I misbehaved, my father punished/would punish me.

    I usually took a gift with me if I went to a friend's house.

    Future Real Conditionals [A future event under a certain condition]

    If Yuki studies hard, she will pass the TOEFL exam.

    I will visit my friend if I have some free time tomorrow.

2. After the review, tell students that they are going to learn about a new type of conditional. Play the song with the lyrics. Ask students to sing along by reading the lyrics (the lyrics should be projected on the board). Repeat this as needed.

3. To help students notice language patterns and use, ask them to discuss in small groups whether the person in the song has $1,000,000 or not and why they think so.

4. Write multiple examples of hypothetical statements about yourself on the board and ask students whether the sentences are real or not. Examples:

   If I had wings, I would fly to my country. (Do I have wings? Can I fly?)

   I would buy a yacht if I were a millionaire. (Am I a millionaire? Can I buy a yacht?)

5. Play the song with the lyrics again and ask students to, within their small groups, compile a list with the things that the person in the song would do if he had $1,000,000. You can help students while they are working on this. Example: "If I had a million dollars, I would buy you a house."

6. After compiling a list with some of the things that the person in the song wishes to have/do, ask students to write complete complex sentences. They need to vary the sentences by starting some sentences with the dependent clause and other sentences with the independent clause. They need to pay attention to the use of commas (these topics should have been covered already). Examples:

   If I had a million dollars, I would buy you a house.

   I'd buy you a fur coat if I had a million dollars.

7. Ask students to circle the verbs in the two clauses and discuss with each other what they have noticed about the patterns (form and use).

8. Help students to arrive at the conclusion that this type of conditional is used to talk about a hypothetical or imagined situation in the present or future, and it is constructed by using the simple past in the dependent clause (the *if* clause) and *would/could* in the independent clause.

   "If ___ simple past___," "___ would/could + base form of the verb ___"

   "___ would/could + base form of the verb ___" "if ___ simple past ___"

9. Students write sentences about things that could or would happen to them under unreal conditions and then share with the class.

CAVEATS AND OPTIONS

The subjunctive mood *were* is not covered in this activity. The use of *were* instead of *was* in hypothetical statements is confusing to students (e.g., If I were you, I would talk to your teacher). The activity could be expanded by providing hypothetical examples using *were* and having students write their own. Two songs that might be used to familiarize students with this structure are "If I Were a Boy," by Beyoncé, or "If I Were a Carpenter," by Johnny Cash.

"Cheap Thrills" by Sia: Identifying Compound-Complex Sentences

Diana Hemmelgarn

Levels	Intermediate to advanced
Aims	Identify and use compound-complex sentences to add variety and complexity to writing
Class Time	1 hour–75 minutes
Preparation Time	10–20 minutes
Resources	Audio or video recording of "Cheap Thrills," by Sia
	Handout of song lyrics

This activity enhances understanding of an advanced grammar skill by (1) using motivational contemporary pop music and (2) providing a catchy "ear worm" as a mnemonic to help students easily remember the elements of a compound-complex sentence, which instructors can tell students to sing to themselves as they take a standardized test. It helps students to identify the grammar target and then importantly also provides a meaningful opportunity to apply it by developing their ideas in an academic writing context.

PROCEDURE

1. Review sentence types: simple, compound, complex, and compound-complex, including independent and dependent clauses. Remind students of the definition of compound-complex sentences.

2. Show the video to students, instructing them to observe the events in the video and to be prepared to discuss what they think the video means.

3. Put students in pairs or small groups, and ask them to describe the events in the video and discuss what they think the possible meaning is (not only one correct answer).

4. Pass out the lyrics and read them aloud together as a class. Discuss any vocabulary that students don't know.

5. Play the video a second time, instructing students to simultaneously listen and read the lyrics. Give students time with their partner to identify the compound-complex sentence.

   Answer: The compound-complex sentences are:
   - "It's Friday night and I won't be long, 'til I hit the dance floor."
   - "I don't need dollar bills to have fun tonight, but I don't need no money as long as I can feel the beat." (Keep in mind that "but" here does not actually indicate an opposite, and that there is a double negative, which is

descriptive grammar—as opposed to prescriptive grammar—because it is certainly used in everyday speech in many dialects.)

6. Instruct students to write a review of the song, including at least two compound-complex sentences of their own. You can determine the length, but 6–10 sentences is a good start. You may also challenge students to replace common words with more descriptive synonyms. You can provide an example song review with all of these features if you choose (see Appendix).

CAVEATS AND OPTIONS

1. When creating the lyrics handout, use size 14 font or bigger with 1.5 spaces or more between lines.

2. One interesting adaptation is to make the lyrics a jigsaw activity. Divide the lyrics by line and cut into pieces. Then have students put the pieces in order as a listening comprehension activity; they can then use those pieces to identify the compound-complex sentence.

3. This activity can be as short or as long as suits your needs. If you are introducing sentence types and clauses, this activity can serve as a skill-building task among a sequence of lessons. It can also be used as a quick no-prep review activity; print the lyrics or project on an overhead and go. You can adapt the writing activity to follow a learning objective for your required course syllabus, or it can be an enjoyable break.

4. This song does not have any explicit lyrics, so it is appropriate for classroom use. Also, although the video is not explicit, teachers should preview first to see if they feel it is appropriate for their student demographic.

APPENDIX: *Short Lesson Example*

Song Review With Compound-Complex Sentences (and five new adjectives)

Sia has become very successful due to her unique sound and catchy beats, which have attracted music lovers from around the world, and she continues to have a strong influence on the entire music industry, writing songs for many other well-known singers. She is known for eccentric choices, such as hiding her face or performing with her back to the audience so that people focus on the music rather than celebrity. *Although her face was unknown for some time, her songs were so entrancing that they gained a large listening audience anyway, and many hit the top of the charts.* Additionally, she chose a central theme of a young girl performing distinctive and mesmerizing dance routines in her videos; essentially, this girl became the known face of Sia. She has also paired this youthful dancer with celebrities, not necessarily to be provocative but to stretch the limits of artistic expression. *Her fresh choices have brought life to a new generation of aesthetic innovation, and after listening to "Cheap Thrills," you may also find yourself chanting "I don't need dollar bills to have fun tonight."*

Note: Compound-complex sentences in italics.

Synonym List

unusual = eccentric

fascinating = entrancing

doing = performing

unique = distinctive

entrancing = mesmerizing

young = youthful

offensive (cause a controversy) = provocative

artistic = aesthetic

invention = innovation

Using Music for Verb Structure Review

Jolene Jaquays

Levels	Intermediate to advanced
Aims	Review verb structures
	Practice listening strategies
Class Time	1 hour
Preparation Time	30 minutes
Resources	Audio and video recording of "Leaving on a Jet Plane," by John Denver
	Handout of song lyrics
	Cloze lyrics worksheet
	Verb structure chart (Online Resource)
	Projector

When teaching listening strategies, it is important to include a combination of both top-down and bottom-up strategies. Listening for contextual information requires different skills than isolating specific grammatical structures (Morley, n.d.). When relaying a story, we often use different tenses to integrate the past, present, and future through the eyes of the storyteller. In this way, students can be exposed to the integration of the various tenses.

PROCEDURE

1. Prior to class, create a cloze handout using the lyrics for "Leaving on a Jet Plane," by John Denver, by focusing on targeted verb forms.
2. Discuss the following prelistening questions:
   - Have you traveled on a jet plane?
   - How did you feel when you were leaving?
   - Did you make plans for your return?
   - Do you know anything about the late singer John Denver? Are you familiar with any of his songs?
3. Watch the first video of "Leaving on a Jet Plane" by John Denver (www.youtube.com/watch?v=vLBKOcUbHR0). It provides a bit of background information about the song.

4. Students discuss the following questions with partners:
   - Who is the singer?
   - To whom is he singing?
   - What is their relationship?
   - What is his overall message?
5. Students report their responses.
6. Listen to the song or watch the second video of "Leaving on a Jet Plane" (www.youtube.com/watch?v=H9qvjRVty7Q). This version includes visuals that help illustrate the vocabulary and meaning of the song.
7. Students find at least one example each of various verb structures and fill in the Verb Structure Chart (Appendix).
8. Students compare answers in small groups.
9. Project the grid on the board and assign each group to provide examples for a specific structure.
10. Replay the song with the lyrics and pause after each new set of lyrics appears. Analyze the reason for using each verb structure. Add missing examples to the projected grid.

CAVEATS AND OPTIONS

1. Depending on the level of the students, the song can either be played straight through, requiring the students to listen and write their responses, or paused after each new set of lyrics appears on the screen.
2. Often, online lyrics contain errors (mechanics, grammar, word choice, etc.). Students can review and detect any errors.
3. This song can also be used to analyze pronoun usage, the lack of stated subject pronouns in imperative forms, and rhythm.
4. Choose another song (e.g., "Counting Stars," by OneRepublic) that has a variety of verb structures for further review or homework.

REFERENCES AND FURTHER READING

Morley, C. (n.d.). Listening: Top down and bottom up. *British Council*. Retrieved from https://www.teachingenglish.org.uk/article/listening-top-down-bottom

Sigurðardóttir, D. (2012). *Language learning through music* (Thesis). Retrieved from Skemman Digital Repository. Retrieved from http://hdl.handle.net/1946/12591

Singing Your Love With Adjective Clauses

Sara Okello, Wendy Wang, and Allison Piippo

Levels	Intermediate to advanced
Aims	Stimulate interest and creativity
	Practice and review adjective clauses in speech when relative pronouns and adverbs are typically deleted
Class Time	30–50 minutes
Preparation Time	10 minutes
Resources	YouTube video of any popular song in which adjective clauses (with relative pronouns and adverbs omitted) are used repeatedly (see Caveats and Options for examples)
	Transcript of song lyrics

Grammaring has been defined as the ability to use grammar structures accurately, meaningfully, and appropriately (Larsen-Freeman, 2003). This focus on form, meaning, and use can help students develop the grammar skills they need to communicate effectively. Songs can be a meaningful, culturally rich medium that can contextualize the grammatical structure (Saricoban & Metin, 2000). By incorporating music into grammar instruction, you give students the opportunity to enjoy grammar while learning to use it in a threefold manner: accurately, semantically, and pragmatically. This activity focuses on the deletion of relative pronouns and relative adverbs in adjective clauses, which is characteristic of speech.

PROCEDURE

1. Warm up: Review adjective clauses that were previously taught and ask students to describe a friend or romantic partner using adjective clauses. Start with "This is the person who . . ."

2. Play a YouTube video of a popular song in which adjective clauses are used repeatedly. In this example, we'll use "You're Still the One," by Shania Twain. Have students listen to the song and discuss how Shania describes the person she loves using the sentence frame: "You are the one who ___") and the six verbs from the chorus (e.g., "You're still the one I run to").

3. Display the lyrics of the song with the adjective clauses highlighted. Ask the students to identify the grammatical structure and its purpose. Review the structure of adjective clauses. Ask students to identify the relative pronouns (e.g., *that, who/whom, which, whose*) and relative adverbs (e.g., *when, where, why*) typically used to introduce adjective clauses. Explain that when relative pronouns act as an object (e.g., "You're still the one I kiss good night"), the relative pronoun can

be omitted. Relative adverbs are often omitted in speech (e.g., The first time [when/that] you touched me).

4. Have students express their love in their own words, changing the relative clauses in the final chorus while retaining the rest of the lyrics. For example:

> "You're Still the One"
> You're still the one I _____
> The one that I _____ (Continue with the rest of the stanza).
>
> "Somebody that I Used to Know"
> You're just somebody that I _____
>
> "The Rose"
> Some say love, it is a _____ that_____
>
> "Everything I Do, I Do it for You"
> Every _____, I do it for you.

5. Play the YouTube karaoke version of the song and have the students sing along using their own lyrics.

CAVEATS AND OPTIONS

1. Some good examples of songs for this activity:
   - "You're Still the One," by Shania Twain
   - "Somebody that I Used to Know," by Gotye
   - "The Rose," by Bette Midler
   - "Everything I Do, I Do It for You," by Bryan Adams

2. This activity can be used to introduce or review adjective clauses where the relative pronoun and adverbs can be omitted. In the song, "You're Still the One," you may want to discuss the use of "ain't" in the second verse and the nonstandard usage of the verb in the sentence "We mighta took the long way" in the first verse.

3. For all songs, preview the videos before showing in class to see if they are appropriate for your students. [Editor's note: You can always 'mute' the video and play only the audio version if the images aren't suitable for your group.]

REFERENCES AND FURTHER READING

Larsen-Freeman, D. (2003). *Teaching language: from grammar to grammaring*. Boston, MA: Thompson-Heinle.

Saricoban, A., & Metin. E. (2000). Songs, verse, and games for teaching grammar. *The Internet TESL Journal, 6*(10).

Songs of Regret

Josefina C. Santana

Levels	Intermediate to advanced
Aims	Practice modals and expressions of regret
Class Time	45 minutes–1 hour
Preparation Time	5–10 minutes
Resources	Board

The objective of this activity is to help students learn by recalling the new structure taught. Music has been shown to be a useful mnemonic tool (Yalch, 1991). This is especially true when the verses are repetitive and when the music is simple, with a clear rhythmic pattern (Wallace, 1991). There is a strong connection between music and memory, and it can be used to help students learn more effectively. For example, creating songs can help students learn a new structure and recall it as needed. Simple songs can also be used to memorize irregular verbs (Santana, 2010).

PROCEDURE

1. Teach the expressions of regret: "should have," "I wish I had . . . ," "If only . . ."
2. Have students work in pairs or groups of three. Ask each team to select a tune they know, or to write a tune of their own.
3. Using that tune, students write a song of regret using the expressions you have just taught. For example, using the tune of "Yesterday," by The Beatles, they can write a song like this:

    Yesterday,
    I shouldn't have eaten so much cake.
    Now I have a really bad stomachache.
    I wish I hadn't
    eaten that cake.
    If only I had eaten
    fruit, instead, etc.

4. Give the students time to rehearse their song. They will present it to the group. They can opt to explain what tune they used and their lyrics, or they can sing for the group if they feel comfortable doing so. You can even have a song competition if the students are interested.

CAVEATS AND OPTIONS

1. The same activity can be used to practice other grammar structures.
2. Some students may not feel comfortable singing in public. Sharing the songs could be on a volunteer basis.

REFERENCES AND FURTHER READING

Santana, J. C. (2010, July–August). Music and memory: What's the connection. *IATEFL Voices, 215*, 9.

Wallace, W. T. (1991). Jingles in advertisements: Can they improve recall? *NA-Advances in Consumer Research, 18*, 239–242.

Yalch, R. (1991). Memory in a jingle jungle: Music as a mnemonic device in communicating advertising slogans. *Journal of Applied Psychology, 76*(2), 268–275.

Grammar Karaoke: Singing Along With *Wh*– Noun Clauses

Wendy Wang, Sara Okello, and Allison Piippo

Levels	High intermediate to advanced
Aims	Help students notice, process, and use Wh– noun clauses
Class Time	30–45 minutes
Preparation Time	10 minutes
Resources	YouTube video of any popular song in which Wh– noun clauses are used repeatedly (see Caveats and Options for examples)
	PowerPoint slide of song lyrics
	Audiovisual equipment with Internet access

Music can be used as an effective tool to teach grammar, particularly complex clausal structures characteristic of speech, such as *wh*– noun clauses (Biber, Gray, & Poonpon, 2011). By introducing a carefully selected song in which *wh*– noun clauses are repeatedly used, you provide students with enhanced input to raise their awareness of the target grammar structure and an opportunity for them to practice using *wh*– noun clauses in speech while having fun.

PROCEDURE

1. Play the YouTube video for the selected song. Here, we'll use "No Matter What," by Boyzone, a popular song in which *wh*– noun clauses are repeatedly used either as subjects or objects.

2. Ask students to share what they heard and guess the main idea of the song.

3. Display the PowerPoint presentation (key words should be highlighted and target grammar structure underlined; e.g., "I can't **deny** what I believe"). Ask students to listen to the song again while reading the lyrics.

4. Discuss in pairs the meaning of the song and how it compares to their original predictions. Then ask students to share their interpretations of the song using questions such as "What kind of relationship is this song about (e.g., family, friendship, love)?" and "How does the author feel about this relationship when others do not approve?"

5. Focus on *wh*– noun clause structure and use: Ask students to circle *wh*– words (e.g., *what, who, where, how*) in each stanza and discuss the structure and functions of *wh*– noun clauses using the following sentence frames:

Wh– noun clause as a subject presented before a verb phrase (VP).

_____ + **is** true. (e.g., *What we believe is true*.)
(VP)

Wh– noun clause as an object after a verb.

I can't **deny** + _____. (e.g., *I can't deny what I believe*.)
(Verb)

6. Divide the class into groups and assign each a different stanza. Play the karaoke version of the song. Each group sings their assigned stanza. The whole class sings the chorus at the end.

CAVEATS AND OPTIONS

1. Some good song examples for this activity:
   - "No Matter What," by Boyzone
   - "What Makes You Beautiful," by One Direction
   - "What Hurts the Most," by Rascal Flatts
   - "Don't Know Why," by Norah Jones
   - "Hello," by Lionel Richie
   - "I Still Haven't Found What I'm Looking for," by U2

2. Teach or review any other target clausal structures characteristic of speech. If you teach a multilevel class, consider providing tiered cloze worksheets to accommodate the needs of your students (e.g., a cloze worksheet with fewer blanks for lower proficiency students, and more for advanced students).

3. If time is available, follow the karaoke sing-along activity with a group singing competition.

REFERENCES AND FURTHER READING

Biber, D., Gray, B., & Poonpon, K. (2011). Should we use characteristics of conversation to measure grammatical complexity in L2 writing development? *TESOL Quarterly, 45*, 5–35.

Song Parodies

Carrie K. Bach

Levels	Advanced
Aims	Practice adapting sentence structures to new contexts
	Develop exposure to the genre of parodies
Class Time	≈ 2 hours
Preparation Time	5–30 minutes
Resources	Music video of a well-known song and a parody of it
	Audio recording of a different song
	Transcript of the lyrics with target phrases bolded (handout or projected)
	Cloze lyrics worksheet
	Video equipment or mobile devices (optional)

This activity allows students to engage with the lyrics of a song and the target language structures of the lesson on a deeper level as they use their creativity to transform the content of the song in their parody of it. Students also gain multimodal literacy skills through creating and performing their song, as well as digital literacy skills if they make a video. The entire project involves *remix culture*, the contemporary culture of appropriating and altering content to serve new, often humorous or parodic, purposes (Hafner, 2015).

PROCEDURE

1. Explain the idea of a parody and give an example by showing a video of a well-known song and a parody of that song (e.g., "Do You Want to Build a Snowman?" and "Do You Wanna Go to Starbucks?" a video, just over 2 minutes, available on YouTube). Students do not need to completely understand the language of the example song and parody; instead, elicit confirmation that students understand parody as a genre.

2. Next, play the song that will be parodied in the remainder of the activity and discuss. Use the transcript with bolded target phrases to draw attention to the language structures that students will be practicing. For example, if you used "Oh Susanna" to target the warning phrase "don't you (+ verb)," you would include the line "Oh Susanna! Oh **don't you** cry for me" on the transcript.

3. Have students write their own parody lyrics for the song, either individually or in groups. To facilitate this process, give students a cloze version of the transcript. The blanks should be placed strategically to allow students to transform the content and story of the song while keeping the target language structure intact.

For example, the cloze transcript would replace the line "Oh Susanna! Oh **don't you** cry for me" with "Oh _____, Oh **don't you** _____."

4. Students either perform their parody song live in front of the class or make a music video for their song using video recorders or mobile phones. In the case of video recordings, the songs could either be emailed or uploaded to a shared drive or class website.

CAVEATS AND OPTIONS

1. Nearly any song can be adapted for this activity, because the purpose of the activity is to change the song into something new. Popular or well-known songs make the activity more engaging.

2. Some students may be shy about singing in front of class, so this activity may be best suited for a group project. In addition, using the video recording option in Step 4 allows some students to be in charge of videography or choreography while still giving all students the opportunity to practice the target language by writing the lyrics for the parody. To provide speaking practice, give these students the job of introducing their video to the class or guiding the class through a reading of the lyrics.

3. This activity can easily be shortened by focusing on only a portion of the original song or by opting for live performances rather than videos of the final product. It can be scaffolded if you give more suggestions about the content of the parody.

4. The activity could also be adapted to a culture class or a content-based class by focusing more on the parody aspect and less on language structures. For example, during a unit on families, the *Lion King*'s "I Just Can't Wait to Be King" could be adapted to "I Just Can't Wait to Be Seen," a song about the plight of an ignored middle child.

REFERENCES AND FURTHER READING

Hafner, C. A. (2015). Remix culture and English language teaching: The expression of learner voice in digital multimodal compositions. *TESOL Quarterly, 49*, 486–509.

Clause Comparison

Allison Piippo, Wendy Wang, and Sara Okello

Levels	Advanced
Aims	Develop oral grammar skills
	Distinguish between different types of clauses
Class Time	30–45 minutes
Preparation Time	20 minutes
Resources	YouTube video of any popular song in which relative clauses and noun clauses are repeatedly used
	Handout of song lyrics
	A computer and projector
	Audiovisual equipment

Complex clausal structures are more often used in speech than previously thought (Biber, Gray, & Poonpon, 2011). Selecting a song in which multiple types of clauses are repeatedly used and having students find and compare the forms allows students to engage in noticing the grammatical forms with a focus on both form and meaning, which aids their acquisition of the target language (Nassaji & Fotos, 2011).

PROCEDURE

1. Select an appropriate song for your students and write discussion questions and answer key. For this example, we'll use the radio edit of Green Day's "Boulevard of Broken Dreams." Students should have received previous instruction in relative and noun clauses.

2. Put students into groups of two or three. Display the discussion questions about the meaning of the lyrics (e.g., What is a "broken dream"? Have you ever had a broken dream in your life?) and have students discuss with their group. Then, watch the YouTube video of "Boulevard of Broken Dreams" and read the lyrics.

3. Students discuss the meaning of the lyrics with their group.

4. Review the two different types of clauses. On the board, make a T-chart with relative and noun clauses as headings at the top. Explain the differences between relative and noun clauses. Have students fill in the chart with the main features of the two types of clauses. Check as a class.

5. Then, pass out the lyrics to students and have groups underline relative and noun clauses in the song. If students have trouble, refer them to the T-chart on the board. You can also direct them to find the part of speech before the clause (e.g., verbs usually come before noun clauses and nouns usually come before relative clauses). Remind students that the relative pronoun may be dropped in some instances.

6. Students label the clauses: R for Relative Clauses and N for Noun Clauses. If students have trouble, direct them to look at the chart they made in Steps 4 and 5.
7. Display the answer key. Students compare their group's responses with the answer key. Answer any questions. Ask students to listen to the song again while reading the lyrics.

CAVEATS AND OPTIONS

1. Some good songs for this activity:
    - "Boulevard of Broken Dreams" [Radio Edit], by Green Day
    - "What Makes You Beautiful," by One Direction
    - "Hello," by Adele
    - "That Thing You Do," by A Newfound Glory
2. This activity can be used to compare any complex oral grammar structures, depending on the song chosen (e.g., gerunds and infinitives, hypothetical conditional clauses and counter-factual conditional clauses).

REFERENCES

Biber, D., Gray, B., & Poonpon, K. (2011). Should we use characteristics of conversation to measure grammatical complexity in L2 writing development? *TESOL Quarterly, 45*, 5–35.

Nassaji, H., & Fotos, S. (2011). *Teaching grammar in second language classrooms: Integrating form-focused instruction in communicative context.* New York, NY: Routledge.

Part VI
Music for Vocabulary

Part VI: Music for Vocabulary

What was the first song you ever learned? Perhaps "Row, Row, Row Your Boat," "Frère Jacques," or "Twinkle, Twinkle Little Star." How long has it been since you've sung it? And one last question: Can you still remember the words? By pairing music and words, chances of remembering both the tune and the lyrics are much greater. Long-term memory of these, or other childhood songs, is almost a given. "Adding rhythm and melody to chunks of language invites rehearsal and transfers words into long-term memory," notes Lake (2003, p. 105). Music with lyrics can provide vast quantities of input to language learners. Indeed, Schoepp (2001) reports on two studies of English as a foreign language learners which "found that music is often the major source of English outside of the classroom. The exposure to authentic English is an important factor in promoting language learning." Using songs that students enjoy can increase the amount of English they are exposed to. The "song stuck in my head phenomenon" may occur, thus providing even more unconscious rehearsal of the language (Murphey, 1990). When songs are spooling through the students' heads, the vocabulary is called to mind along with the tune. Leith (1979), a language teacher who used 30–40 songs in his conversational French class each semester, found that "if the students like a song, they usually memorize it, whether asked to or not" (p. 543). For learning vocabulary, songs are a bonanza.

The first contribution in this chapter comes from Ross Sundberg, Walcir Cardoso, and Tiago Bione. Though it's not a typical in-class activity, it was placed at the beginning of the chapter because it is a very useful starting point for determining the suitability of the lexical level of a song's lyrics for your students. This is accomplished with an online tool called VocabProfile, which will enable you to choose song lyrics best suited to your students' level.

Another consideration for selecting songs for vocabulary activities is the congruence of the music to the words used in the songs. Jensen (2000) found that

> when music induces various moods, students are more likely to pay attention to words that match that induced mood. This may help explain why we tend to better remember words that are congruent with their music accompaniment, such as movie soundtracks. (pp. 73–74)

Music, even without lyrics, can help students learn vocabulary, as Emily Herrick exemplifies in an activity that encourages students to talk about the emotions evoked by music, and has students create similes, metaphors, or comparisons. As she also notes, movie soundtracks can work well in activities like hers in which students are meant to find congruence between the music and the words they use to talk about it. Ha Hoang's activity enhances awareness of metaphor and helps learners build lexical networks incorporating metaphor-related vocabulary. Sally La Luzerne-Oi uses a song's theme to provide context and as a springboard for a discussion about time. Timothy R. Janda, Friederike Tegge, and Sibel Taşkin Şimşek find sound uses for cloze activities.

Şimşek's activity takes the cloze a bit further–letting the students be the creators and take responsibility for leading the activity. Priscila Leal's activity, in which students seek answers from each other to complete the task, also fosters such student autonomy. Music can lighten the atmosphere and make it easier for students to learn from each other. The aims of Leal's activity are to develop independent learning strategies and build community by helping students realize that they can learn from each other.

Kevin McCaughey's call-and-response activity helps automatize vocabulary through an engaging method of repeating, Laura Murphy puts a musical spin on running dictation, Deniz Şalli-Çopur adapts the game of bingo to a musical theme, and Gene Thompson's activity helps activate vocabulary acquisition in beginner learners. Longtime music educator Brewer (1995) says: "Music greatly affects and enhances our learning and living!" (para. 4). We can't agree more. Learning thousands of words which are required for successful academic work is a feat of memory, and music has a proven track record in assisting memorization and retention (Jensen 2000; Lake, 2003).

> The more educators use music to assist in the learning of other material, the more quickly and accurately the material will become embedded. Instead of relying strictly on lecture, educators who use more movement, singing, and music will improve learning efficiency and retention. (Jensen, 2000, pp. 74–75)

All the activities in this chapter strike us as fun—almost a gamification of learning vocabulary. We hope you'll have fun selecting appropriate music and playing it in your classroom. Game on!

REFERENCES

Brewer, C. B. (1995). Music and learning: Integrating music in the classroom. New Horizons for Learning. Retrieved from http://education.jhu.edu/PD/new horizons/strategies/topics/Arts%20in%20Education/brewer.htm

Jensen, E. (2000). *Music with the brain in mind: Enhance learning with music.* San Diego, CA: Corwin Press.

Lake, R. (2003). Enhancing acquisition through music. *The Journal of the Imagination in Language Learning and Teaching*, 7, 98–106.

Leith, W. D. (1979). Advanced French conversation through popular music. *The French Review 52*(4), 537–551.

Murphey, T. (1990). The song stuck in my head phenomenon: A melodic DIN in the LAD? *System*, *18*(1), 53–64.

Schoepp, K., (2001). Reasons for using songs in the ESL/EFL classroom. *The Internet TESL Journal*, 7(2).

Graded Music: Analyzing Lyrics by Vocabulary Level

Ross Sundberg, Walcir Cardoso, and Tiago Bione

Levels	All
Aims	Help teachers choose songs with level-appropriate vocabulary for the classroom
Class Time	To be completed outside of class
Preparation Time	15 minutes
Resources	Internet access
	Song lyrics

Research has demonstrated that learners need to understand about 98% of what they hear to comprehend a message well and for learning to take place (Nation, 2006). For that reason, we have used 98% as the guideline in the procedure for this activity. This way, we can treat the song lyrics somewhat like graded readers, where students can work through material while ensuring exposure to a high number of commonly used words in the target language. Fortunately, songs are often short and repetitive, offering learners an opportunity to tackle shorter vocabulary lists and build fluency through repeated exposure.

PROCEDURE

1. Select a song that you would like to use in your class, one that you would like to assess in terms of vocabulary appropriateness for your students' proficiency level.

2. To analyze your song's lyrics in terms of its vocabulary profile (e.g., the distribution of words based on frequency bands), go to www.lextutor.ca and click on "Vocabprofile." Under "VP-Compleat," select the corpus you would like to use (e.g., "BNC-COCA-25" for English).

3. Locate the lyrics you would like to analyse and copy and paste them into the dialog box on the Lextutor page that is already open.

4. Some of the words in the lyrics may be easily understood but not be categorized properly. For example, slang words that are not part of the corpus *and* that students are likely to know (e.g., "cool," which is used in many languages as an English borrowing) do not need to be counted as L2 terms and may show up as "offlist" items (i.e., words that are unusual, a proper name, or part of specialist vocabulary). You can recategorize words by double-clicking them in the lyrics, after which they will reappear in the "RECAT" box below the dialog box where the lyrics were pasted.

5. Click "submit_window" for access to the percentage breakdown of types and tokens that are among the 0–1,000 (K-1); 1,001–2,000 (K-2); and so on most frequent word families in English (see Appendix for a sample; a "token" is every occurrence of an item, whether or not it is the same as one that occurred previously). For example, an easy song would have at least 98% of its lyrics fall within the K-1 group (1,000 most frequent word families), thus indicating that 2% of its words have the potential to be easily learned (Nation, 2006). As fewer and fewer words are a part of the most frequent word families, the vocabulary in the song will be progressively more difficult for learners to comprehend. For low-intermediate groups, we recommend selecting songs with 98% of the lyrics falling into the 2,000 (K-2) most frequent words. Collecting a list of songs with their corresponding percentage of words within the K-2 level will provide an excellent graded list of music and ensure students work with vocabulary that matches their level of proficiency.

CAVEATS AND OPTIONS

1. There is more to selecting songs for pedagogical use than vocabulary frequency, including learners' interests, speech clarity, grammar coverage, and familiarity with language variety. Accordingly, based on these factors, you will have to discern in the end whether or not the music is appropriate for your particular teaching context.

2. To expand this activity and give students opportunities to learn new words, you could create listening and fill-in-the-blank activities using potentially learnable words (i.e., those that are in higher-numbered lists [ascending from K-1] and are therefore less frequent, as analyzed by Lextutor's Vocabprofile).

REFERENCES AND FURTHER READING

Engh, D. (2013). Why use music in English language learning? A survey of the literature. *English Language Teaching, 6*(2), 113–127.

Milton, J., & Alexiou, T. (2009). Vocabulary size and the Common European Framework of Reference in Languages. In B. Richards, H. Daller, D. Malvern, P. Meara, J. Milton, & J. Treffers-Daller (Eds.), *Vocabulary studies in first and second language acquisition* (pp. 194–211). Basingstoke, United Kingdom: Palgrave Macmillan.

Nation, I. (2006). How large a vocabulary is needed for reading and listening? *Canadian Modern Language Review, 63*(1), 59–82.

Nation, P., & Newton, J. (2009). *Teaching ESL/EFL listening and speaking.* New York, NY: Routledge.

Van Zeeland, H., & Schmitt, N. (2012). Lexical coverage in L1 and L2 listening comprehension: The same or different from reading comprehension? *Applied Linguistics, 34*(4), 457–479.

APPENDIX

Here is a screenshot from Lextutor's analysis of the song "First," by Cold War Kids. Looking at the cumulative token percentage on the far right, we can see that about 95% of the lyrics fall into the 2,000 most frequent words in English. However, this analysis also indicates that knowledge of the first 5,000 most frequent English words (K-5 Words) is required to understand 98% of the lyrics, thus indicating that this song is more appropriate for students at a more advanced level (see Table 1).

Freq. Level	Families (%)	Types (%)	Tokens (%)	Cumul. token %
K-1 Words :	88 (86.27)	100 (85.47)	347 (92.29)	92.29
K-2 Words :	7 (6.86)	7 (5.98)	10 (2.66)	94.95
K-3 Words :	4 (3.92)	4 (3.42)	8 (2.13)	97.08
K-4 Words :	1 (0.98)	1 (0.85)	1 (0.27)	97.35
K-5 Words :	2 (1.96)	2 (1.71)	2 (0.53)	97.88

The following table shows the typical vocabulary sizes recommended for students at various proficiency levels in English (for details, see Milton & Alexiou, 2009):

TABLE 1. TYPICAL VOCABULARY SIZES

Levels by the Common European Framework of Reference for Languages	Assumed Vocabulary Size: English	K-Word Level recommendation
A1	0–1,500	98% within K-1
A2	1,500–2,500	98% within K-2
B1	2,750–3,250	98% within K-2 or K-3
B2	3,250–3,750	98% within K-3 or K-4
C1	3,750–4,500	98% within K-4
C2	4,500–5,000	98% within K-5

Activating Learner Recognition of Vocabulary Through Music

Gene Thompson

Levels	Beginner
Aims	Be introduced to key vocabulary
	Demonstrate recognition of key words or phrases in connected speech
	Be introduced to music sources, with scaffolding, before engaging in more complex activities
Class Time	≈ 15 minutes
Preparation Time	15 minutes
Resources	Audio recording of the song
	Up to 4 vocabulary cards for each student

Many techniques for the use of music rely on students recognizing key words and phrases from a song. The activity introduced here provides a means for students to demonstrate recognition of vocabulary and phrases in connected speech. It provides students with a mastery experience (i.e., demonstrated successful recognition) that can be used to introduce key words or phrases and highlight key vocabulary and terms when introducing songs as input texts. By monitoring student performance, you can evaluate whether the input songs are at an appropriate level for your learners.

PROCEDURE

1. Prepare up to four cards for each student, each card with one key vocabulary item from your selected song. An example for use with beginner students learning basic vocabulary and classroom language is the Beatles song "Hello/Goodbye," which has a range of basic words and phrases useful for introducing and reviewing classroom language.
2. Start by distributing two cards to each student.
3. Ask students to listen to the song, and raise the card they have when they hear their word.
4. Play the song and monitor student performance. After confirming that students can interact with the song, provide two new cards to each student.
5. Play the song again and ask students to raise the correct card when they hear their words. With four cards, things can get quite unruly as students attempt to change between cards.
6. Review the key vocabulary from the song.
7. Move on to practice opportunities or more detailed inference activities.

CAVEATS AND OPTIONS

1. Vary this activity to match a number of situations in which noticing is important for subsequent activities. Develop it by asking students to sing the words as they hear them.

2. Integrate further activities. For the example introduced in this activity from "Hello/Goodbye," ask students to make dialogues and/or role-plays using the key vocabulary in language use situations.

3. Add a cloze activity in which students should try to rebuild the song without listening.

4. For more advanced learners, use this activity to introduce key vocabulary needed for further activities, such as discussion activities about the message of the song. For example, highlight key words in John Lennon's song "Imagine" to be noticed by learners; this would later be useful in discussions about the message of the song.

5. Finally, this activity can be used to help learners recognize verb tense change over songs, such as the change in tense during Eric Clapton's song, "Wonderful Tonight."

Acknowledgment: I'd like to acknowledge Dr. Diane Johnson of the University of Waikato, New Zealand, who introduced this technique to me and provided permission for me to outline it here.

Hi De Ho: Vocabulary Call-and-Response

Kevin McCaughey

Levels	Beginner to intermediate
Aims	Repeat and become familiar with new vocabulary, especially as found in vocabulary lists and textbooks
Class Time	5–10 minutes
Preparation Time	30 minutes for the first time; 2 minutes afterward
Resources	A link to a video recording of "Minnie the Moocher," by Cab Calloway (optional)
	Audiovisual equipment (optional)

Acquainting students for the first time with word lists can be tedious. Harnessing the rhythms of musical phrases will engage students more than the traditional "repeat after me" approach, and it allows for more repetition and more practice—without the tedium. Cab Calloway's song features a call-and-response section in which Cab calls out phrases like "Hi De Hi De Hi De Ho." The audience then replicates the phrases, melody, and rhythm. An Internet search for the song title, the singer, or just "Hi De Ho" will lead to video recordings. Play the video for the class if possible. That way, students will understand the process and the spirit of call-and-response. For the classroom, the teacher will do the call and students the response. All you need is your voice and a little courage.

PROCEDURE

1. Identify a set of new vocabulary words or phrases.

2. Fit the words or chunks into musical phrases based on the "Hi De Ho" melody, or a melody of your preference.

3. Sing the phrases to the class (call); the class sings them back (response). At this point, you've finished the first stage. You've provided repetition of new words and given students the chance to try them out on their tongues, but the real fun starts in the next stages.

4. Expand, improvise, and play. "Hi De Ho" will work with any set of words: a list of foods, adjectives to describe personality, or specialized vocabulary. Let's say the class is learning about cars. You call, "Steering wheel, yeah, steering wheel . . ." The class responds. Next: "Steering wheel and a spare tire . . ."

    In the original song, the initial "Hi De Ho" riff evolves, with the caller scrunching in extra syllables. You can—and should—do this, too; like so: "Steering wheel, spare tire, hood and trunk . . ."

5. Add context. You can provide further information about the vocabulary, putting it into phrases or full sentences:

> The trunk is in the back . . .
>
> The hood is in the front . . .
>
> You can open up the hood . . .
>
> You'll find the engine underneath . . .
>
> Some people call the hood a bonnet, yes they do . . .
>
> Some people call the trunk the boot, yeah, it's true . . .

6. Add movement, wherever possible, reinforcing meaning through mime: "I've got my hands on the steering wheel . . ." Show this action; students repeat it during their response.

CAVEATS AND OPTIONS

1. Familiarity with the song "Minnie the Moocher" by Cab Calloway will help you with this activity.

2. The basic call-and-response form of "Hi De Ho" is simple: too simple to engage learners for more than a couple of minutes. However, the process is expandable and flexible, as we've seen. In theory, you could prepare your calls in advance, but the appeal of the activity is that it requires virtually no preparation. So, I prefer to improvise. Improvising leads to some flubs, but the spontaneity makes for more fun.

3. You might provide some musical accompaniment to activate the rhythm: Play a keyboard, ukulele, or guitar. (The "Hi De Ho" chorus in "Minnie the Moocher" is all one chord: E minor.) Or you can download a karaoke version of the song from the Internet.

4. Of course, other melodies can work just as well as "Hi De Ho." For young learners, you may find success with familiar melodies like "Head, Shoulders, Knees, and Toes" or "Happy Birthday."

5. Weeks down the road, once students are familiar with the task, they can work in groups and fit new vocabulary into the melody themselves. Then each group can lead a short call-and-response session.

Cloze Clues

Timothy R. Janda

Levels	High beginner to high intermediate
Aims	Learn new vocabulary in context
	Improve reading and listening skills
	Use lexical and structural clues to predict targeted vocabulary
Class Time	15–30 minutes
Preparation Time	30–45 minutes
Resources	Audio recording of a song
	Cloze lyrics worksheet

Both reading and listening comprehension occur within the context of a text. Similarly, vocabulary is best learned in context—and in this case, the context of a song. Cloze exercises require students to use their understanding of structure and meaning and their background knowledge to make predictions and problem solve in reading. The use of multiple domains, in this case reading and listening for cross-checking, mutually reinforces learning.

PROCEDURE

1. Create a cloze worksheet from the transcript of any song, usually leaving one blank per line of the song and numbering the blanks.
2. At the bottom half of the page (or, if preferred, vertically in two columns) for each numbered blank, write a brief clue that will help students to guess the meaning of the word, which they will later corroborate by listening to the song. Depending on the needs or focus of the class, clues can take almost any form imaginable, such as

   - synonyms (e.g., another word for X),
   - antonyms (e.g., the opposite of X),
   - grammatical descriptions (e.g., the past participle of X),
   - brief definitions (e.g., the ordinal form of the number one),
   - easily completed collocations (e.g., "_____ Christmas!"),
   - parts of speech (e.g., the adjective form of beauty), and
   - even simple completion exercises (e.g., "Is this yours?" "Yes, it's _____!")

   Photocopy and distribute one copy to each student.

3. Using both the clues and the context of the song itself, have students fill in the numbered blanks with the words they think they will hear.
4. Play the song and have students check their answers.
5. Repeat as necessary until all answers are correct.

CAVEATS AND OPTIONS

1. If the purpose of the class is to practice listening comprehension, have students fill in the blanks while listening to the song and then go back and use the clues to check or help them fill in items they might have missed.
2. Often, song lyrics allow students to employ other strategies to problem solve, such as rhyming, which can further reinforce both listening and reading/phonics skills.

The New Year Class

Deniz Şallı-Çopur

Levels	Low intermediate to intermediate
Aims	Recognize word forms such as nouns, verbs, and adjectives
Class Time	1 hour
Preparation Time	25–30 minutes
Resources	Teacher-made Bingo cards
	Audio recording of the song "This Year," by Chantal Kreviazuk
	Cloze lyrics worksheet (optional)

Getting language learners to enthusiastically participate in a writing activity is not an easy job, and setting creative tasks for writing is a challenge for most teachers. Through this activity, the song is used not only for a game, but also to help students write their expectations and plans for the near future. Instead of writing a paragraph, a list, or a message to themselves, rewriting the song lyrics also encourages them to use their creativity.

PROCEDURE

1. Show students a list of vocabulary items all taken from the song but in jumbled order, and ask them if there are any words that they do not know. If there are unknown items, explain them.

2. Ask students to categorize the words according to their part of speech. (The vocabulary items, in alphabetical order, are: April, ask, energy, fall, February, feel, find, fly, fun, get, have, incredible, January, learn, line, love, March, masterpiece, May, one, paint, people, pinnacle, planets, reach, real, recognize, stop, top, year). Some words may be in two categories such as "love" or "top."

3. After categorizing the words, each student takes one Bingo card, which has five columns and three rows (15 boxes). Each student fills the boxes in the card using the words (nouns, adjectives, verbs) from the given list in any order they wish. The only rule is that they need to write nouns in the first row, adjectives in the second, and verbs in the third. They should write only one word for each box.

4. Ask students to listen to the song and cross out the words on their Bingo card when they hear them in the song. The person who crosses all five words in any of the rows calls out *Bingo*! (Check to see if all of the words in the Bingo row are in the right category.) After the first Bingo is made, the class continues listening to the song to cross out the words in the other two categories. If no one can make a Bingo when the song ends, they listen to it again. It is possible to have three different students making a Bingo for each of the three rows (nouns, adjectives, and verbs) or one student winning in all of the rows.

5. After the Bingo, give the students the song lyrics as a cloze activity (with about 10 blanks). They should try to complete the blanks in pairs with the words on their Bingo cards first and then listen to the song again to check their answers. (You can prepare two or three different cloze worksheets targeting different parts of speech for the omitted words, if desired).

6. Ask students to rewrite the lyrics according to their plans for the New Year. They may change any word or line they like, as long as they are loyal to the melody of the song. The students should write at least three things they plan to do or change in their lives for the coming year. Their papers can be placed in a time capsule to be opened at the end of the term or month, or on the next New Year's Eve.

CAVEATS AND OPTIONS

1. Some students may find it difficult to identify the vocabulary items while listening to the song. In order to help them recognize the words, ask them to listen to the song once before they start the Bingo game.

2. This activity can be used with any song that has a variety of easy vocabulary items and a fast rhythm. However, the content of this song is appropriate for the topic of the class and the writing task.

The "Happy Friday" Song Project

Sibel Taşkin Şimşek

Levels	Low intermediate to advanced
Aims	Improve listening skills and vocabulary
	Learn vocabulary in a natural and meaningful context
	Develop autonomy
	Increase engagement and performance in both receptive and productive skills
	Lift the atmosphere in class and bring about a boost of energy
Class Time	15 minutes
Preparation Time	≈ 15 minutes for both the student and the teacher
Resources	Audio and video recording of the song
	Audiovisual equipment
	Gap-fill lyrics handout (student created)

Learners can have a sense of monotony during the last minutes of the week; to help them avoid this feeling, the "Happy Friday" song project is designed to be achievable by all students. This activity takes up the final 15 minutes of the last class of the week. In this project, instead of you choosing the song and creating the task, your students are asked to choose songs of their own preference to create a feeling of involvement and for students to take responsibility for their own learning. (See an example of the assignment on the *New Ways in Teaching with Music* companion page www.tesol.org/newwaysmusic)

PROCEDURE

To keep the learners motivated until the final 15 minutes of the last lesson on Fridays, the simple procedures of the project, done on a voluntary basis, are as follows:

1. At the beginning of each week, preferably on Monday, choose a volunteer.

2. That student chooses a popular song and on Tuesday sends the video clip link and the lyrics to you. This is to make sure the student is on task and will prepare a song for Friday.

3. If the students in a class have different cultural backgrounds, then it is a good idea for you to preview the song to avoid offense that could be caused by explicit lyrics or visuals. Therefore, before the volunteer student starts preparing the activity, you need to approve the song.

4. The same student prepares a gap-fill activity and brings the printouts to class on Friday.

5. In the last 10–15 minutes, the class listens to the song and completes the task.
6. After they complete the gap-fill activity, together with the volunteer student, the answers are checked.
7. They watch the video clip and sing the song together.
8. Post both the gap-fill activity students create and the name of the song and the artist on the class blog or wiki if there is one.
9. As a follow up, in groups students either discuss the meaning of the song or prepare a poster. Alternatively, the follow-up can be done as a journal task, allowing students to reflect on the song over the weekend.

CAVEATS AND OPTIONS

1. Although the project has simple steps, the way of presenting the project is very important. You should give your students the impression that it is not something obligatory, nor is it something imposed on them, but the intention is to create a positive finish to the week.
2. Make sure that their song choices are suitable in terms of level and content, but do not give feedback on the task they prepared because it is not their job to create a perfectly designed gap-fill activity. Instead, allow them to listen and enjoy the lyrics to finish the week with a nice atmosphere.
3. After a few songs and activities, they may start commenting on how to choose a song and how to create a gap-fill activity for a song. Here are the suggestions from my students on how to choose a good song and create good material:

   > 1. Choose a song at a suitable level that can be understood easily.
   > 2. Do not delete words that are repeated somewhere else in the lyrics.
   > 3. Do not choose a song that everyone knows by heart.

4. Let students enjoy the songs in the activities from time to time or regularly like we did in the last minutes of the week, which will help them be filled with positive feelings when leaving school for the weekend.

REFERENCES AND FURTHER READING

Harmer, J. (2001). *The practice of English language teaching* (3rd ed.). Harlow, England: Pearson Education.

Links that can be shared with the students: www.lyricsmode.com, www.metrolyrics.com, www.lyricsfreak.com

See www.tesol.org/teachingwithmusic for an example of instructions and a first lesson.

This Song Is as Sad as a Wet Puppy

Emily Herrick

Levels	*Intermediate*
Aims	*Develop and reinforce vocabulary, particularly adjectives used to describe feelings*
	Use similes, metaphors, and comparative forms
Class Time	*Variable*
Preparation Time	*10–20 minutes (for students as homework)*
Resources	*Any method of playing music for individual students or student groups, such as a mobile phone*

PROCEDURE

1. After introducing vocabulary used to express emotions or grammatical structures used for comparison, assign students to bring a favorite song, even one in their native language, with or without words.

2. Divide students into groups or pairs and have them play excerpts from the songs they brought or play the songs in their entirety if there is time.

3. Have each student write "A" on the front of a piece of paper and "B" on the back. On side A of the piece of paper, have each group or pair make a list of adjectives they could use to describe the mood created by the song, as well as create similes and metaphors describing the mood of the songs. On side B, they write the name of the song. On a separate piece of paper, students list the songs they described in random order. It is helpful if they also include a link to the song so that the other group can quickly find it on their devices.

4. Students then exchange papers with another group. As they listen to the songs on the list, they try to match each song with the descriptions on side A before turning the paper over to discover if their guesses were correct.

CAVEATS AND OPTIONS

1. Allowing students to use a thesaurus or online dictionary can increase their exposure to richer vocabulary.

2. This activity works best with a small class because it can be time-consuming with a large class.

3. For a large class, rather than have students bring songs, you bring several songs reflecting a variety of emotions and play these. Movie soundtracks work well.

Do You Know *X*?

Priscila Leal

Levels	Intermediate
Aims	Develop independent learning strategies
	Build community
Class Time	≈ 1 hour
Preparation Time	15–30 minutes
Resources	Music video with subtitles or audio recording of selected song
	Handout of song lyrics
	Audiovisual equipment (optional)

Songs often address universal themes and evoke emotional responses, making them a meaningful resource for language learning. In addition, fragments of songs tend to stick in our minds. By focusing on what is being said (content) and how it is being said (pronunciation and grammar), students can use songs as authentic sources of vocabulary and grammar in context. A variety of popular songs can be used to focus on different vocabulary and grammar in context.

PROCEDURE

1. Select the music video of a popular song and prepare a handout with its lyrics. Preselect which grammatical feature(s) to focus on based on the song. For example, if you choose Pharrell Williams's song, "Happy," you might focus on phrasal verbs ("feel like"), conditional sentences, or modals.

2. Play the music video (or the audio recording) in class. Give students a copy of the lyrics so that they can read them as they listen to the song, and play the music video again. Invite students to sing along.

3. Ask students to circle any unfamiliar vocabulary or expressions in the lyrics. Then, pair students and have them compare their lists. Partners ask each other if they know the meaning of a word or expression the other student circled by asking, "Do you know *X*?" (*X* being the unfamiliar word). If the partner knows, he or she can share it and check the word off the list; otherwise, the word is saved for the next regrouping.

4. After pairs have gone through all the words or expressions in their lists, rearrange the groups into trios or quartets, depending on classroom size. Ask the new groups to compare their lists, explain to each other the meaning of any remaining unfamiliar words or expressions, and to check these words off their lists.

5. As a whole group, address any remaining unfamiliar words. Invite students to check the meaning by using an online dictionary such as wordspy.com or www.urbandictonary.com for more up-to-date interpretations. (Editor's note: Be aware that Urban Dictionary is user generated and contains slang, profanity, and adult content.)
6. Based on your preselected grammatical features, ask students to identify and underline those features in the lyrics. Help students analyze the grammar in context and its features in relation to the intention and meaning (e.g., What do the conditional sentences in the lyrics have in common? What are the differences between the modals in the lyrics?)

CAVEATS AND OPTIONS

1. Variations of this activity include selecting from shorter, slower tempo songs for beginner levels with lots of chorus repetition, to longer, faster paced songs for more advanced levels.
2. While secondary and adult learners may discuss the theme of the song and make inferences related to their lives or life experience, younger learners may pay attention to connected speech, draw pictures of the content, and sing along.

REFERENCES AND FURTHER READING

Lems, K. (2001). *Using music in the adult ESL classroom*. ERIC Digest. Retrieved from http://files.eric.ed.gov/fulltext/ED459634.pdf

Chunking Song Lyrics

Laura Murphy

Levels	Intermediate
Aims	Build vocabulary and develop listening skills
	Process new language in chunks for better retention
Class Time	≈ 45 minutes
Preparation Time	15–20 minutes
Resources	Audio recording of a selected song
	Handout of song lyrics (or projector)
	Scissors and tape
	2 cut-up copies of the lyrics handout

Chunking language phrases is an effective way to develop fluency and make meaningful connections with new vocabulary words. Chunking also helps students remember new words and grammatical structures grouped together, thus facilitating easier language acquisition. Furthermore, as a variation to running dictation, this activity enables students to build their listening skill as their partner dictates the lyrics to them; it also fosters cooperative group work.

PROCEDURE

1. Select an audio recording of a song that has examples of targeted grammatical structures or vocabulary, or contains a similar theme to content being presented in class.

2. In class, play the song one time without showing the lyrics, so students have an idea of the rhythm, intonation, and stress patterns.

3. Print several copies of the song lyrics in a large font (e.g., 24 pt). Cut up part of the song so that you have several copies of the same three to five lines and display them on the wall outside or at the back of the classroom. Place them at a distance from one another so that students are not jostling each other to be able to read the lyrics. Arrange the students into pairs—partner A and partner B.

4. Ask partner A to step outside to memorize in chunks the lyrics posted on the wall, leaving electronic devices, paper, and writing utensils in the classroom: they are not allowed to take pictures of the lyrics or write them down. Partner A will return to partner B in the classroom to retell what he or she can remember. Partner B writes down what partner A dictates. Partner A continues going back to the posted lyrics outside until all of the posted lyrics have been told to and recorded by partner B.

5. Remove the first set of lyrics posted outside and display another part of the song.

6. Switch roles and ask partner B to go outside the room to memorize in chunks and retell the lyrics to partner A, who is now in the classroom.

7. Continue until partner B has dictated all of the lines and had partner A write them down.

8. Give all students a copy of the lyrics and ask them to check their spelling. Or, show the lyrics on the projector for them to self-check. Then ask the students to identify and review any targeted grammatical structures or vocabulary in the lyrics.

9. Play the song for them to listen to and encourage them to sing along or mouth the words while listening.

CAVEATS AND OPTIONS

1. If you have a large class, you may need to make more copies of the lyrics to display on the wall so that all students can easily see a copy during this activity.

2. Provide a cloze handout of the chunked lyrics being memorized. This enables the students to fill in the missing parts of the song and see their lyrics within the context of the whole song.

3. For a final activity extension, divide the class into two groups and play the song a third time. The first group sings the first stanza of the song, and the second group sings the second stanza, so that the two groups alternate singing stanzas, which encourages a feeling of competition as each group strives to sing louder than the other group.

Listening Between the Lines

Ha Hoang

Levels	Intermediate to advanced
Aims	Build awareness of metaphoric reasoning and metaphorical language
	Learn the skill of developing ideas using metaphor
	Learn the skill of building lexical networks using metaphor
Class Time	≈ 30 minutes
Preparation Time	5 minutes
Resources	Audio recording of a song that contains an overall metaphor
	Handout of song lyrics (or projector)

Metaphor is shown to underlie daily thinking and speech (Lakoff & Johnson, 1980), and it can be used to help learners conceptualize their learning process and foster their reflective thinking (Berendt, 2008; Wan & Low, 2015). Raising second language learners' awareness of metaphor is an innovative method in second language instruction (Holme, 2004; Littlemore & Low, 2006). A great amount of research (see Hoang, 2014, for a review) has shown that learners who are aware of metaphor can learn words more effectively and remember them longer than those who are not.

PROCEDURE

1. Select a song that contains an overall metaphor (e.g., "Life Is a Highway," by Rascal Flatts, or "Firework," by Katy Perry).

2. Write the overall theme (the overall metaphor) of the song on the board and elicit ideas related to the theme (termed "metaphorical extensions") from the students. For example, for the metaphor *firework*, students may give answers like *ignite*, *burst*, *shine*, etc.

3. Play the song and ask students to listen for the words and phrases related to the theme. For example, in Katy Perry's "Firework," each individual is likened to a firework. Students will hear words and phrases such as *ignite*, *shine*, *shoot across the sky*, and many more.

4. Give students the lyrics or display the lyrics.

5. Discuss how a metaphor can help build a cluster of ideas or a network of vocabulary. For example, a business can be seen as a person: It can be said to *be in its infancy*, *grow*, *break down*, *die*.

6. Ask students to work in groups and think of a metaphor and its extensions for the lesson/focus of the day to further strengthen the awareness of metaphoric reasoning and metaphorical language. For example, you may want to ask

students to think about their writing topic as an overall metaphor and develop an outline by using the extensions of the metaphor.

CAVEATS AND OPTIONS

1. Use this activity to introduce or end a theme-based reading or writing lesson.
2. Start with the lyrics and build up the theme metaphor from the words and phrases from the song.
3. As a follow-up activity or project, especially for younger learners, ask students to bring songs, which are related to the theme of the lesson, to class to analyze the metaphor and metaphorical extensions used in the songs. This can be assigned as group work.

REFERENCES AND FURTHER READING

Berendt, E. (Ed.). (2008). *Metaphors for learning: Cross-cultural perspectives*. Philadelphia, PA: John Benjamins.

Hoang, H. (2014). Metaphor and second language learning: The state of the field. *TESL-EJ, 18*(2).

Holme, R. (2004). *Mind, metaphor and language teaching*. Basingstoke, United Kingdom: Palgrave Macmillan.

Lakoff, G., & Johnson, M. (1980). *Metaphors we live by*. Chicago, IL: The University of Chicago Press.

Littlemore, J., & Low, G. (2006). *Figurative thinking and foreign language learning*. Basingstoke, United Kingdom: Palgrave Macmillan.

Wan, W., & Low, G. (2015). *Elicited metaphor analysis in educational discourse*. Philadelphia, PA: John Benjamins.

About Time

Sally La Luzerne-Oi

Levels	Intermediate to advanced
Aims	Learn time expressions
	Exchange cultural information about time
Class Time	45 minutes–1 hour
Preparation Time	15 minutes
Resources	Audio recording of "Does Anybody Really Know What Time It Is?," by Chicago
	Handout of song lyrics
	Discussion questions (See Appendix)

English uses many expressions incorporating time, and an understanding that the concept of time varies from one culture to another is important. "Does Anybody Really Know What Time It Is?," by Chicago, is ideal for introducing a discussion on both pertinent topics.

PROCEDURE

1. Tell students they are going to hear a song about time. The question they should try to answer after listening is "What does the singer think about time?"
2. Play the song. Ask the question "What does the singer think about time?" Play the song at least one more time to confirm students' answers or to help them answer the question if they could not.
3. Hand out the lyrics and discuss them.
4. Form small groups of students and ask them to discuss the questions in the handout.
5. To end the activity, ask a spokesperson from each group to report on the group's discussion.

CAVEATS AND OPTIONS

1. If you have a homogeneous class, tell students to answer Discussion Questions 2 and 3 (Appendix) based on other countries/cultures they know.
2. Alternatively, you can start with a whole class discussion of Questions 2 and 3 (Appendix), giving examples if students are unable to do so.

APPENDIX

Discuss these questions with your classmates.

1. Do you usually arrive to an appointment on time, ahead of time, or late? What about a gathering with friends?
2. In your country/culture, if you have an appointment at 9 am, what time should you arrive? If you have a gathering with friends at 8 pm, what time should you arrive?
3. What time does school start/end in your country? What time do businesses open/close?
4. How do you know what time it is? Have you ever worn a watch?
5. How do you spend your time on weekends?
6. What do you make time to do every week?
7. Has someone or something ever wasted your time? Explain.
8. Do you take your time doing homework?
9. When do you lose track of time?
10. Here are some common expressions. Do you agree with them? Why or why not?
    - Time flies when you're having a good time.
    - Time is money.
    - Time heals all wounds.

Teaching Collocations, Phrasal Verbs, and Idioms Through Songs

Friederike Tegge

Levels	Intermediate to advanced
Aims	Learn formulaic sequences (collocations, phrasal verbs, idioms)
	Become familiar with poetic sound devices (e.g., alliteration)
Class Time	20–35 minutes
Preparation Time	≈ 20 minutes
Resources	Gap-fill lyrics worksheet
	List of target expressions
	Audio recording of a particular song

Formulaic sequences such as collocations, phrasal verbs, and idioms make up large parts of a language, and using them correctly allows speakers to appear more fluent (Pawley & Syder, 1983). Second language learners, however, frequently struggle to acquire formulaic sequences and use them correctly. Teaching with songs can assist the acquisition of such multiword units. Firstly, many lyrics contain a comparatively high number of formulaic expressions, as they are meant to evoke commonly shared experiences and feelings using few words (Murphey, 1990). Secondly, songs draw attention to the structural side of language with their melody, rhythm, and use of poetic sound patterns, potentially leading to increased memorization (Tegge, 2015). Such a memory effect can be enhanced by explicitly pointing out and drawing the learners' attention to the sound patterns (Boers, Lindstromberg, & Eyckmans, 2014).

PROCEDURE

1. Choose a song that contains a certain number of formulaic sequences, such as collocations and idiomatic expressions, that you would like your students to learn. While the formulaic sequences will be new to the learners, the individual words should be familiar.

2. Prepare a gap-fill activity. Delete the entire formulaic sequence to highlight its unity. For example, in Bill Withers's "Lean on Me," delete "swallow your pride" from "So swallow your pride," and "carry on" from "I'll help you carry on." If this is too challenging for your learners, only delete one or two words. In that case, the gaps should target words that are less salient and less concrete. For example, in "If you need a hand," delete the more abstract "need."

3. Listening 1: Hand out the gap-fill worksheet. Play the song for the first time. The learners listen for the missing words and fill in the gaps.

4. Discuss the answers of the gap-fill activity.

5. Listening 2: Play the song a second time. Learners check the answers and attempt to understand the words they could not hear previously.

6. Provide a list of the selected formulaic sequences and discuss their meaning. Let students deduce the meaning from context before you explain. If the expressions have metaphorical meaning, discuss both the literal and the figurative senses. If possible, you can even act out a physical activity.

7. Discuss the structure of target expressions. Highlight sound patterns such as rhyme, alliteration, assonance, and consonance in the formulaic sequences. In Dolly Parton's "9 to 5," for example, the words "get" and "credit" in the expression "get the credit" display semirhyme, and the expression "the tide's gonna turn" alliterates (tide/turn).

8. Listening 3/Singing: Encourage learners to sing along while you play the song for a third time. The spoken or, rather, sung output can trigger further processing of the sound patterns and supports deeper entrenchment of the lyrics in memory.

9. Practice target expressions: Learners write their own sentences using the target expressions. This can be done individually or as team or group work. It can also be given as homework.

CAVEATS AND OPTIONS

Combine this activity with tasks encouraging memorization of the entire text. Memorizing text beyond certain target words and highlighting sound patterns across lines and sentences can help learners remember the selected sequences. For example, in The Police's "Every Breath You Take," end rhyme can aid memorization of several collocations: "Every breath you take, every move you make, every bond you break, every step you take."

REFERENCES AND FURTHER READING

Boers, F., Lindstromberg, S., & Eyckmans, J. (2014). Is alliteration mnemonic without awareness-raising? *Language Awareness, 23*(4), 291–303.

Murphey, T. (1990). *Song and music in language learning.* Bern, Switzerland: Peter Lang.

Pawley, A., & Syder, F. H. (1983). Two puzzles of linguistic theory: Nativelike selection and nativelike fluency. In J. C. Richards & R. W. Schmidt (Eds.), *Language and communication* (pp. 191–225). New York, NY: Longman.

Tegge, F. (2015). *Investigating song-based language teaching and its effect on lexical learning* (Unpublished doctoral dissertation). Victoria University of Wellington, New Zealand. Retrieved from http://researcharchive.vuw.ac.nz/handle/10063/4577

Part VII

Music for Cultural Exploration

Part VII: Music for Cultural Exploration

It is almost redundant to discuss the relationship between music and culture, for how could they ever be separated? Virtually no culture is without music, and music can't help but reflect the culture from which it originates. As U.K. professor and entrepreneur Vikas Shah has written, "Music is one of the most primal and fundamental aspects of human culture" (Shah, 2015). The same intrinsic interconnectivity can be argued for the relationship between language and culture as between language and music. The nine activities in this chapter creatively triangulate: culture, music, and language.

In Crystal Bock-Thiessen's "Weekly Worldly Warm-Up," students use language to explore music from any culture in the world while developing discussion skills and world knowledge. "Community Radio Collaboration" by Emily Herrick provides students with an opportunity to explore any musical genre broadcast in their community by getting out of the classroom and into a local radio station.

Students can deepen their understanding of the challenges of intercultural communication through Kevin Knight's "Music Video for Cultural Exploration" by learning how to anticipate and appreciate communication style differences.

Students use their creativity and critical thinking skills to reflect on, discuss, and share their views on social issues that can affect people in any location on the planet in "Make a Music Video With a Social Message," by Sean H. Toland and Simon Thomas, and "What's in a Song? From Peace to Protests: Culture Abounds," by Joshua Wedlock.

Timothy R. Janda's "American History Through Folk Songs" incorporates higher level reading skills by having students analyze lyrics within a historical context, and "America's National Pastime," by Constance Leonard, uses music to teach idioms as well as the sport of baseball. Elizabeth J. Lange uses national anthems as a lens for viewing different countries' cultures in "National Anthems." In "Looking at the Great Depression Through Song," by Jacqueline Nenchin, students have an opportunity not only to learn about history but also to express their own experiences living in another culture.

Music may be part of what makes us human. Levitin (2007) explains:

> Whenever humans come together for any reason, music is there: weddings, funerals, graduation from college, men marching off to war, stadium sporting events, a night on the town, prayer, a romantic dinner, mothers rocking their infants to sleep, and college students studying with music as background. (p. 6)

It seems only natural that music would find a comfortable home in a language classroom where culture is explored.

REFERENCES

Levitin, D. (2007). *This is your brain on music: The science of a human obsession.* New York, NY: Penguin Group.

Shah, V. (2015). The role of music in human culture. *Thought Economics.* Retrieved from https://thoughteconomics.com/the-role-of-music-in-human-culture

Looking at the Great Depression Through Song

Jacqueline Nenchin

Levels	Low intermediate
Aims	Develop an understanding of the Great Depression and relate it to the problems faced by current U.S. residents
	Create a 4-line verse based on personal experiences in America
Class Time	≈ 90 minutes
Preparation Time	40 minutes
Resources	Audio recording of "This Land Is Your Land," by Woody Guthrie
	Handout of song lyrics
	PowerPoint sideshow with images related to song lyrics

Music is universal, and together with song lyrics it can perform a unifying role in helping introduce an unfamiliar cultural or historical topic to students and build context for future study of that topic. Music is also motivational for many students, so it can be used to increase student involvement and aid in the learning of new vocabulary.

PROCEDURE

1. Locate an audio recording of Woody Guthrie's "This Land is Your Land," which addresses the cultural and historical topic of the Great Depression, and think about how the song connects to the topic. (You can find a video recording on YouTube at www.youtube.com/watch?v=XaI5IRuS2aE.)

2. Introduce the name and background of the song and the singer-songwriter.

3. Provide the students with a copy of the lyrics and optionally the music. Preteach any difficult or unfamiliar words. Play the song for the class once while students listen attentively. Play the song again with the PowerPoint images and discuss the meaning of the lyrics and their relationship to the topic, the Great Depression. (You can find images of the Franklin Delano Roosevelt Memorial at www.nps.gov/frde/index.htm.)

4. Students will write their own verse about their experiences in America to add to the song. Model the process for them. Provide students with a template, which they may use if they need scaffolding. For example:

> I've *verb (past participle)* and *verb (past participle)* and *verb (past participle)*_____
>
> To the *adjective noun* of the *adjective noun*,
>
> And all around me the *noun helping verb* + *verb* (past continuous tense),
>
> "This land was made for you and me."

5. Give students 20–30 minutes to brainstorm, write, and illustrate their verse.
6. Students can share their verses orally with the class and together create a new version of the song, which they can perform.

CAVEATS AND OPTIONS

1. Because songs reflect the values and beliefs of a people, you can find songs to illustrate many important events covering different topics.
2. Use different versions of songs by different singers to illustrate how and why the original song may have been changed over time. Though the product of this activity is a written one, the activity itself involves all four skills and use of the students' lexico-grammatical resources.

REFERENCES AND FURTHER READING

Google Images of the Great Depression. (n.d.). Retrieved from https://www.google.com/search?hl=en&site=imghp&tbm=isch&source=hp&biw=1299&bih=639&q=great+depression+photos&oq=Great+Depression&gs_l=img.1.1.0l10.13093.21065.0.25136.16.12.0.4.4.0.258.1379.9j1j2.12.0....0...1ac.1.64.img..0.16.1405...0i7i30k1.O6vhTdDpaJQ#imgrc=EFPt9WGAlx8KOM%3A

Guthrie, W. (1992). This land is your land. In W. Hyman & L. H. Diefenbacher (Eds.), *Singing USA: Springboard to culture* (pp. 6–8). Boston, MA: Heinle and Heinle.

NPR Staff. (2012, July 5). Woodie Guthrie's indelible mark on American culture. *Talk of the Nation*. Retrieved from http://www.npr.org/2012/07/05/156301144/woody-guthries-indelible-mark-on-american-culture

Woody Guthrie Center. (2016). Retrieved from http://woodyguthriecenter.org

Weekly Worldly Warm-Up

Crystal Bock-Thiessen

Levels	Intermediate to advanced
Aims	Learn about a variety of world music, culture, and geography
	Enhance partner and group discussion skills
	Express and support opinions
	Warm up for the day's lesson
Class Time	25 minutes the first time, 10–15 minutes after
Preparation Time	≈ 10 minutes
Resources	Variety of world music CDs (or Internet access)
	Handouts (Appendices)
	World map (optional)

Music is said to be the world's common language, because it is something enjoyed, produced, and shared by almost every culture. Listening to a variety of musical selections from all over the world gives students a chance to broaden their cultural horizons in a way they might not explore on their own. Additionally, the breadth of musical selection that is easily accessible via personal collections, online, and from libraries helps retain interest and promote expression through the shared enjoyment of music.

PROCEDURE

1. When introducing the activity, ask students to get into groups and talk about their favorite kinds of music.
   a. Why do they like a particular artist or musical style?
   b. What makes us favor a particular kind of music?
   c. Why and how is music important to us as humans?
2. Hand out the "Musical Terms and Vocabulary" sheet (Appendix A) and have students take note of any terms unfamiliar to them. In groups, have them write their own reminders regarding the words' meanings, and then keep the paper in a binder or folder for subsequent reference. (This works best as a weekly warm-up series.)

Afterward, introduce them to the Weekly Worldly Warm-Up activity:

1. Hand out a "Discussion Chart" (Appendix B) to each student (can be printed three to four to a page in order to save paper).

2. Choose a song (3–5 minutes) from anywhere in the world to play in class (see Caveats and Options for suggestions). Encourage students to just listen for at least the first minute before writing anything down on their Discussion Chart. Before the song finishes, students should be filling out their Discussion Charts in preparation for the discussion.

3. After the music has finished, give students a minute or two to finish before placing them into pairs or groups of three.

4. Using the Discussion Chart as a guide for conversation (and not something from which to read), students should discuss the selection with each other and make guesses as to which part of the world the song is from.

5. Finally, reveal where the song and/or the artist(s) originated, using a map if desired. You can keep a list of Weekly Worldly song titles and artists in the classroom or on the class website so students may further access any of the music that they enjoyed.

CAVEATS AND OPTIONS

1. The collection of music available from Putumayo World Music CDs and its website (www.putumayo.com) work great for this activity, but don't forget about surprising regional variations and mixes from within a particular country or between widely different styles (e.g., French rap from Burkina Faso; the tribal, funky beats of the American group Rusted Root; American bluegrass or Japanese hip hop; connecting folk with modern, or traditional with contemporary).

2. This is a great way to move students beyond what they expect from a particular country or culture, even furthering their understanding of the world through expanded musical exposure. After a few weeks of this activity, you might consider giving each student a chance to send you their own interesting piece of music for the Weekly Worldly Warm-Up for their classmates to discuss. Encourage them to choose something that might be surprising or different even to those who come from their own country.

APPENDIX A: *Musical Terms and Vocabulary*

These can be adjusted for level.

Word/term	Definition	My Own Reminder/Example
Rhythm	Regular, repeated sound, like the beat of a drum	
Tempo	The speed of a musical piece	
Genre	A category or type of music	

Rhythm	**Tempo**	**Genre**	**Feeling/Mood**
Syncopated	Fast/Upbeat	Country/Bluegrass	Calm/Peaceful
Gentle	Moderate	Pop/Rock	Lively
Strong	Slow/Mellow	Rap/Hip Hop	Energetic
Irregular	Changing	Traditional	Sad/Depressed
		Folk	Emotional
			Romantic

APPENDIX B: *Discussion Chart*

Describe the rhythm, style, and tempo. What do you think the genre is?	What is the feeling or mood of the music? Describe how it makes you feel and why.	What are your impressions of this music? Have you ever heard anything similar?	What language do you think this music is in? What country do you think it's from?	Would you add this song to your music playlist? Why or why not?

Community Radio Collaboration

Emily Herrick

Levels	Intermediate to advanced
Aims	Learn about American culture through music with an integrated skills approach
	Learn field research skills
Class Time	1 week–several weeks
Preparation Time	Variable; this project will take many hours to develop
Resources	Willing radio stations within your community
	Various classroom handouts (teacher created)

Almost everyone knows popular music, but fewer people know roots music, the music that popular music grew out of and which has deeper connections to the peoples and communities that gave birth to it. This activity takes students out of the classroom and into a local radio station to explore roots music that may be representative of the communities they are studying in.

PROCEDURE

1. Identify radio programmers/DJs specializing in various types of American roots music (Native American, gospel, blues, zydeco, bluegrass, etc.) and approach them about the project. Community, campus, or public radio stations may be good contacts.

2. Prepare classroom and homework activities to introduce your students to each genre available on the radio in your community. This would most likely include identifying sample songs you could play in class, along with short readings about the music and related cultures and musicians.

3. Introduce students to the various genres over several class periods.

4. Assign students individually, in pairs, or in small groups to interview relevant programmers/DJs in more depth about the musical genre they are interested in.

5. Students prepare both written and oral reports that provide a deeper or broader look at the genre of music they researched.

CAVEATS AND OPTIONS

This project is as variable as the communities in which it may take place. It also relies on the commitment and availability of programmers/DJs and is very labor intensive for instructors the first time through.

American History Through Folk Songs

Timothy R. Janda

Levels	Intermediate to advanced
Aims	Improve cultural knowledge and reading skills
	Study song lyrics within historical contexts
Class Time	≈ 1 hour
Preparation Time	15–30 minutes
Resources	Audio recording of a historical folk song
	Handout of song lyrics, key vocabulary items, and discussion questions (teacher created)

Recognition of the written word is reinforced through hearing the word spoken or sung. Learning about and gaining familiarity with the culture of the target language through an exploration of its history contributes to learners' functional competence. Focusing on textual evidence to support an opinion helps students focus on critical thinking skills.

PROCEDURE

1. Select an audio recording of a historical folk song (nearly any folk song with a historical precedent can serve as an object of study) and create or locate a transcript of the lyrics, a list of key vocabulary items, and a brief set of questions that require students to identify and discuss key aspects of the song. Distribute one copy to each student.

2. Review the key vocabulary through any appropriate means, such as discussion or matching words with definitions, synonyms, or antonyms.

3. Listen to the song several times while reading a transcript of the lyrics.

4. Have students answer comprehension questions about relevant topics expressed in the song. The answers often take the form of a definition, process description, or narrative:

    - They can name the setting (the approximate time and place) and the event or phenomenon described in the song.
    - If the song tells a story, ask students to identify main characters and typical components of a narrative, such as the situation, conflict, and resolution.
    - If the song describes a process (e.g., the building of the first transcontinental railroad or transporting goods using the Erie Canal), ask students to define the process and its significance or give a description of how it works.

- Ask students to identify the attitude or point of view expressed by the singer in the lyrics and to cite evidence supporting their opinions.

   Students may work alone, in pairs, or in small groups to complete the task.

5. After some discussion, you can repeat the process of reading the lyrics while listening to the song for students to gain a deeper understanding of the song. Answer questions to clarify doubts about meaning, and solicit further insights and observations.

6. As a follow up, you may want to ask students to research and write about or discuss the event/phenomenon described in the song. Alternatively, ask students to compare the ideas expressed in the song to similar or related events or phenomena in their own cultures.

CAVEATS AND OPTIONS

1. It is best to find a song whose history is easily researched, and it's a bonus if it has been recently rerecorded by a popular or contemporary artist. For example, one of my favorites is Thomas S. Allen's "The Erie Canal Song," which may hold relevance for aspiring structural engineers and was recently rerecorded by Bruce Springsteen.

2. If applicable, you may want to provide students with additional information about the writer of the song, though you will want to stop short of saying too much because, as much as possible, it is the students' job to use the lyrics of the song to identify the song's historical and cultural context.

3. To help students practice listening skills, combine this activity with cloze or fill-in-the-blank exercises, or you can withhold and then later hand out a transcript of the lyrics.

REFERENCES AND FURTHER READING

Blood, P., Patterson, A., & McWhirter, K. L. (2004). *Rise up singing: The group singing songbook*. Bethlehem, PA: Sing Out.

Rise Up Singing is a rich source of folk songs—1,200 in all—organized into categories such as America, ecology, farm and prairie, hard times and blues, and work, and it includes brief explanations and background. The Smithsonian Folkways website (www.folkways.si.edu/folkways-recordings/smithsonian) is another rich source of material and information.

Music Video for Cultural Exploration

Kevin Knight

Levels	Intermediate to advanced
Aims	Create cultural awareness and generate discussion
Class Time	≈ 20 minutes
Preparation Time	15 minutes
Resources	A computer with Internet access and a projector or large screen
	The Behind the Mic multilanguage video recording of "Let It Go," from *Frozen*

The video of the multilanguage version of "Let It Go," from the Disney movie *Frozen* (available on YouTube from www.youtube.com/watch?v=BS0T8Cd4UhA &app=desktop), helps participants in this activity to do the following: 1) Clearly visualize cultural differences around the world. The learners can see that the singers have different languages and ways of expression. 2) Consider the challenges that can be involved in communicating with individuals of different nationalities in different locations around the world. 3) Begin to understand how culture and language are interconnected. 4) Enjoy and appreciate cultural differences worldwide. 5) Become motivated to use music and videos for learning a new language.

PROCEDURE

1. Tell the class that you are going to show them the music video. Elicit with a show of hands how many of the participants have heard the song or seen the music video.

2. Show the music video to the class. It is not necessary to print out or discuss the lyrics.

3. Divide the participants into small groups. Ask the groups to discuss how the cultures of the singers might differ. Ask them to list as many differences as possible, such as

   - national language(s)
   - greeting styles (handshake, kiss, hug, bow, etc.)
   - display of emotions (acceptable vs. unacceptable)
   - voice in speaking (loud vs. soft)
   - eye contact (polite vs. impolite)
   - use of names (given name vs. family name)
   - clothing (formal vs. casual)
   - leadership and decision-making (individual vs. group)

- business meetings (formal vs. informal; socializing before or after meeting)
- typical workdays and working hours
- traditional food/drink and eating utensils (chopsticks vs. fork and spoon)
- important holidays and festivals
- popular sports, entertainment, and recreation
- communication (cell phones, texting, email, face-to-face)
- orientation to time (punctual vs. late)
- social roles of men and women
- values and beliefs
- legal and political systems

4. Give the participants 10 minutes to list the differences.
5. Elicit the differences from each group, and write them on the board.
6. In view of the cultural differences on the board, elicit from the students (as a class) intercultural communication challenges.

CAVEATS AND OPTIONS

1. As an alternative, use the video recording of another multilanguage version of a popular song in which the singers are clearly of different nationalities.
2. If this music video is shown in connection with business training on-site at a company, be prepared to explain to a supervisor your reason for showing such a video. Using this video, you can also ask the following:
   a. Describe the personal qualities and leadership style of the ideal leader for a global team consisting of members from different countries.
   b. In view of cultural differences and differences in languages worldwide, are all of the singers viewing the song in the same way?
   c. How can such music videos help you to improve your pronunciation and enunciation?

REFERENCES AND FURTHER READING

Knight, K. (2015, February 10). Disney music for business English training [Blog post]. Retrieved from http://blog.tesol.org/disney-music-for-business-english-training/

National Anthems

Elizabeth J. Lange

Levels	Intermediate to advanced
Aims	Develop listening and speaking skills based on independent research
	Develop an appreciation of different countries' cultures and history in relation to their national anthems
Class Time	≈ 2 class sessions, several days apart
Preparation Time	≈ 20 minutes
Resources	Electronic devices with Internet access
	Interview question handout (Appendix A)
	Research template handout (Appendix B)

A national song is the heart and soul of a country, inspiring feelings of national pride and patriotism when sung or played on important occasions. Understanding more about other countries' national songs can give valuable insights into different countries' rich history and cultural heritage. Furthermore, by listening to the songs and hearing the related information, students may gain a deeper appreciation of the importance of the anthems to the people of that country.

PROCEDURE

1. As a warm-up for the assignment, talk about national anthems in general: their significance and how they raise feelings of national pride and nostalgia—even tears—when played at events such as the Olympics. Follow with questions about the national anthem of the country where they presently are, such as whether they know the title; who wrote it and when; whether they know some key words; if they can sing it; and the song's background, history, and meaning.

2. In pairs, have students interview each other about their country's national anthem using the "Interview Questions" handout (Appendix A).

3. Tell students they will be doing research and giving a presentation about a different country's anthem. Have each student in the class choose an anthem and complete the "Research Template" (Appendix B) for homework. Tell the students that if the words to the song are in another language, they need to find an English translation to share with the class.

4. Once the students complete the template, set a class presentation day and instruct students to practice their speeches, utilizing key points or an outline to aid them; they will not be permitted to read the information during the presentation.

5. While students are presenting, have the audience listen and take notes. By listening to the songs and hearing the related information, they may gain a deeper appreciation of the importance of the anthems to the people of that country.

CAVEATS AND OPTIONS

Have students interview each other in rotating pairs or groups on the national song they researched. This can help students gain confidence before presenting.

APPENDIX A: *Interview Questions*

1. Do you know how to sing your country's national anthem?
2. Do you like this song?
3. Can you tell me anything about this anthem?
4. When was it written?
5. What are key words in this song?
6. When and where is it usually played or sung?
7. Who wrote the song?
8. Who composed the lyrics?
9. What is the first line of the song?
10. What is the main idea of the whole song?
11. Did this national song have a background story before it was composed?
12. If the answer is yes, can you tell me?
13. What's your own comment about this song?
14. Have you also done some research on another country's national anthem?
15. If no, which country's national anthem would you like to do research on?
16. If yes, which country's national anthem is it?
17. Do you know how to sing this country's national anthem?
18. Now, repeat questions 1–13 about this second country's national anthem.

APPENDIX B: *Research Template*

Country:

Title of national song:

Key words:

When (and where) usually played:

Name of writer:

Name of composer:

When written:

First few lines (or stanza) of the lyrics:

Main idea of the whole song:

Summary of the song's background:

Other information:

Comments:

America's National Pastime

Constance Leonard

Levels	Intermediate to advanced
Aims	Explore the U.S. culture, history, and importance of baseball
	Learn common phrases and idioms that have been derived from baseball
Class Time	2 hours
Preparation Time	30 minutes
Resources	Audio or video recording of "Take Me out to the Ball Game"
	Lyrics to display or distribute
	Paper "bases" and tape
	Idioms handouts (Online resource)

Historically, music and language have been intertwined; using a popular song in the classroom will build students' cultural knowledge and vocabulary. It can also break down barriers and serve as a motivator.

PROCEDURE

1. Explain the basic rules of baseball, which can be found online if needed.

2. Divide the class into two groups. Play a review baseball game in the classroom. Create simple bases using plain paper taped to the floor. Label each base. Review a recent lesson in any skill area with questions that each team who "goes to bat" must answer correctly to progress along the bases. These could be questions on a reading; vocabulary that students produce from a definition, a synonym, or putting a word in a sentence; error correction; or using a modal correctly. "Three strikes and you're out!"

3. Play "Take Me out to the Ball Game," sing along several times with expression, and examine the cultural aspects. Explain what "peanuts and Cracker Jack" are and discuss their cultural significance. Elicit what culturally important snacks are available at sports events in the students' countries.

4. Introduce the first idiom in the song: "Three strikes you're out."

5. Elicit sports idioms the students might know in English and/or their first language. Introduce more baseball idioms (see Appendix A).

6. Practice idioms in pairs with the "List of Idioms for Class" handout (Appendix A). Have students fold this handout in half so they see only the idiom or the meaning. Students can help each other learn the idioms by one partner reading the idiom and the other saying the meaning, or vice versa.

7. Play a second baseball game using the "List of Idioms for Class" (Appendix A).
8. Assign idioms for homework: one word each or the entire worksheet (Appendix B).

CAVEATS AND OPTIONS

1. This activity can easily be adapted for any level. Younger learners can focus on the chorus and a few idioms; adult learners can discuss the culture and history of baseball in depth.
2. Distribute peanuts and Cracker Jack if possible and appropriate. (Does anyone have nut allergies?)

REFERENCES AND FURTHER READING

Norworth, J. (2009). *Take me out to the ball game.* New York, NY: Little, Brown Books for Young Readers.

Thompson, R., Wiles, T., & Strasberg, A. (2008). *Baseball's greatest hit: The story of "Take me out to the ball game."* New York, NY: Hal Leonard Books.

Make a Music Video With a Social Message

Sean H. Toland and Simon Thomas

Levels	Intermediate to advanced
Aims	Raise awareness of social issues
	Enhance critical thinking skills
	Develop listening and presentation skills
	Expand vocabulary
	Participate in collaborative learning
Class Time	90 minutes–2 hours
Preparation Time	30 minutes
Resources	"No Guns Allowed" music video
	Internet-connected devices for each student or group of students
	Handout of several songs' lyrics, some cut up
	Video analysis chart handout (Appendix A—Online Resource)
	Music video plan handout (Appendix B—Online Resource)
	6 envelopes
	Timer/stopwatch
	Projector

Studying music videos can be an excellent springboard to get English language learners to sharpen their critical thinking skills and discuss important social issues. In addition, incorporating music videos into an EFL/ESL lesson can spark students' cultural curiosity and motivational fires as well as enhance the language learning process. This activity requires the learners to critically examine a music video, discuss their observations, and then brainstorm ideas for an original music video with a social message that they would like to create for their favorite recording artist or group. Afterward, the duos make a mini-presentation to their classmates.

PROCEDURE

1. Obtain the lyrics for six songs (using, e.g., www.metrolyrics.com). See Caveats and Options for suggested songs. One song will be used as a class example. The remaining songs are for group activities.

2. Prepare the class activity example by printing one set of the lyrics for "No Guns Allowed," by Snoop Lion featuring Drake and Cori B., for each group and cutting them into five parts.

3. Print out two copies of the lyrics for the remaining five songs for the group activities. One copy is the answer key. Cut the second copy into five parts. Label each part with a letter A through E and put the parts in an envelope. Make one copy of the "Video Analysis Chart" (Appendix A) for each student. Copy "Our Music Video Plan" (Appendix B) as a handout for each group.

Class Activity

1. Divide the class into groups. Write the following phrases on the board: "social issues" and "images that represent the issue." Discuss their meanings and provide students with an example (e.g., air pollution–smoke from a factory chimney).
2. Give groups 5 minutes to brainstorm ideas. Each team must write down one social issue and two images on the board.
3. Bring the groups' ideas together. Provide corrective feedback and elicit more ideas for images.
4. Provide each group with the cut-up lyrics for the example song. Play the example video. Ask students to put the lyrics in the correct order.
5. Provide corrective feedback.
6. Discuss the topics in the headings of the "Video Analysis Chart" (Appendix A) and elicit ideas.
7. Distribute the "Video Analysis Chart." Select volunteers to read each category from the "No Guns Allowed" example. Compare ideas, review difficult vocabulary, and answer any questions.
8. Watch the video one more time. Check comprehension by instructing students to call out when they see the ideas identified in the example.

Group Activities

1. Assign one video and distribute an envelope containing the song lyrics to each group. Students must: watch the music video twice on their mobile devices, put the lyrics in order, and examine the video and complete the "Video Analysis Chart."
2. Bring groups together. Tell learners they must learn about other teams' videos. They will walk around the classroom asking and answering questions about their respective videos. Model questions with a student volunteer (e.g., What images did you see?). Remind the class this is a communicative activity and not a copying exercise.
3. After a set amount of time, bring groups together. Ask each team to report the social issue they noticed in their assigned video. Provide corrective feedback and answer questions.
4. Distribute the "Our Music Video Plan" handout (Appendix B) to each team. Review each item on the chart. Give students 15 minutes to work with a partner to create an original music video idea for their favorite musician to highlight one social issue.

5. Each duo must make a mini-presentation about their music video concept.
6. Bring the class together to discuss the social issues that students identified and their music video ideas.

CAVEATS AND OPTIONS

1. Suggested songs include:
   - "No Guns Allowed," by Snoop Lion featuring Drake and Cori B. (gun violence)
   - "If I Were a Boy," by Beyoncé (gender roles)
   - "Borders," by M.I.A (global refugee crisis, tolerance)
   - "Diamonds from Sierra Leone," by Kanye West (child labor, war diamond industry)
   - "Earth Song," by Michael Jackson (environmental issues)
   - "I Still Love You," by Jennifer Hudson (same-sex marriage, LGBT rights)

   [Editors' note: Preview song lyrics for appropriateness for your students.]

2. At each stage of this activity, you can make modifications for different English proficiency levels. For example, preintermediate learners might need more time to complete their music video plans. Mini-presentations can then be done during the next lesson. More advanced learners can write a song to accompany the video that they would like to make.

What's in a Song? From Peace to Protests: Culture Abounds

Joshua Wedlock

Levels	Intermediate to advanced
Aims	Increase cultural knowledge and familiarity
	Improve analytical and discussion skills
	Develop a clearer understanding of how different linguistic features (e.g., metaphor, simile, slang) can be used
Class Time	50 minutes–1 hour
Preparation Time	≈ 30–45 minutes
Resources	Audio recording of selected songs
	Handout (see Appendix)

By using song to explore culture and society, we can transport our students to a different time and place in order to help them feel and experience the history, culture, or social commentary associated with a certain song, artist, or genre. This approach to teaching culture can make a seemingly boring topic come alive and facilitate learning in a fun and enjoyable way. (I dare you not to tap your foot to Stevie Wonder's (1981) "Happy Birthday," which was written to honor Martin Luther King, Jr.).

PROCEDURE

1. Select an appropriate song (or series of songs if you would like to do an entire unit on a certain topic or theme) that has had an immense social or political impact, or one that is about a culturally significant event or person. You should possess pertinent background information relevant to the song. See Caveats and Options for song suggestions.

2. Prepare a level-appropriate introduction passage about the song, the artist, and the significance of the event or person being depicted. Include the artist's name, the name of the song, a selection of focus questions, and the song's lyrics (See Appendix).

3. Have the students read the introduction passage and discuss their initial thoughts in small groups or pairs. Your students may also use this step to uncover any new vocabulary, linguistic features, or grammar structures that need clarifying.

4. Play the song in class and encourage the students to discuss any possible meanings or what they think the cultural relevance of the song is. For example, if the song is John Lennon's (1971) "Imagine," the students might discuss a world without religion or without poverty. In this section of the class, you may need to act as a facilitator and ask questions to guide the students to not only the more obvious meanings, but also to any hidden or underlying meanings.

5. A homework activity could involve the students researching a song of their own choosing (possibly from their own culture) that has cultural, political, or social significance. The students can then either prepare a short talk or paper in English outlining the song's significance.

CAVEATS AND OPTIONS

1. Possible song selections include:
   - "A Change Is Gonna Come," by Sam Cooke
   - "Blowin' in the Wind," by Bob Dylan
   - "Sunday, Bloody Sunday," by U2
   - "Imagine," by John Lennon
   - "War," by Edwin Starr
   - "Get Up Stand Up," by Bob Marley
   - "Do They Know It's Christmas?," by Band Aid
   - "Fight the Power," by Public Enemy

   [Editors' note: Preview song lyrics for appropriateness for your students.]

2. Assuming your class enjoys this activity, you may decide to do a "music week" to analyze and discuss several songs dealing with the same subject, person, or event (e.g., human rights, war and peace, protest songs).

REFERENCES AND FURTHER READING

Carducci, R., & Rhoads, R. A. (2005). Of minds and media: Teaching critical citizenship to the plugged-in generation. *About Campus*, *10*(5), 2–9.

Lee, J. H. (2015). Using popular music as a teaching tool: A literature review. *Asia-Pacific Journal of Multimedia Services Convergent with Art, Humanities, and Sociology*, *5*(1), 99–106.

APPENDIX: *Sample Handout: John Lennon's (1971) "Imagine"*

Title: "Imagine"

Artist: John Lennon

Year: 1971

Focus Questions

1. Were there any significant events taking place in 1971?
2. What do you think is the message or meaning of this song?
3. Is this song still relevant? Why/Why not?
4. Why do you think John Lennon wrote this song?

Background

Often cited as Lennon's greatest song, this peace anthem contains lyrics that encourage the listener to imagine a world without war, a world without borders, and a world without the divisions of religion and nationality. It also encourages the listener to consider the possibility that people should be living a life unattached to material possessions.

Add Lyrics Here:

Part VIII

Music for Integrated Skills

Part VIII: Music for Integrated Skills

It could easily be argued that all of the activities in this book (and, in fact, all language teaching activities everywhere) are integrated skills activities. It is nearly impossible to separate the receptive skills (listening and reading) from the productive skills (speaking and writing), or to separate listening from speaking, or reading from writing. Of course, vocabulary and grammar combine to make up any utterance. Each activity in this chapter addresses at least three of the six language areas included in this book: listening, speaking, reading, writing, grammar, and vocabulary. Several also incorporate cultural exploration or critical thinking skills as aims.

Eleanora S. Bell and Xiaowei Shi, and Mike Hammond combine well-known written stories with their musical versions. Ha Hoang's activity uses ballads and student drawings to teach speaking, writing, and grammar, while Ruth Ann Marotta and Theresa McGarry tap the emotional connections between songs and memories to reinforce both grammar and vocabulary skills. In activities provided by Joyce Cunningham, Thomas Fast, and Lisa G. Harris, students explore social issues while developing their abilities in writing, listening, and speaking. Thomas Fast's second activity in this chapter combines listening for both gist and detail with learning prepositions and descriptive writing. Rebecca Palmer's activity addresses language skills from spelling to examining the differences between formal and informal language. Friederike Tegge's "Song Dictogloss" tackles grammar, vocabulary, listening, and speaking. For teachers looking for a fresh way to present comparatives and adjectives while students write poems or lyrics to express their wishes, Hayriye Ulaş Taraf's activity will be of interest.

Integrating language skills has been compared to weaving together different strands of a tapestry (Oxford, 2001). "This approach stresses that English is not just an object of academic interest nor merely a key to passing an examination; instead, English becomes a real means of interaction and sharing among people" (p. 5), Oxford explains. What could be more natural than to weave music into the tapestry?

REFERENCE

Oxford, R. (2001). Integrated skills in the ESL/EFL classroom. *ESL Magazine, 6*(1). Retrieved from http://files.eric.ed.gov/fulltext/ED456670.pdf

Song Dictogloss

Friederike Tegge

Levels	All
Aims	Raise awareness of linguistic forms
	Review grammar
	Practice and entrench familiar vocabulary, collocations, and idiomatic expressions
	Listen for detail
	Speak in peer interaction
Class Time	15–30 minutes
Preparation Time	15 minutes (or longer if you need to find a suitable song)
Resources	Audio recording of a selected song
	Song lyrics to hand out or display

A dictogloss combines dictation with the memorization of longer stretches of language (see Harmer, 2015, p. 380). Asking learners to re-create the text verbatim raises their awareness of linguistic structure. You further encourage this focus on form during peer interaction (in small groups or team work) and finally when you have students compare the re-created versions with the original lyrics.

Playing a song rather than reading a text is a musical, enjoyable variation of the conventional dictogloss. Presenting language in the format of song lyrics also draws the listeners' attention to the structure of the language; it encourages a focus on how something is said rather than just on what is being said. In addition, songs support the memorization of text through rhythm; rhyme; and the use of poetic devices such as repetition, alliteration, and assonance (See Tegge, 2015). Finally, many songs further aid memorization because they are repetitive.

PROCEDURE

1. Your selected song should be suitable for your students' proficiency levels, contain the desired target language, and be clearly enunciated. The song should not contain completely unfamiliar vocabulary. However, this cannot always be avoided. Any unknown words should be introduced in a preteaching activity.

2. Before playing the song (or a part of it), explain the concept of a dictogloss to students: A dictogloss is like a dictation: Students write down the exact words of the text they have heard. However, unlike a dictation, they cannot write while listening. Instead, they attempt to re-create the text verbatim after they have listened to it.

3. Listening 1: Play the song (or a part of it) and make sure that students do not take notes.

4. Depending on the length of the selected section, give students 2–4 minutes to write down as many of the song lyrics as they remember.

5. Listening 2 (optional): Play the song a second time. Again, the students cannot write while they listen. Once they have finished listening, they add more to their version of the lyrics and correct mistakes they have made previously.

6. Give students in small groups 3–5 minutes to compare their texts and to produce a more complete and accurate version together. Encourage discussions about grammar and vocabulary.

7. Listening 3: Play the song a third (or second) time. Again, students cannot write while listening.

8. Again, give the students in small groups 3–5 minutes to improve their text and to re-create the original as accurately as possible.

9. Show the original lyrics and let students compare their versions with the original. Discuss mistakes and differences and point out underlying grammar points, collocations, or idiomatic expressions.

CAVEATS AND OPTIONS

1. The "Song Dictogloss" activity can be adapted to all proficiency levels by way of choosing a song suitable for the target learners and varying the length of the song section used—from only a few lines to the whole song.

2. It can be challenging to find a song that suits your learners and your purpose and that is clearly enunciated. Build up a song library over time and keep a record of target levels and particular teaching goals.

3. Many songs can be clearly linked to a certain theme. A few suggestions of authentic songs are:
   - "If I Had a Million Dollars," S. Page and E. Robertson (intermediate; if-clauses; dreams and wishes)
   - "The Lion Sleeps Tonight" (1961), S. Linda, H. Peretti, L. Creatore, G. D. Weiss, and A. Stanton (beginner; simple sentences in present tense, adjectives, prepositions; lullabies, jungles)
   - "Moon over Bourbon Street," Sting (high intermediate to advanced; idiomatic expressions; vampires).

REFERENCES AND FURTHER READING

Harmer, J. (2015). *The practice of English language teaching*. Harlow, United Kingdom: Pearson Education Limited.

Tegge, F. (2015). *Investigating song-based language teaching and its effect on lexical learning* (Unpublished doctoral thesis). Victoria University of Wellington, New Zealand. Retrieved from http://researcharchive.vuw.ac.nz/handle/10063/4577

All I Want to Be . . .

Hayriye Ulaş Taraf

Levels	Beginner to low intermediate
Aims	Practice a list of new adjectives
	Practice comparative structures
	Develop sublistening skills, such as listening for specific information
	Improve a sense of rhythm and harmony while writing original lyrics
	Develop speaking skills
	Engage in guided writing and express life wishes
	Engage in a peaceful, nonthreatening classroom atmosphere
Class Time	≈ 1 hour
Preparation Time	15–20 minutes
Resources	Audio recording of the song "Everything at Once," by Lenka
	Gap-fill handout of song lyrics (teacher created)

The literature (Canning-Wilson & Wallace, 2000; Hemei, 1997; Katchen, 1996; Wright, 1976) suggests that exposure to contextualized examples of grammar structure and vocabulary pieces, especially with the use of audiovisual materials, can contribute to foreign language learners' mastering grammar rules and vocabulary items.

Contextualizing grammar teaching necessitates using the language in real-life contexts or with authentic materials, and songs can be considered one of the most powerful tools to catch learners' interest. The lyrics of the song, "Everything at Once," by Lenka, include many examples of the comparative structure "as . . . as" and a rich variety of adjectives, like in these lines: "as sly as a fox, as strong as an ox; as fast as a hare . . ." Moreover, songs may play a vital role in creating a positive environment in the second language classroom due to their motivating effect.

PROCEDURE

1. Make two gap-fill exercises of the lyrics. Versions A and B should have different gaps from each other.

2. Announce to students that they are going to listen to the first verse of the song "Everything at Once," by Lenka, without a copy of the lyrics.

3. Play only the first verse of the song in class and ask the students to find and tell each other what the adjectives in the verse are.

4. Discuss the meaning of the lyrics in the first verse and tell the students they are going to learn how to use the comparative structure "as . . . as."

5. Give half the students handout A, and the other half get handout B. Tell the students the handouts have different gaps from each other.

6. Play the song and ask them to listen to the full song and fill in the gaps in the lyrics. Ask them to read their answers aloud to the class.

7. Ask the students to try to guess the meanings of the adjectives they don't know.

8. Write a few adjectives with their opposites randomly on the board, and ask the students to match them.

9. Then, draw students' attention to the comparative structure "as . . . as," often used in the song, and teach the structure.

10. Ask students to write a poem or further lyrics for the song using "as . . . as" about what they want to be. Provide students an example of lyrics you created. For example:

    As happy as a child, as colourful as a butterfly
    As calm as the sea, as innocent as a baby
    All I wanna be (All I want to be)
    All I wanna be is everything

11. Students can share their lyrics in small groups or with the class.

CAVEATS AND OPTIONS

1. Use this activity to teach other subjects, such as animal vocabulary, by teaching students how to describe animals. You can also teach articles (*a*, *an*, *the*); there are many examples of them in the song.

2. Instead of using this activity for grammar and vocabulary teaching, use it as a warm-up activity, enabling students to do creative writing, or use it as you would any text for reading practice. Using the lyrics as a reading text, ask students how the song writer feels and what he or she wants to change about him- or herself. For creative writing exercises, you can teach your students to create similes.

3. To further practice adjectives, have students make and throw adjective paper balls. Ask students to take out two pieces of paper and write an adjective on one and its opposite on the other. Then, ask them to crumple these sheets into paper balls and throw them toward the board. Group students and ask them to stand up, rush to unfold the paper balls, and find adjectives and match them with their opposites. Finally, tell students the group that collects and matches the most adjectives with their opposites will be the winner.

REFERENCES AND FURTHER READING

Canning-Wilson C., & Wallace, J. (2000). Practical aspects of using video in the foreign language classroom. *The Internet TESL Journal*, 6(11).

Hemei, J. (1997). Teaching with video in an English class. *Journal of English Teaching Forum, 35*(2), 45–47.

Katchen, J. E. (1996). Video in ELT—Theoretical and Pedagogical Foundations. In *Proceedings of the 2002 KATE (The Korea Association of Teachers of English) International Conference* (pp. 256–259). Taipei, Taiwan: The Crane Publishing Company, Ltd.

Wright, A. (1976). *Visual materials for the language teacher*. Essex, United Kingdom: Longman Wilson.

Drawing a Tale

Ha Hoang

Levels	High beginner to low intermediate
Aims	Develop narrative speaking and/or writing
	Learn past tenses and chronological order
Class Time	≈ 1 hour
Preparation Time	15 minutes
Resources	Audio recording of a ballad that narrates a story with many details/scenes
	Pins or tape
	Handout of song lyrics (optional)
	A sketched picture (teacher created; optional)

Learning outcomes are higher when you deepen the learning process (Craik & Tulving, 1975). By using the dual system of image and words (Paivio, 1971), by drawing pictures themselves, and by listening to music, learners are exposed to the language in focus in four different ways. This repeated exposure to the language in focus in different modes deepens the learning process and thus enhances retention.

PROCEDURE

1. Select an audio recording of a ballad that contains a fairly complex story line (e.g., Johnny Cash's "Ballad of the Teenage Queen" or Conway Twitty's "Don't Cry, Joni").

2. Play the song in class for the students to follow the story line (i.e., the events in the correct order of time). Discuss the lyrics to draw students' attention to the focus of the activity (i.e., past tense or chronological writing). Students do not need to see the lyrics at this stage.

3. Show students a picture you've drawn of the beginning of the story or of a character in the song. Give them 15–20 minutes to work in pairs or small groups to draw pictures describing the rest of the story.

4. Pin the pictures on the wall for students to look at and retell/rewrite the story in pairs using the language focus of the activity.

5. Play the song again (you may want to give the students the lyrics at this stage) for students to check whether they have narrated the story and used the language in focus correctly.

CAVEATS AND OPTIONS

1. Ask the students to work in groups to listen to different parts of the song and draw the pictures, then retell/rewrite the story in the correct order.

2. Use two different songs. Students work in groups of four. Within each group, students work in pairs, listen to the two songs separately on their own devices or in the computer lab, and then draw pictures. They exchange pictures with the other pair to retell/rewrite the story using the language focus of the activity. Students then listen to the song together to check their language.

3. As a follow-up task, students can write a small play based on the song and act it out.

REFERENCES

Craik, F., & Tulving, E. (1975). Depth of processing and the retention of words in episodic memory. *Journal of Experimental Psychology: General, 104,* 268–294.

Paivio, A. (1971). *Imagery and verbal processes*. New York, NY: Psychology Press.

Tying It Together: Music, Reading, and Writing

Eleanora (Nonie) S. Bell and Xiaowei (Vivian) Shi

Levels	Intermediate
Aims	Provide cultural background for a short story
	Develop reading and vocabulary skills
	Write a narrative
Class Time	≈ 145 minutes
Preparation Time	15–30 minutes
Resources	Audio recording of "Tie a Yellow Ribbon Round the Old Oak Tree"
	Handouts (Online Resource)
	Copies of story
	Internet access
	Projector

In this activity, the lively music draws weak readers into the story. Students, catching the human interest, read with more enthusiasm. The activity develops students' vocabulary in multiple ways: The cloze listening exercise reinforces noting parts of speech, guessing meaning from context uses observation and deduction to extend vocabulary and reading skills, and creating conversations and narratives further practices key vocabulary. Strategic observation questions push students to interpret and analyze information from the text and relate the concepts to their own lives. Writing a dialogue or retelling the story to a loved one helps students personalize the narrative, providing a transition to writing their own experiences.

PROCEDURE

Prereading Activities (≈ 45 minutes)

1. Divide students into groups of three to five. Each table group discusses the following group discussion questions:

    a. What is the longest trip you have ever taken?

    b. Do you talk to strangers who sit next to you on public transportation, such as buses or planes?

    c. Please share with your classmates an interesting story that has happened on a trip.

2. Introduce the physical features and cultural meaning of oak trees and yellow ribbons (i.e., oak trees grow tall with many branches and yellow ribbons indicate military families are waiting for the safe return of loved ones), asking if students have noticed these in their community.

3. Students listen to the song "Tie a Yellow Ribbon Round the Old Oak Tree" (available at www.youtube.com/watch?v=7NCZ4l8FCFc), completing the cloze exercise from Appendix A and discussing their answers as a group.

4. Use sample questions to lead students in noticing and interpreting the song lyrics. Raise the following questions:
    a. Why is the whole bus cheering when they see the oak tree?
    b. What is the relationship between the main character and the bus passengers?
    c. Why do they care, and why they are excited about what they see?

Reading Activities (≈ 30 minutes)

1. Split the short story "The Yellow Ribbon," by Pete Hamill (available at www.townsendpress.com/uploaded_files/tinymce/Library%20Excerpts/tenreal.pdf), into three sections.
    - Part 1: From the beginning of page 3 to the top of page 5.
    - Part 2: From the first full paragraph on page 5 to the end of last full paragraph on page 6.
    - Part 3: From the beginning of last paragraph on page 6 to the end of the story on page 7.

    Assign each one of the reading's three sections to a group of students, the last section to the most proficient readers. Direct students to read the story for more detailed answers to the prereading questions from Step 4 in the Prereading Activities. To save time, assign this as homework.

2. After students have completed the reading, hand out the "Vocabulary List" (Appendix B). Move around room, clarifying unfamiliar words. Each group only needs to work on the words in its assigned reading portion.

3. Remind students to consult the dictionary as needed and to guess the meaning of other unfamiliar words from the context of the reading.

Postreading Activities (the following class session; ≈ 55 minutes)

1. After reading the story, each homework group meets to discuss its portion of the story. Circulate, verifying students' comprehension of the text and vocabulary.

2. Students move to mixed groups (with at least one representative of each reading portion) and recount what has been read and understood of the story.

3. Ask students to note the places named in the text, indicating the path of the trip on a projected map (available at www.google.com/maps/d/edit?mid=zajV67qVSkWI.kiOn69ueE70s).

4. Explain that Howard Johnson Hotels are a chain of inexpensive American hotels with an iconic architectural style still visible in some communities. Project an image of one, if you'd like.

5. Use the "Postreading Discussion Questions" (Appendix C) to help students identify with the experience described in the song lyrics, thereby enhancing reading comprehension. Prior to discussion, explain the following:
   a. What it means to say "I've done my time"
   b. What it means to "cheer"
   c. What it means to not be able to "bear" something

Writing Activity (≈ 15 minutes)

1. Recap the story of the song "Tie a Yellow Ribbon Round the Old Oak Tree" and direct students to think of a song that is important to them, possibly a patriotic, childhood, or romantic song.
2. The students write a personal narrative describing when they first heard the song, why it was special to them, and how it has impacted their lives.
3. Assign students to write in class or for homework, possibly providing a writing rubric. If the writing is done in class, it could require an additional 45–60 minutes.

CAVEATS AND OPTIONS

1. Each student may draw two scenes from his or her homework reading on two separate pages. In class, mixed groups (with a student representing each reading section) put the pictures together in the order of the story's events.
2. Each mixed group of students marks a map with the stops from their section of the story of the bus trip.
3. Partners write and role-play a dialogue based on the story.

REFERENCES AND FURTHER READING

Kilusf. (2006, October 11). Tie a yellow ribbon round the old oak tree [Video file]. Retrieved from https://www.youtube.com/watch?v=7NCZ4l8FCFc

Hamill, P. (1996). The yellow ribbon. In *Ten real-life stories* (pp. 3–7). West Berlin, NJ: Townsend Press. Retrieved from http://www.townsendpress.com/uploaded_files/tinymce/Library%20Excerpts/tenreal.pdf

"Nobody's Home"

Joyce Cunningham

Levels	Intermediate to advanced
Aims	Participate in active listening, discussion, reflection, and writing on real-life problems in society through a content-based approach
Class Time	90 minutes–2 hours
Preparation Time	≈ 30 minutes
Resources	Video recordings of "Nobody's Home," by Avril Lavigne (one with lyrics and one without; see References and Further Reading)
	Audiovisual equipment
	Gap-fill lyrics worksheet (teacher created)
	A download from Maketreks of the interviews with two homeless men (optional; see References and Further Reading).

In light of natural and manmade disasters such as earthquakes, tsunamis, and wars, introducing the plight of people caught in disasters draws on students' prior knowledge and stimulates them to consider causes and possible solutions for homelessness. Many students enjoy songs by Avril Lavigne but may not be familiar with her more serious side. The video for her song "Nobody's Home" can serve as an opening onto problems facing homeless people, such as drug and alcohol abuse.

PROCEDURE

1. Small groups brainstorm problems facing the homeless in their cities or societies.

2. View the video "Nobody's Home" by Avril Lavigne (available at www.youtube.com/watch?v=NGFSNE18Ywc), initially without sound. In small groups, have students identify problems experienced by street people in the video. You may stop the video at several points or wait until the end of the video to elicit predictions about what might happen to the young woman.

3. Distribute a gap-fill worksheet. Groups listen, fill in the blanks, and compare answers. Correction can come from watching another video of the same song in which the words are shown as screen lyrics (available at https://www.youtube.com/watch?v=3tCeSyewAJk). This will familiarize students with an example of video lyrics (see Caveats and Options, Item 4).

4. Students choose to discuss either the older or younger woman and divide into small groups accordingly. They brainstorm and discuss reasons and possible solutions for homelessness and write a letter to the woman they chose. The letters are posted on the wall of the classroom or on a blog. Small groups then choose another group's letter to read and respond to, thus heightening interest about homelessness.

5. Discuss the videos with questions such as:
   - What are some possible meanings of the song title?
   - Avril Lavigne is shown almost entirely in black and white in this video. Why do you think her appearance differs from that of her usual videos?
   - In your group, decide on a different ending to this video.
   - What are possible ways to help homeless people?

CAVEATS AND OPTIONS

1. In groups, students with lower proficiency describe the actions of the young woman during the course of a day, either in the past or present tenses. Groups are changed several times so that the descriptions become longer and more complete.

2. Consider challenging lower level groups to depict problems in the video and decide on several key words to explain each situation. Indeed, learning that engages more senses can heighten interest and memory. Allen (2008) points out, "Adding drawing to the lesson allows those more visually oriented students to remember the information better . . . while everyone seems to enjoy the process."

3. Role-play several of the scenes by imagining and discussing what may have gone on before or after a scene (e.g., at the store, the washroom or in the car).

4. Consider having students make their own digital photo stories by matching key words of the song with pictures and/or images selected from the Internet. Teachers can download Microsoft's free Photo Story www.microsoft.com/en-us/download/details.aspx?id=11132. Small groups select, edit, and organize digital photos or images to create a visual story about an aspect of the song that interests them. Learners then present their projects to the class. Lems (2016) states that this procedure, while "creative and interpretive, also requires clear understanding of the vocabulary in the song and an ability to find images to support the understanding."

5. Two informative videos of homeless men shed light on the possible causes of becoming homeless (available on YouTube at www.youtube.com/watch?v=O5LZPuREnyg and www.youtube.com/watch?v=yaxeMUETyi0). Higher level students can do a listening retell. Assign one of the two interviews to each half of the class. Students take notes (either guided or free). Pair each student with another student who watched the same video. Partners then retell the information to each other to check their notes. Then, students exchange information with a new partner who saw the other video. Short, paired dictations taken from one of the interviews can render this activity more accessible to lower proficiency learners.

REFERENCES AND FURTHER READING

Allen, R. (2008). *Green light classrooms: Teaching techniques that accelerate learning.* Thousand Oaks, CA: Corwin Press.

Lems, K. (2016, July 26). Learning English through music in the digital age. *TESOL Video News.* Retrieved from http://newsmanager.commpartners.com/tesolvdmis/issues/2016-07-26/4.html

It's Not Easy Being Born This Way

Thomas Fast

Levels	Intermediate to advanced
Aims	*Develop listening skills (gist and detail)*
	Develop critical thinking skills (infer, analyze, apply, create, etc.)
	Gain cultural understanding of racism
	Recognize the use of music as a tool for social change
	Gain understanding of metaphor as a literary device
Class Time	*1 hour+*
Preparation Time	*30 minutes–1 hour (including worksheet preparation)*
Resources	*Audio or video recording of "It's Not Easy Being Green," by Kermit the Frog*
	Audiovisual equipment
	Gap-fill handout (teacher created)
	Images of Kermit the Frog and Sesame Street

This activity introduces students to a song that is simultaneously simple and profound. The lyrics provide students with listening and critical thinking practice. The song can also provide a greater understanding of the complexity of race and culture, which students can compare with their own cultural situations. Finally, the lyrics promote self-reflection.

PROCEDURE

1. Introduce Kermit the Frog, Sesame Street, and the title of the song, "It's Not Easy Being Green," with visual aids. Have the students discuss the possible meaning of the song, based on the title and visuals. Elicit feedback.

2. Listen for gist. Ask students to listen to the song, noting any keywords, phrases, or hints (e.g., singer's tone of voice) that suggest the meaning of the song. Ask students to share their findings with their neighbors.

3. Pass out the gap-fill handout, which should focus on selected target language, and go over any difficult vocabulary in the lyrics (e.g., *blend*).

4. Listen for detail. Have students fill in the gaps in the lyrics. Repeat the song as necessary. Allow students to compare their answers between listenings.

5. Postlistening discussion: Have students answer the following questions in pairs or small groups:

a. Who is the song for? (children)

   b. What style of song is this (children's song/folk/blues)

   c. What is Kermit trying to say? (All skin colors are beautiful)

   Provide feedback as needed. Elicit the idea that green is a metaphor for skin color and/or the qualities that we are born with—and that we are all born beautiful. Perhaps talk about how this song was written in 1970 at the height of the U.S. Civil Rights movement.

6. Now have students write their own version: "It's not easy being _____."

CAVEATS AND OPTIONS

1. If using video, I recommend not showing it to the students for the first listening. Wait until students have a better grasp of the lyrics.

2. If time allows (or for homework), the students write their own lyrics to the melody, turning a potentially negative aspect of their own lives into a positive. Use the example: *It's not easy being left-handed*.

3. As a follow-up activity, you may wish to compare "It's Not Easy Being Green" to Lady Gaga's song, "Born This Way." Possible discussion questions could be:

   a. Who is this song for?

   b. What style of music is this?

   c. Who does "H.I.M." refer to?

   d. What is Lady Gaga's message?

   e. How is this song similar to or different from "It's Not Easy Being Green?"

"Tom's Diner"

Thomas Fast

Levels	Intermediate to advanced
Aims	Develop ability to read for gist
	Develop listening skills (for detail)
	Develop descriptive writing skills
	Develop critical thinking skills (infer, analyze, apply, create, etc.)
Class Time	1 hour+
Preparation Time	30 minutes (including worksheet preparation)
Resources	Audio or video recording of "Tom's Diner," by Suzanne Vega
	Descriptive devices worksheet (Appendix)
	Handout of song lyrics

This activity introduces students to a catchy song that is simultaneously simple and profound. The lyrics provide students with compelling examples of descriptive writing (as well as the present continuous tense). Some of the more poetic passages provide critical thinking practice as well.

PROCEDURE

1. Introduce the topic of descriptive writing: What language tools do we use to write descriptions? (adjectives, words associated with the five senses, prepositions of location).
2. Pass out the lyrics handout and the "Descriptive Devices" worksheet (Appendix), and go over any difficult vocabulary.
3. Ask students to read the lyrics, noting any keywords, phrases, or hints that suggest the meaning of the song. Ask students to share their findings with their neighbors.
4. Play the song and listen for detail, noting the singer's cadence and phrasing. Repeat the song as necessary.
5. Postlistening discussion: Have students answer the following questions in pairs or small groups:
   - Where is she?
   - What is she doing?
   - Who does she see? What are they doing?
   - What is she thinking?
   - How is she feeling? How do you know?
   - What is your interpretation of the "midnight picnic" lyric?

6. Descriptive writing:
    a. Ask students to complete the "Descriptive Devices" handout.
    b. Note that very few adjectives are used in the song. Also note lyrical devices that typically would not be used in other writing (e.g., use of "and" in the song).
    c. Instruct students to write a description of an important place in their life, using vivid adjectives, prepositions of location, and the five senses. (This could be homework.)
    d. Share student writing in groups and with the class.

CAVEATS AND OPTIONS

I recommend familiarizing the students with the song in the following order:

1. Read the lyrics. (Don't even tell them it's a song at first. Just tell them it is a person describing a place.)
2. Listen to the original a capella version of the song.
3. Next, play the better known dance track version of the song for an enthusiastic response from the class.
4. As a final activity, you could have students sing the song for motivation and pronunciation practice.

APPENDIX: *Descriptive Devices*

1. Which of the five senses does the singer use to describe her environment?

    sight   sound   touch   taste   smell

2. Underline the prepositions of location that are used in the song.

    | above | before | far from | opposite |
    | across | behind | from | outside |
    | after | below | in | over |
    | against | beneath | in back of | past |
    | ahead of | beside | inside | throughout |
    | along | between | near | under |
    | among | beyond | next to | |
    | around | by | on | |
    | at | close to | on top of | |

3. Imagine a place in your life. Write four original sentences to describe it. Use prepositions of location (above). In addition, use your senses as well as vivid adjectives.

Content Connection: Environment and Climate Change

Lisa G. Harris

Levels	Intermediate to advanced
Aims	Practice listening, speaking, and critical thinking skills
Class Time	≈ 1 hour
Preparation Time	30 minutes
Resources	Computer with Internet connection
	Projector
	Video recording of "Mercy Mercy Me (The Ecology)," by Marvin Gaye
	Printout of song lyrics
	Cloze lyrics worksheet (teacher created)
	Photo of Marvin Gaye

The environment and climate change are relevant and popular content themes in ESL/EFL textbooks and classrooms worldwide. This activity includes a range of activities using multiple modalities and incorporates a variety of listening opportunities, rich discussion questions, and critical thinking exercises, all of which will enhance and connect content and build students' listening and speaking skills.

PROCEDURE

1. Choose a music video with lyrics for "Mercy Mercy Me (The Ecology)," by Marvin Gaye. There are several good ones available on YouTube.

2. Prepare a cloze with the song lyrics, eliminating five to eight clearly enunciated content words (e.g., *blue skies, oceans, fish, animals*) that are well-spaced throughout the song.

3. Begin the activity by reading the following sentences as a dictation:
   - We're going to listen to a song by a famous American singer.
   - This singer was born in Washington, DC, in 1939.
   - He began singing in church at the age of 4.
   - During his career, he sang, wrote songs, played instruments, and produced music.
   - He had many popular songs in the 1960s, 70s, and 80s.
   - He was shot and killed by his father one day before his 45th birthday in 1984.

4. Display background information and prelistening vocabulary (Appendix A) on the overhead and discuss. You can also show a photograph of Marvin Gaye (available on the Internet).

5. Play the song one time with sound only (no video). The song is instrumental after 1:50, so you can stop it or turn down the volume and continue with class at that point to save time.

6. Elicit responses about what students heard and their predictions of the song's meaning.

7. Distribute the cloze lyrics worksheet, and play the song again (no video). Students listen and complete the cloze.

8. Show the music video and the lyrics on the overhead.

9. Put students into small groups to discuss the "Postlistening Discussion Questions" (Appendix B). Then have groups share their answers with the class.

CAVEATS AND OPTIONS

1. Make the dictation more student centered and active by doing a running dictation or a dictogloss.

2. To incorporate technology into the dictation, have students use their cell phones (if available) to record the sentences and play them back to their partner.

APPENDIX A: *Background Information*

"Mercy Mercy Me (The Ecology)" by Marvin Gaye

- This song was the number one rhythm and blues song in August of 1971.
- Marvin Gaye was a leading artist with Motown Records (the same record company that launched Michael Jackson's musical career).
- He received numerous honors and awards for his music.

Prelistening vocabulary

- *Mercy*: compassionate treatment
- *Mercy me*: an uncommon expression used to show feelings such as surprise, compassion, fear, or sadness
- *Ain't*: slang contraction for am not, is not, are not
- *Mercury*: a chemical element (Hg)
- *Radiation*: a form of energy that comes from nuclear reactions and can be harmful to living things

APPENDIX B: *Postlistening Discussion Questions*

- What is this song about?
- Why do you think Marvin Gaye wrote about this topic in 1971? Do we have some of the same concerns today? Explain with examples.
- What does Line 4 of the song mean? "Poison is the wind that blows from the north and south and east." Explain your answer.

- What does the singer-songwriter mean when he sings, "Things just ain't what they used to be?" Be specific with your answers.
- Who or what does "she" refer to in this line: "How much more abuse from man can she stand?"
- Why do you think he named the song "Mercy Mercy Me?"
- If you could rename this song, what name would you give it and why?
- Why do you think he ended the song with "My Lord . . . My sweet Lord?"

Songs and Memories for Expanding Vocabulary and Grammar

Ruth Ann Marotta and Theresa McGarry

Levels	Intermediate to advanced
Aims	Interpret and construct song lyrics in order to share background and experience
	Engage in peer review
Class Time	50 minutes
Preparation Time	30 minutes–1 hour (foundational lesson)
Resources	Audio recording of a song about a place or past time
	Printout of lyrics for projecting
	Projector

This activity evokes the neurological benefits of music and linguistic benefits of lyrics (Lems, 2001) while engaging your students as whole people with histories. It provides a scaffolding context for learners who may not be ready to write long poems or other extended works but can write expressively and interpret the writing of other writers and students. In the deeply engaging form of music, this activity provides a fresh review of grammatical concepts and emotional reasons for writing.

PROCEDURE

1. Prepare or locate a recording of a song about a place or a past time with a section that can be rewritten by replacing some of the phrases. In "The House That Built Me," sung by Miranda Lambert and written by Tom Douglas and Allen Shamblin, the first verse would be a good choice. The phrases in bold could be replaced:

   I know they say you can't go home again.
   I just had to come back one last time.
   Ma'am I know you don't know me from Adam.
   But **these handprints on the front steps** are mine.
   And **up those stairs, in that little back bedroom**
   Is where I **did my homework** and I **learned to play guitar**.
   And I bet you didn't know **under that live oak**
   My favorite dog is buried in the yard.

2. Begin by showing the students the list of the phrases you have identified and telling them that they are phrases from a song about someone's memory of a meaningful place. The students then read over the phrases and discuss what kind of place and memory the artist might be thinking of.

3. Play the part of the song that the phrases came from, in this case the first verse, while showing the lyrics. Discuss anything interesting about the lyrics; for example, here you might discuss the idiom "don't know someone from Adam." Then give the students a little more specific information; in this case, you would say that the song is about a house the artist lived in as a child, and the students are going to rewrite this part of the song to make it about a place from their own past—a residence, familiar playground, or so on. Show them the lines of the song with blanks where the phrases to be replaced occur, labeled with the kind of phrase that should go there, as in this example, and let them fill in the blanks.

> But _____ (noun phrase) _____ (prepositional phrase) are mine.
>
> And _____ (prepositional phrase), _____ (prepositional phrase)
>
> Is where I _____ (past tense verb phrase) and I _____. (past tense verb phrase)
>
> And I bet you didn't know _____. (noun phrase or noun clause)

4. Then each student will read aloud their rewritten verse. The other students should listen, and after each reading they may write down their favorite detail from the sketch, and one or a few words that express their interpretation, such as "fun" or "writer sounds nostalgic." If there are fewer than 10 students, you can do this as a class; if there are more, small groups may work better.

5. If the students are in groups, bring the class back together. Ask each student to name his or her favorite of the other students' compositions, read the detail noted, and briefly describe the interpretation.

6. Finally, play the original song as you show the lyrics, and finish with a group discussion on the mood of the song and the phrases that help to create it.

CAVEATS AND OPTIONS

1. If a student is shy about sharing a personal experience, an option may be to write about the experience of someone they know or have heard about, or to just make something up.

2. You may prefer to let students hear the whole song before they do the writing. This may be particularly motivating for learners with strong musical and/or aural skills.

3. Showing videos associated with songs may also be motivating, particularly for more visual learners.

4. Some learners may need a review of verb phrases, noun phrases, and prepositional phrases.

REFERENCES AND FURTHER READING

Lems, K. (2001). *Using music in the adult ESL classroom. ERIC Digest.* Retrieved from https://eric.ed.gov/?id=ED459634

Sing Our Song

Rebecca Palmer

Levels	Intermediate to advanced
Aims	Practice listening skills, spelling, pronunciation, capitalization, and punctuation
	Discuss the differences between formal and informal English
Class Time	40–50 minutes
Preparation Time	20–30 minutes
Resources	Computers or electronic devices with Internet access (one device for each group)

For some ESL students, spelling and pronouncing words in English is tough because of the irregularities of English sound and spelling patterns (Schneider & Evers, 2009). These irregularities are especially challenging for learners whose native languages use different orthographies and phonologies (Shoebottom, 2016). Students who speak Arabic often have trouble spelling vowel sounds, particularly short vowel sounds. Chinese students often have difficulty knowing how to break apart multisyllabic words because their dialects are based on one-syllable words, and they have a smaller number of vowel sounds. For some students, consonants can be hard; they do not hear the difference between consonant sounds such as [l] and [r] or [b] and [p]. Instead of having students do worksheets or mindless drills to practice spelling and pronunciation, singing and transcribing songs can help students practice in an enjoyable way.

PROCEDURE

1. Brainstorm ideas about a topic students have studied recently.
2. Assign students to pairs or small groups.
3. Have each group use a computer, cell phone, or tablet to find the lyrics and music to a song related to one of the ideas from the brainstorming activity, with the provision that each song's lyrics need to be appropriate for sharing in an academic class.
4. Each small group should write down the lyrics to a part of the song they have chosen. Because many groups will be presenting in the end, groups should choose only 8–15 lines from the song, perhaps some stanza or section of the song that is important, repeated, or makes sense alone. Each group should practice singing this section of their song until they can teach the words and music to another group.
5. As one small group sings their song section, another small group must write down the lyrics. If the listeners fall behind, they may ask the singing group

to stop or go back. They might even try using recording phrases such as *stop*, *rewind*, *play*, and *fast forward* to control the pace of the singers.

6. The groups should switch roles, and the other group should teach the first group their song, and, following the same procedure, the new listening group should write down the song lyrics.

7. When both groups are done, each group should check each other's lyrics, looking for correct spelling, capitalization, and punctuation and give points: no errors = 15 points; 1–2 errors = 10 points; 3–4 errors = 5 points; 5+ errors = 1 point.

8. When finished, the two groups should each practice the song they have been taught.

9. When the groups are ready, they will present the song they have learned to the whole class in a sing off. The group that sings the words and music the best scores 15 more points. The group with the song most related to the topic gets 10 more points.

10. After the song presentations, close the activity by asking students to spell some of the words from the songs that were difficult to pronounce and talk about their spelling/sound patterns, as well as the differences between formal and informal forms of words, as some of the songs may use casual forms such as "singin'" for *singing* and "ya" for *you*. Note also any capitalization and punctuation rules that the songs used and how these rules help or hinder transcriptions.

CAVEATS AND OPTIONS

1. Direct your students to online song training sites for ESL students that have music and lyrics for songs: YouTube is great if your school allows it, or try one of these three sites:
   - lyricstraining.com
   - esl-bits.net (click on Songs-Listen, Read and Sing Along at the bottom of the home page
   - efl.net (click on comaudio/songs)

2. Rather than singing the song for another group in person, the singers can make a video of themselves singing a section of the song to give to another group. That will make it easier for the listeners to stop, rewind, and play the song at a speed with which they can keep up. Students can use iMovie, MovieMaker, or PhotoPeach to make short videos to share. Again, the listening group needs to transcribe the words to the song, practice performing it, and present it in a sing off.

REFERENCES AND FURTHER READING

Schneider, E., & Evers, T. (2009). Linguistic intervention techniques for at-risk English language learners. *Foreign Language Annals, 42*, 55–76.

Shoebottom, P. (2016.) Language differences. Retrieved from http://esl.fis.edu/grammar/langdiff/index.htm

Studying Literature With Music

Mike Hammond

Levels	High intermediate to advanced
Aims	Develop reading skills and vocabulary
	Explore comparisons between literature and song lyrics
	Improve skills in understanding inferred meaning
	Develop writing skills in both summary and response (opinion) writing
Class Time	3 class meetings (1+ hour per class)
Preparation Time	30 minutes
Resources	Copy of lesson plan (Appendix)
	Online readings or paper copies of Edgar Allan Poe's poem "The Raven" and story "The Tell-Tale Heart"
	Lyrics and audio of Alan Parsons Project songs "The Raven" and "The Tell-Tale Heart"
	Audiovisual equipment

In this activity, students experience a story through two separate media: the original poem/story and a song that interprets the poem/story. Students use comparative skills to gain stronger recognition of paraphrasing, summarizing, and opinion expression. Students also gain an understanding of the conversion of old stories to modern forms.

PROCEDURE

1. Have students read all of "Background on Author, Poem, Story, Music Group, and Songs" (Appendix, Part 1) and answer all comprehension questions.
2. Check and discuss answers in class.
3. As homework, have students read "The Raven" (available at www.poetry foundation.org/poems-and-poets/poems/detail/48860) and highlight vocabulary that is difficult or seems outdated.
4. Discuss vocabulary in class.
5. Do "Music Lesson: 'The Raven'" (Appendix, Part 2) in class, and listen to the song. (The lyrics are available for projection at http://www.azlyrics.com/lyrics/alanparsonsproject/theraven.html.)
6. Students write summary of song and reading (in-class or homework).

7. Have students read "The Tell-Tale Heart" (available as a text and as a recorded reading at learningenglish.voanews.com/a/tell-tale-hear-edgar-allan-poe/2972675.html) as homework, noting any vocabulary words that are difficult or seem outdated.

8. Discuss vocabulary in class.

9. Do "Music Lesson: 'The Tell-Tale Heart'" (Appendix, Part 3) in class, and listen to the song. (The lyrics are available for projection at http://www.azlyrics.com/lyrics/alanparsonsproject/thetelltaleheart.html.)

10. Students write response to reading and song prompt.

CAVEATS AND OPTIONS

1. Depending on time and student levels, the lesson could be done over two to three class meeting days.

2. The assignment on the conversion of the original story into music could be used as an assessment in addition to providing paraphrasing and summarizing practice.

3. Themes of the poem and short story are of the dark horror genre; this lesson could be done as part of a Halloween theme.